Who Killed Richard Oland?

Who Killed Richard Oland?

A real-life murder mystery

JANICE MIDDLETON

FORMAC PUBLISHING COMPANY LIMITED
HALIFAX

Formac Publishing Company Limited recognizes the support of the Province of Nova Scotia through the Department of Communities, Culture, Tourism and Heritage. We are pleased to work in partnership with the Province of Nova Scotia to develop and promote our cultural resources for all Nova Scotians. We acknowledge the support of the Canada Council for the Arts.

Canada NOVA SCOTIA   Canada Council   Conseil des Arts
                       for the Arts   du Canada

Cover design: Tyler Cleroux
Cover image: Dennis Oland

Library and Archives Canada Cataloguing in Publication

Title: Who killed Richard Oland? : a real-life murder mystery / Janice Middleton.
Names: Middleton, Janice, author.
Description: Includes bibliographical references.
Identifiers: Canadiana (print) 20230237800 | Canadiana (ebook) 20230237819 | ISBN 9781459507234 (softcover) | ISBN 9781459507241 (EPUB)
Subjects: LCSH: Oland, Richard—Death and burial. | LCSH: Murder—New Brunswick—Saint John. | LCGFT: True crime stories.
Classification: LCC HV6535.C33 S3532 2023 | DDC 364.152/30971532—dc23

Formac Publishing Company Limited
5502 Atlantic Street
Halifax, Nova Scotia, Canada
B3H 1G4
www.formac.ca

Distributed in Canada by:
Formac Lorimer Books
5502 Atlantic Street
Halifax, NS, Canada
B3H 1G4
www.formaclorimerbooks.ca

Printed and bound in Canada.

For Paul, my partner in all that matters, and
for Paige and Meghan, with love.

Contents

Dramatis Personae   9

Preface   15

Chapter One: The Murder   17

Chapter Two: The Victim   20

Chapter Three: The Investment Gone Wrong   23

Chapter Four: Richard Oland's Last Day   26

Chapter Five: The Prime Suspect — Dennis Oland   35

Chapter Six: A Body Is Found   38

Chapter Seven: The Funeral   52

Chapter Eight: An Accomplished Yet Ornery Man   56

Chapter Nine: The Investigation   68

Chapter Ten: Dennis Oland's Arrest   74

Chapter Eleven: The Quiet Man   82

Chapter Twelve: Theory of the Case   92

Chapter Thirteen: Plenty of Suspects   97

Chapter Fourteen: Six Generations of Brewers   101

Chapter Fifteen: Dennis Oland's Preliminary Hearing   110

Chapter Sixteen: The First Trial: Setting the Scene   128

Chapter Seventeen: The First Trial: The Pathologist   137

Chapter Eighteen: The First Trial: The Brown Jacket   145

Chapter Nineteen: The First Trial: The Money   152

Chapter Twenty: The First Trial: An Incredible Verdict   158

Chapter Twenty-One: The Appeal and the Beating   160

Chapter Twenty-Two: The Retrial: A Tainted Jury   169

Chapter Twenty-Three: The Retrial: New Evidence
for the Defence   177

Chapter Twenty-Four: The Retrial: A Key Witness   192

Chapter Twenty-Five: Questions about "Red Mafia"
Involvement   196

Chapter Twenty-Six: The Rich and the Dead   210

Chapter Twenty-Seven: Investigation Failings:
A Deeper Look   220

Chapter Twenty-Eight: The Lawyers and the Bill   228

Chapter Twenty-Nine: Reasonable Doubts   234

Chapter Thirty: Psychology and Money   240

Chapter Thirty-One: Dennis Oland Speaks Out   247

Chapter Thirty-Two: The Mystery Lives On   255

Postscript   262

Author's Note   272

Timeline   273

Sources   317

Acknowledgments   322

Index   325

Dramatis Personae

The Olands and the In-Laws

Lisa Bustin (Oland) – Richard and Connie Oland's daughter and Dennis's sister.

Jack Connell – Connie's brother, Richard Oland's brother-in-law, Dennis Oland's uncle.

Andrew Oland – Dennis's cousin and the oldest son of Derek Oland. Currently Moosehead Breweries Ltd. president and CEO.

Connie Oland – Richard Oland's wife of forty-six years.

Dennis Oland – Richard Oland's only son, accused, tried, convicted and acquitted of his father's murder. Dennis was a securities trader and financial advisor at CIBC Wood Gundy in Saint John.

Derek Oland – Richard's older brother and Moosehead's executive chairman. The family patriarch.

George Bauld Oland (George B.) – Grandfather of Richard Oland, Sidney's older brother and oldest son of W.C. The New Brunswick patriarch who managed Oland brewery operations and established Moosehead in 1947.

Lesley Phinney Oland – First wife of Dennis.

Lisa Oland – Second wife of Dennis, now divorced.

Mary Frink Oland – Wife of P.W. Oland and mother of Derek, Richard and Jane.

Philip Warburton (P.W.) Oland – Father of Derek and Richard and the last Oland to act as a hands-on brew master.

Richard Henry Oland – Born in 1941 into the top echelon of New Brunswick society, Oland was a scion of the Moosehead Breweries family, a global brand with roots in the Maritimes dating back to 1867. The family is in its sixth generation of continually operating Canada's oldest independent brewery.

Tom Oland – A member of the Saint John Oland clan who was interviewed by police and the media following the murder.

Jacqueline Walsh (Oland) – Richard and Connie Oland's daughter and Dennis's sister.

The Rest

Bill Adamson – Maureen's husband.

Maureen Adamson – Richard Oland's personal assistant of thirty-seven years.

John Ainsworth – Owner of the building at 52 Canterbury Street and operator of Printing Plus, the ground floor print shop, Oland's landlord.

Hilary Brock - An Oland neighbor in Rothesay and a wealth advisor with Canada National Bank Financial, with whom Richard Oland had invested more than $1 million. Brock and Oland were having an affair at the time of Richard's murder.

David Brooker – Head of the Saint John Police Force's Major Crime Unit and part of the Richard Oland murder investigation.

John Cardwell – Former Can Sugar President and the man who initiated the project. Also vanished after Richard Oland's murder. He was apparently a friend of Oland who sponsored his membership in the exclusive Union Club.

Preston Chiasson – Man who called 911 to alert police of Oland's death. He was in the print shop below Oland's office when summoned by Maureen Adamson after she found Richard Oland's body.

David Coles – Halifax media lawyer who successfully challenged the trial judge's publication ban.

Bruce Connell – Police chief at the time of Oland's acquittal in July 2019; said he would not reopen the investigation unless significant new evidence came to light.

Constable Stephen Davidson – Oland case investigator who interrogated Dennis Oland the day after the murder.

Dr. Albert Fraser – Forensic toxicologist who was a witness at the first trial.

Alan D. Gold – One of Canada's top criminal defence lawyers and lead counsel for Dennis Oland's defence.

Cheryl Johnson – Saint John family lawyer who was working late in her Gorman Nason office across the alley from Far End Corporation when she overheard two men shouting.

Mike King – Staff Sergeant (Retired) who was a constable when he testified that his former supervisor McCloskey had taken him into his office prior to Dennis Oland's preliminary hearing and urged him not to reveal that McCloskey had entered the crime scene.

Michael Lacy – Another of Oland's defence lawyers during the appeal and second trial.

Judge Ronald LeBlanc – A former Crown prosecutor from Bathurst, NB and presiding judge for Dennis Oland's preliminary hearing (forty days from May 12, 2014, to December 12, 2014).

Gerry Lowe – Local politician, businessman and union leader. Key witness in Dennis Oland's retrial.

Constable David MacDonald – A Saint John police forensics expert involved in the murder investigation. He visually inspected Dennis Oland's coarsely woven brown linen jacket for blood but found nothing.

Barry MacKnight – Retired Fredericton Police Chief hired as an independent investigator by the New Brunswick Police Commission to perform a professional conduct review of McCloskey and King.

Inspector Glen McCloskey – Member of the Saint John

Police Force who, although not officially part of the investigation team, took a strong interest and viewed the crime scene several times early on the day the body was found — without donning any protective gear. When Bill Reid retired, by then Deputy Chief McCloskey was appointed acting-chief for the summer and first two months of the Oland trial.

Robert McFadden – Richard Oland's fulltime accountant since 1987.

Gary Miller – Prominent New Brunswick criminal defence lawyer on Dennis Oland's defence team.

Justice Terrence Morrison – New Brunswick lawyer appointed a judge in 2008. Presided over Dennis Oland's retrial — his first murder trial.

Dr. Ather Naseemuddin – Pathologist for the province of New Brunswick.

Constable Greg Oram – Police officer who wandered about the crime scene with Inspector McCloskey, although he too was not needed at the murder site. He later ran the police polygraph tests for the investigation.

Bill Reid – Saint John Police Chief at the time of the murder. Retired in 2015 after thirty-seven years with the force.

Sean Rocca – Saint John police officer who conducted "improper" background checks on jurors.

Rick Russell – Saint John Police team's lead investigator into the murder of Richard Oland.

Diana Sedlacek – Real estate agent and interior decorator, Richard Oland's long-time mistress.

Jiri Sedlacek – Retired executive with multinational footwear manufacturer Bata Corporation. Husband of Diana.

Anthony Shaw – Worked at Printing Plus when the murder took place.

Sgt. Mark Smith – Head of the Saint John Police Force's forensics unit.

Bill Teed - The Oland family's long-time friend, neighbour and lawyer, and a member of Dennis Oland's defence team.

Paul (P.J.) Veniot – Retired Crown prosecutor asked by the Office of the Attorney General to take over the case in August 2015. Veniot was assisted at the first trial by co-Crowns **Patrick Wilbur** and **Derek Weaver.**

Justice John (Jack) Walsh – Legal expert in DNA who presided over Dennis Oland's 2015 jury trial for second-degree murder.

Brian Wentzell – RCMP forensic expert stationed in Halifax who investigated the murder scene, as well as Dennis's car and clothing, for blood splatter.

Preface

Believing others should be grateful for his know-how was Richard Oland's default mode. Life with Dick was a memorable time, even a good time for some — but not all. Could his pointed condescension and careless cruelty drive someone to lash back at him?

Whatever one might say about Dick, he didn't deserve to die like that.

CHAPTER ONE
The Murder

Multi-millionaire Richard Oland — "Dick" to all and man-about-town — was at his desk with his back to the door when two men entered the office with a quick knock and caught him by surprise. It was Oland's first day back at his investment firm in the heritage business district of Saint John, New Brunswick, after a holiday spent salmon fishing on the Miramichi River. The sixty-nine-year-old, working late and alone in the two-room office on the second floor at 52 Canterbury Street, was not expecting visitors.

Oland kept his schedule tightly organized, even marking in leisure time, and he frowned impatiently at the interruption. The older man who did the talking he recognized vaguely as someone he knew. The other man, who hung back slightly and stayed silent, was a stranger, and Oland passed over the quick introduction with polite indifference. This man, of average height and well-muscled in a black T-shirt and black athletic pants, moved restlessly around the office, past the desk where Oland was standing to peer out the window through the venetian blinds.

The demand for payment to cover investors' losses from a failed business venture focused Oland's attention on the spokesman. The conversation quickly escalated, becoming a shouting match. Oland was incensed by what he considered to be an outrageous request, turning red-faced with anger. A lawyer working at her computer after hours in an office building across the alley looked up at hearing the two men's loud voices.

From the corner of his eye, Oland glimpsed the other man moving and spotted the hammer, the shaft rising. His expression changed to alarm, and he threw up his arms to block the weapon. Too late to stop the arc of the blow, the strike smashed through, breaking his fingers.

The man stepped back, easily avoiding Oland's desperate attempts to fend off the assault. Swinging the hammer in a big circle, the assailant brought it down, fast and hard and accurately in a perfect curve. It was a two-headed steel hammer with a sharp blade and a round, flat head weighing under a pound, a common drywaller's tool — lightweight by construction standards but devastatingly effective in cracking a skull. The second strike landed precisely on the left side of Oland's head, slicing through his thinning hair and scalp, cutting deep into his brain.

Oland, immediately unconscious, fell spread-eagled to the floor face down, legs apart, arms bent wide, his glasses tumbling to rest on the hardwood floor in the widening pool of his blood. The attack did not stop there. More blows rained on his head and neck in furious succession from the sharp blade and then the round end, dozens of times, sending blood and brain matter flying in all directions, spattering the office walls and furniture, soiling the papers on the desk. The copper smell of blood permeated the space as he lay dying. In five minutes, his heart stopped.

Retreating to the hall, the attacker stepped onto a large plastic garbage bag that was laid out flat like a bath rug. He wiped his head, hands, and arms with a damp towel from a plastic bag he had stashed by the office door. He stripped off the blood-soaked clothing and shoes. Soon he was dressed in a fresh black T-shirt, the lightweight black running shorts he had on under the pants and a fresh set of track shoes.

As he pulled the bag closed around the bloody clothing and the weapon, his accomplice opened the back door to the alley where a car waited for their escape. A third man on watch behind the street door on Canterbury mounted the stairs and bolted the steel door behind them. Then he headed back down and left by the street door, walking casually towards the city's centre.

The air conditioning hummed and the fluorescent ceiling lights in the office burned all night, an unusual occurrence. Richard Oland, notorious for his frugality and miserly ways, never left the lights on or the air conditioning running. A clear and warm summer night in the industrial port city of Saint John, there would have been a few pedestrians and the occasional car passing by on the one-way street. But no one noticed the brightly lit office, including the police who patrolled the area at regular intervals.

This scenario above is a reconstruction based on the evidence at the crime scene and the grisly nature of the killing. According to experts in organized crime, it seemed to be a contract murder. There were no witnesses, so no one except the perpetrators can say.

CHAPTER TWO

The Victim

Born into the top echelon of New Brunswick society, Oland was a scion of the Moosehead Breweries family, a global brand with its roots in the Maritimes dating back more than 150 years. The family is in its sixth generation of continuously operating Canada's oldest independent brewer, known as Moosehead Breweries since 1947, headed by Richard's older brother Derek, the family patriarch and chairman of the board.

Richard was the second son and not his father's choice to succeed him at Moosehead. Outmaneuvered in an acrimonious battle for the top job by Derek, he left the company at age forty as executive vice-president in 1981 and pursued a career in transport trucking and property development.

John Travis was fresh out of university when he joined

Richard Oland's Brookville Transport firm as sales and marketing manager. Oland had just thirty-five drivers then. Travis worked alongside him for a dozen years as he built the company into a fleet of more than five hundred truckers:

> *Dick was a doer. He had an insatiable drive to innovate, question everything, to try and find a better solution to problems from shipping rates to equipment design. If our opinions weren't shared, we aired our differences, and it wasn't brought up again.*

Travis, now an investment advisor and branch manager at CIBC Wood Gundy in Saint John, is a longtime Oland family friend. He was Dennis Oland's supervisor at Wood Gundy at the time of Dick's murder. He recalled an incident when his boss and mentor invited himself along on a week-long business trip to the United States, starting in Boston. "As we were flying into Logan Airport, Dick starts searching his pockets and his briefcase. Then he turns to me and says, 'I don't have my wallet.'"

Travis used his credit card to pay for everything all week.

In 1997, Oland sold the company, and Travis was thrown out of work when the new owners fired half the staff. One day when he was between jobs, Oland called to see if he was up for a road trip. Dick was in the market for a new BMW, and he wanted Travis to come along and keep him company. "'Come car shopping with me,' he said, so I did. Dropped everything." Over five days in search of the best deal, "We must have hit every (BMW) dealership on the East Coast. We had a great time." Did Travis have the chance to take a model out for a spin? "No."

As a high-profile citizen of Saint John and an honoured philanthropist with a net worth of thirty-seven million dollars, Dick wore bespoke suits and a special-edition Rolex on his wrist that he won in a 2010 international yachting race sponsored by the Swiss watchmaker.

He and Connie, his wife of forty-six years, lived in an expensively restored ancestral mansion in the leafy enclave of Rothesay, a wealthy residential community of eleven thousand people just outside Saint John. Their son Dennis, who became the chief suspect in his father's death, and his wife lived next door in the twenty-two-room Tudor house where Dick grew up. Their two daughters, Lisa and Jaqueline, married locally and also settled in Rothesay. John Travis was a neighbour. What was once a cottage community of summer homes on the Kennebecasis River is now home year-round to an extraordinary number of millionaires and billionaires, many of whom are descendants of New Brunswick's founding industrialists. The average Rothesay homeowner's net worth is north of two million dollars.

When Dick didn't come home for dinner that night, neither his wife Connie nor their house guest, Connie's brother Jack Connell, thought about calling him. Used to his frequent absences and knowing he had a board of directors meeting at chocolatier Ganong Bros. Ltd. in the town of St. Stephen the next morning, they assumed he had decided to drive down the evening before. He'd stay over in a hotel in the town a little over an hour away from Saint John on the Bay of Fundy coast.

CHAPTER THREE
The Investment Gone Wrong

As a leading citizen and Saint John promoter, Richard Oland was a natural cheerleader for a plan to revive sugar refining, a traditional industry on the city's waterfront after 'Lantic Sugar, Canada's largest sugar refinery, closed its Saint John plant in 2000 — after nearly nine decades of continuous operation. 'Lantic Sugar had taken over ownership of its competitor, St. Lawrence Sugar of Montreal, in 1984 and then expanded and upgraded to consolidate its operation. But by 2000, the company abandoned its Saint John home; it could serve the national market from its expanded Montreal refinery. Saint John lost 180 jobs as a result of the shutdown.

Local Saint John businessman John Cardwell, one of 'Lantic's managers, thought there was room for a competitor in the market. He quit his job to lead the new venture, Can Sugar Inc., which was set up to reopen and operate the refinery. In keeping with his role as a promoter and booster of economic development for the city, Richard Oland assisted Cardwell and the new plant's majority owner-investors, a Russian/Ukrainian group. The investors contributed $17.5 million for the new operation.

Richard Oland helped the project along by making introductions to the city's economic development agency, Enterprise Saint John; the local branch of the Royal Bank of Canada; provincial government officials; and federal officers at The Atlantic Canada Opportunities Agency. The funding agencies contributed a further eight million dollars to the project, and the province loaned Can Sugar $1.5 million. Local companies were happy to see the refinery start up again and provided millions in goods and services.

The company started operations in 2003 by importing vast quantities of raw cane sugar to be refined. Much of the imported sugar proved too coarse to refine for human consumption; the refinery was producing a fraction of its expected volumes. By the end of its first year in business, Can Sugar had run out of money. No one stepped up to offer the financing that was needed to keep it operating, and Can Sugar entered bankruptcy proceedings.

Richard Oland helped with these, his accountant working on closing out the books. Local firms that had acted as suppliers to the new company lost out. The Russian/Ukrainian owners lost their $17.5 million. Government funders lost their money too. John Cardwell lost his life savings - over three hundred thousand dollars. Oland eschewed investing in startups as a rule so had no money in the project.

After the refinery was dismantled and its assets sold off,

the raw sugar inventory was taken to Jamaica, where it was made into ethanol, an alcohol-based fuel produced by the fermentation of sugarcane juice and molasses.

CHAPTER FOUR

Richard Oland's Last Day

Richard Oland viewed his romantic extra-marital relationship with Diana Sedlacek, real estate agent and interior decorator, as a diversion that spiced up his life and kept him current on the news around town. Her unwavering attention, care and devotion to his well-being had been steady for the last eight years. She spoke openly to her real estate colleagues about their trips and the things they did on the weekend. She let it be known she expected to marry him.

It was simple, really. She was attracted to Dick's world of power and money; he liked her for the way she made him feel. They wanted a lot of the same things and the freedom to enjoy them — to do what they wanted, when they wanted; or truth be told, in the way *he* wanted.

Diana and her husband Jiri Sedlacek moved to New

Brunswick from Toronto in late 2003. Jiri was a retired executive with multinational footwear manufacturer Bata Corporation. Diana had met Jiri, twenty-four years her senior, in Toronto, marrying him in 1989. On arrival in Saint John, they enrolled their teenage son in Rothesay Netherwood School, where he graduated in 2005. Netherwood is a small, independent, co-ed boarding and day school for Grades six to twelve with a worldwide reputation for excellence. The Sedlaceks cited the school as their reason for moving out east.

For Diana, the move meant coming home. She was born in Saint John, one of five children to Lina Arsenault and John Virgin, a welder who worked in the port repairing ships for Saint-John Drydock and Shipyard Ltd., an Irving company. For the dockworker's daughter and the brew master's son, sexual intimacy was heightened by the thrill of doing something forbidden. Oland concealed contact details for Sedlacek on his iPhone under the photos of three male colleagues to prevent embarrassing pop ups. Diana kept her relationship with Dick a secret from Jiri.

Their daily dialogue began around breakfast time, and they would text and, less frequently, call to talk throughout the day until bedtime. Once or twice a week, usually on Sunday after church, they met at a downtown hotel suite that Dick kept available for some personal time. At sixty-three, Diana was a fit and slender blonde, six years younger than Dick. She dressed well and was sophisticated but at the same time she was raunchy, uninhibited sexually and affectionate.

Wednesday, July 6, 2011, dawned hot and humid, Oland's first day back at Far End Corporation after a two-week guys-only fishing trip with friends on the Miramichi River in northern New Brunswick. Dick and Diana's correspondence began with a text from Diana about an upcoming trip to Portland, Maine. Not exactly a destination calculated to generate romantic fantasies, but Dick needed some boat parts and Portland was the place to get them.

Like Saint John, Portland has a venerable history and an Old Port district known for its nineteenth-century architecture and nightlife. The biggest city in Maine, its 66,215 population mirrors the 67,580 of Saint John (as of 2023). Portland's port is the largest tonnage seaport in New England; Saint John is the biggest port in New Brunswick. Portland's marine industry still plays an important role in the city's economy, with a busy waterfront that supports fishing and commercial shipping — and parts for sailing yachts enough to captivate Richard Oland's heart.

That morning, Oland was seated at the breakfast table when Sedlacek messaged at 9:08 a.m.: *Morning Lixxxx on Golden Gun. Drvn 2gy---Did Zu find note? re Our Trip?*

9:09 a.m.: he texts back: *Have in [office] just up kkk.*

9:10 a.m — Diana: *Kisssss wen U get ther text it—— mmm kisss.*

Putting the phone aside, Dick turned to talk with his brother-in-law Jack Connell, who had just sat down with him. They were joined by Connie. Forty minutes later, he had a call from his personal assistant Maureen Adamson, reminding him that he had a meeting in a half-hour.

Far End Corporation, named after Dick and Connie's historic home Far End, rented modest office space on the second floor of a late-Victorian three-storey red-brick building in the historic section of uptown Saint John. The city's core is referred to as uptown rather than the usual downtown because the city is built on a hill. Far End Corporation's large multi-paned windows look down on Thandi, a trendy restaurant on the opposite side of Canterbury Street that specializes in a fusion of Indian and Thai cuisine. The

Trinity Royal Heritage Conservation Area is a rundown section of ornate brick low rises pocked with empty lots after buildings were razed in the 1970s. However, the district is gentrifying slowly and the rather forlorn architecture that remains houses some upscale shops and businesses.

On the ground floor beneath Far End was Printing Plus, a business operated by Dick's landlord, John Ainsworth. A punk rock band rented the third floor from Ainsworth for practice space. Young men were often lounging about at the street door joking around and sharing cigarettes. On the northwest side, the building next door was a former garage, at that time turned into storage space. The southeast side was vacant land awaiting development, meanwhile serving as an unpaved parking lot.

Oland's fulltime accountant, Robert McFadden, was waiting at the office along with Maureen Adamson, Oland's personal assistant. Both were staunchly loyal friends to Oland and had been with him for decades. McFadden's handwritten to-do list for the day contained six items, the final one being "the Will," which Oland wanted to review. Other items included filing the corporation's 2010 tax return, negotiating a lease for a new office, reviewing Oland's life insurance policy and finalizing work contracts relating to the new sailing yacht Oland was having built in Spain.

Financial advisors Gordon Graham and Barry Prosser had booked an appointment with Oland and McFadden to discuss Oland's life insurance policy, which was coming up for renewal in a few months. The two men hoped to sell him a new package, and Oland had agreed to taking the required medical tests to see if he could get a better rate. Far End Corporation was the beneficiary of his existing policy, which would pay out death benefits of eight million dollars.

Oland was the sole owner and director of Far End as well as a real estate company, Kingshurst Estates Limited. Both were subsidiaries of a numbered holding company also owned by Oland. His son Dennis and McFadden were co-executors of the estate. On his father's death, Dennis would become president of the holding company and director of the two subsidiaries, Far End and Kingshurst. McFadden would be secretary and treasurer of the holding company and president and treasurer of the two subsidiaries.

Under the terms of Oland's existing will, a straight-forward document that had remained unchanged since 1996, the Rothesay house Far End, along with all its furniture and fixtures, was to go to Connie; it had been her child-hood home. After funeral expenses, any assets realized plus the companies were to go to Connie in a spousal trust. She would receive income from the residual, and if that was "insufficient," she could receive more money from the capital at the discretion of the trustees, Dennis and McFadden. Upon Connie's death, the trust would dissolve, and the three Oland children would share the residual estate equally.

Any changes Oland was considering to his will would not have cut anyone out or favoured one beneficiary over another. As his wealthy friends were doing, Oland planned to set up a family trust to reduce the taxes payable upon his death. Rather than making bequests to individuals, he had in mind to set up an auction of his possessions to avoid fights for his belongings among his family. A bidding war did not occur to him, but it would to others when they learned about his terms.

It was noon before Oland got back to Sedlacek. He texted her at 12:01 p.m about Portland, Maine, on one of three possible dates for the trip. *3 options all ex St. Stephen nb. Option 1 lv jul 11 return Jul 15 11 am; Option 2 lv 15 pm return 3:00 jul 19; Option 3 lv Jul 20 at 4 pm return 24th. All should be 4 nites, would prefer option 2 or 3.* Sedlacek was driving when she received the message and pulled over to the side of the road to text a reply. *I agree 2 or 3 let me think.*

Lunch for Oland was a takeout pizza brought to him by Adamson. He shared it with McFadden's son, Galen, hired as an intern for the summer to help around the office and scan documents into Oland's computer system. The job meant stacks of bankers' boxes filled with records were piled all around the normally neat office. Oland restricted his wife to two thousand dollars a month to maintain their household, but he had state-of-the-art equipment for his investment business and for tracking the money markets, including a direct phone line to his son's office.

At work a few streets away at his CIBC Wood Gundy office, Dennis, a securities trader and financial advisor, reminded his daughter in a text sent at 12:45 p.m. to thank her grandfather for his donation to her high school basketball team to help send them to a meet in Newfoundland.

At 1:57 p.m., Sedlacek texted Oland, *Let's leave at Noon on Fri. 15th we can arrive early enough in Portland--so leave 15th come back on 19th. Kisses*

Busy clearing a backlog of work that had built up over the two weeks he'd been away, Oland didn't get around to reading Sedlacek's message. He had one million dollars on account with CIBC Wood Gundy that was managed by Dennis. At 2:41 and 2:51 p.m. Dennis sent emails to his father concerning a stock split and a RRIF (Registered Retirement Investment Fund).

At 4:42 p.m., apparently forgetting about checking Sedlacek's text message selecting July 15 for their trip,

Oland made entries to his electronic calendar regarding trips to Portland Maine for all three dates, July 11, 15 or 20. Two minutes later — as was his daily workday habit — he disconnected his fully charged iPhone 4 from his computer and put it aside on his desk, allowing calls and texts to go directly to voice mail.

Closed-circuit security cameras at the entrance to CIBC Wood Gundy in Brunswick House at the end of King Street caught Dennis leaving at 5:08 p.m., impeccably dressed in a dark sports coat and lighter-coloured pants. At 5:26 p.m., Thandi's security camera clocked his silver VW Golf parking on the west side of Canterbury Street across from the green street door at No. 52. A modest brass plaque mounted on the wall to the right of the door identified Far End Corporation.

Business for the day concluded, McFadden and Galen left the office together for home. Their departure is recorded on Thandi's camera at 5:30 p.m. McFadden nodded to Bill Adamson, Maureen's husband, who was parked curbside on Canterbury Street. As he waited for Maureen, Adamson saw Dennis enter the street door to Oland's office building. He noticed he was carrying a red reusable grocery bag with something, not heavy, in it. Maureen joined Bill in their car at 5:45 p.m. Talking about her day, she mentioned that Dennis had come by to discuss genealogy with his father.

Dennis mistakenly sent his sister Lisa a text message at 6:12 p.m., that was meant for his wife, also named Lisa, saying he was at his father's office doing "history stuff" and was heading for home. He was again caught on Thandi's security camera. The video showed him walking on Canterbury Street. His jacket and light-coloured pants were clean, and he appeared unruffled, his face calm. He opened the rear hatch of his car and deposited the red reusable grocery bag.

The silver Golf headed southwards on Canterbury, a one-way street, but then Dennis looped back around in a return trip to Far End Corporation. He later stated that he had gone back to retrieve a family camp visitors' book for his uncle Jack Connell. His father had borrowed it a year ago, and Connell was asking for its return. Adamson had finished scanning it into the computer file for the genealogy project on the family history that Dennis and his father had undertaken. Titled "The Island Camp," the log was a record of several generations of visitors to a summer camp owned by the Connells. As Dennis had earlier promised Connell he would deliver it home, he'd decided he had to go back for it.

When he arrived at Far End, Dennis found his father standing next to the boardroom table, presumably getting ready to go out. They took a few minutes leafing through the log together, reminiscing about the years gone by and laughing about some of the entries. "Dick had to go home to shovel shit," read one entry written by Connie. Her then boyfriend had a summer job at a horse stable. "For five dollars a week," Dick chortled.

About twenty minutes later, at 6:44 p.m., Diana texted Dick, *U there??* from her home on Darlings Island. Cellphone records were submitted in court showing a call to Oland's iPhone had pinged off a Rothesay tower at 6:44 p.m. on July 6, 2011, near the Renforth Wharf — where Dennis stopped on the way home after visiting his father.

It was not answered. Subsequent calls and texts did not reach the phone, indicating to Oland's carrier Rogers that it was switched off after 6:44 p.m. Once turned off, a cellphone cannot emit any signals and ceases communicating with any nearby cellphone towers.

In the next half-hour Sedlacek phoned Oland five times. She sent another text at 7:19 p.m., extremely irate: *You've turned your phone off?! Why!!!!!??????? Your not at office & don't tell me you have a 'Bus' mtg cause U don't --So tell the fucking truth!!! Cause I'm sitting here not doing suspicious things & I hav a lot of men who would love 2 b with me!!!!!! Do stop this fucking around! And answer the damn phone! I wil call at your house.*

This text and subsequent texts, along with a dozen or so unanswered calls she made over the course of the evening failed to connect with Oland's iPhone and went to voice mail. She also rang the Far End office landline phone at 7:15 p.m. and 8:01 p.m. and left a message. She threatened, "I will call your house."

At 11:12 p.m., Sedlacek sent the last text of the evening, *Pathetic!*

Diana and Jiri testified they were both at home all evening on July 6, 2011, at their six-acre property on Darlings Island on the Kennebecasis River, an eighteen-minute drive northeast of Rothesay.

It turned out that Oland's iPhone was turned off from July 6, 2011, at 6:44 p.m. until July 9, when it was turned on and sent back a "roaming error" message to the caller, a Rogers technician assisting the Saint John police in search of the device. A roaming error meant it was live but out of Rogers' service jurisdiction. Though the police in 2011 should have been able to locate the phone anywhere in the world, according to tech experts who do these searches with police, the Saint John police investigators never found or located Richard Oland's iPhone 4.

CHAPTER FIVE

The Prime Suspect — Dennis Oland

A middle-aged couple in their car in the parking lot at the Renforth Wharf sipping coffee and enjoying the view of the wide and peaceful Kennebecasis River witnessed a man walk briskly onto the wharf around the time that Sedlacek sent her 6:44 p.m. text to Richard Oland's cellphone. They did not see him throw anything into the water. The woman said she saw him pick something up and put it in a red bag.

Dennis readily volunteered he had been to the wharf on his way home; he said he was checking to see if his kids, who took kayak lessons there, were still swimming as they often did. They were not, so he continued home.

Dennis Oland told police he did not really remember picking anything up, but keeping the wharf area clear of litter was automatic for local boat owners like him. He guessed it might have been a beer can.

In any case, had he taken his father's cellphone and thrown it into the water as the police later suspected, it would not have been in working order on July 9 as the Rogers technicians discovered.

Amidst Diana Sedlacek's efforts to reach her lover by phone, Dennis was going about his routine business. Around 7:30 p.m. on July 6, Dennis was recorded on video shopping at two different stores in Rothesay — at Kennebecasis Drugs and then at Cochran's Country Market, where he and wife Lisa were videoed chatting with Dennis's aunt, Jane Toward. Dennis, dressed casually in golf shirt and shorts, cradled a melon in his left arm as he paid at the counter for their groceries.

There was no police evidence, at least produced in court, of Richard Oland's activities after 6:20 p.m. on July 6, 2011. However, there was anecdotal evidence of activity at the Far End offices. Saint John family lawyer Cheryl Johnson was working late in her office across the alley from Far End Corporation when she overheard two men shouting. She provided a statement to police in the early days of the investigation to the effect that she had heard raised voices coming from the vicinity of Oland's office at about 7:40 p.m. that Wednesday. Inexplicably, she was never called to testify at Dennis Oland's trial by either the prosecution or the defence.

When I contacted her in 2016 about what she heard on July 6, 2011, Johnson declined to talk about it. She answered my phone call in a cheerful and strong voice, but when asked about the argument she overheard at Richard Oland's office that evening, Johnson responded in a strangled, barely audible voice, "I'm sorry. I'm not interested." Then she put the phone down. She sounded terrified.

Richard Oland's autopsy found traces of alcohol in his urine, indicating he had left his office and had a drink after Dennis had departed. There was no alcohol kept in his office according to Adamson and McFadden. However, alcohol was readily at hand at his private club around the corner from his office, the Union Club at 125 Germain Street.

The police made it known that Dennis Oland was the last known person to see Richard Oland alive. Eight years passed before it became public that a witness saw an unidentified man leave the street door at 52 Canterbury a few minutes before 8:00 p.m. on the night of Oland's murder. Local politician Gerry Lowe said he provided the information about the sighting to the Saint John police in the days immediately after the killing, but he was not called to testify until 2019.

CHAPTER SIX
A Body Is Found

New Brunswick, one of four Atlantic provinces, has a population of fewer than 800,000 and is known for the beauty of its wilderness. Driving the Trans-Canada Highway through its endless forests is a reminder of how the continent must have looked to the first European settlers in the 1700s. The famous Reversing Falls caused when the Bay of Fundy tidal bore collides with rapids at the mouth of the Saint John River, expansive parks of salt-water marshes, lakes and ancient volcanic rock attract a million visitors a year from around the world.

French explorer Samuel de Champlain landed at the mouth of the Saint John River on June 24, 1604, the feast day of St. John the Baptist, and gave the river its name. Richard Oland died in Saint John on July 6, 2011, beaten to death with a hammer. More than 416 years separate these two events that each had a major impact on the province.

Saint John is a blue-collar, post-industrial community with a shrinking population of about 70,000 people as of 2022. That means a shrinking tax base and steadily shrinking services, including the city's police force. The oldest incorporated city in Canada, it was created by Royal Charter in 1785 by King George III of England, its colonial master. Suffering from the effects of globalization for the past three decades, Saint John has enjoyed a small growth spurt recently as Canada's third largest port by tonnage. Its deep harbour on the Bay of Fundy, ice-free year round, and easy transportation links to other parts of North America keep the city going and offer hope for the future. The Oland family's Moosehead Breweries is as much a part of that future as it is an important part of the city's past.

Saint John and its surrounding communities are closeknit — places where everyone knows or knows of everyone else (and their business), and people tend to leave their doors unlocked. On the warm, sunny morning of July 7, 2011, Maureen Adamson stepped out of her husband's car shortly before 9:00 a.m., gave him a cheerful goodbye and headed to work. She put her key in the door at 52 Canterbury Street; the door was unlocked. As the shared entrance to several offices, it was sometimes left open, so finding the street door unlocked was not unusual. No surprise there.

Carrying a tray with two cups of steaming Tim Hortons coffee in one hand, the solid greying woman in her late 50s slowly climbed the twenty-three steep stairs to the second floor, where a landing led to two offices and a shared bathroom. Turning into the investment firm Far End Corporation, she found the glass-paned French door was slightly ajar. That was a surprise. Normally she was the first to arrive in the morning, unlock the office, and turn on the lights and air conditioning. The last one out at night shut down and locked up.

And there was a most appalling smell. Sickening. Inside she saw two trousered legs splayed on the floor, the pants' fabric riding up, displaying two milk-white calves. The black leather loafers, black socks and pale shins seemed thin and frail. Stunned, she set the coffee down on the boardroom table in the centre of the office. Fearing the worst, she turned and rushed down the stairs to the print shop on the ground floor for help.

Preston Chiasson, a friend of one of the employees there, followed the shocked woman back up to the office. Chiasson called 911. It was 8:54 a.m. Paramedics arrived quickly, but it was clear that Richard Oland was beyond help. One of the city's leading citizens, in his business clothes, had been dead for hours, lying face down in a huge pool of blood.

The brutal murder of the autocratic businessman, one of the most powerful men in Atlantic Canada, sent shock waves and rampant speculation throughout the community and across the country. The violent crime index for Saint John is below that of all other Maritime cities and well below that of most cities across the country. If you want to take the measure of a community, look at its elected officials. Conservative Party representatives tell you the people are self-reliant and slow to change. The murder of a member of an establishment family shattered the law-abiding self-image of this small-c conservative city as a place of stability and constancy. Saint John is a shipping and shipbuilding hub that usually elects a large-C Conservative Member of Parliament. In 1993, when only two Conservatives under

Prime Minister Kim Campbell were elected nationwide, Saint John elected one of them. Elsie Wayne, for those with long memories, was the only non-Liberal elected in the Maritimes. If Richard Oland wasn't safe in going about his daily business here, who was?

Whatever the effect on the community at large, the sheltered life of an elite family of New Brunswick society ended abruptly that morning with the grisly discovery of Oland's battered body by his personal assistant Maureen Adamson. Far End accountant Bob McFadden, hoping to avoid the police uproar and questions from curious media and bystanders, headed for the golf course, only to find most everyone there had already heard the news. They asked him, "Do you have something to tell us, Bob?"

Shirley McAlary, former mayor of Saint John, said "Something like this doesn't happen in Saint John often. The whole family is very well known. It has led to speculation and a lot of talk among everyone in the city. This is very disturbing. People are very concerned."

Oland was brought down by his assailant in a hail of forty-five savage blows. His skull was completely shattered. Bits of brain matter were found on his back. The attack left blood and matter for three metres around the body on every wall, and spatter was visible on Oland's desk, his computer, some filing cabinets and an empty pizza box in the garbage can under the desk that had tipped over in the attack. The police quickly concluded that the murder was personal, and that the assailant knew the victim.

Dr. Ather Naseemuddin, the province's pathologist, counted fourteen fractures in Oland's cranium, which had been pounded in so badly on the left side that it had a fist-sized concave area spanning ten centimetres (about the length of the long edge of a credit card) in length, seven centimetres across, and two centimetres deep, penetrating the brain. The bones of his eye sockets were "like a cracked eggshell." His fingers were broken in trying to defend himself.

Despite this, in police photos taken of the crime scene amidst all the gore, there was no apparent blood staining his light gray ergonomic office chair, which had a tall back, neck, and head support. This would tend to discredit the prosecution's theory that Oland was ambushed from behind while he sat unaware in that chair. It rested on a floor protector and had wheeled castors for easy movement. In the crime scene photos, it is shoved away from the desk, which faced the windows, where Oland would sit with his back to the rectangular room. A black cloth backpack leaned against the near right corner of his desk. The boardroom table in the middle of the room was cluttered with files amidst stacks of banker's boxes — part of Oland's project to store his paper records digitally on his computers.

Yachtsman and world traveller Richard Oland lived an enviable and flamboyant life. In a perfect example of life imitating art, he was the virtual embodiment of the archetype character in the 1897 narrative poem *Richard Cory* by Edwin Arlington Robinson, an American poet and three-time Pulitzer Prize winner. Songs, plays and other poems have been based on the Robinson poem, including Paul Simon's 1966 song *Richard Cory*, in which Simon adds how his factory employees envy him even though he kills himself. As the chorus goes, *Oh I wish that I could be Richard Cory*. Simon's song about workers want was covered by seven other singers as diverse as Van Morrison and Paul McCartney.

In a 1976 play called *Richard Cory*, based on the poem, A. R. Gurney Jr. asks the question, "Who Killed Richard

Cory?" The play is an attempt to expand Robinson's poem, and in so doing, to explain the mysterious death. The play, the poem and the song describe a businessman with vast holdings in the community he dominates, whose success is built on political connections, inherited wealth, philanthropy and civic involvement — a resume resembling Richard Oland's. Cory owns the town's major employer. The poem's final stanza reveals that despite his wealth and status, Cory to everyone's surprise kills himself. While Richard Oland was brutally murdered, certain striking parallels remain. As two stanzas taken from the poem illustrate.

> *Whenever Richard Cory went downtown,*
> *We people on the pavement looked at him:*
> *He was a gentleman from sole to crown,*
> *Clean favored, and imperially slim.*
>
> *And he was always quietly arrayed,*
> *And he was always human when he talked;*
> *But still he fluttered pulses when he said,*
> *"Good morning," and he glittered when he walked.*

Oland's penchant for extramarital affairs was an open secret. At the time of his death, he was involved in the eight-year affair with Diana Sedlacek, as described above. This coincided with a liaison with his son's first wife, Lesley Phinney Oland. According to local scuttlebutt, Oland paid to help Lesley get her real estate licence after her marriage with Dennis ended. Then "one thing led to another," as the old saying goes. At the time of his murder, he was also seeing a family friend, Hilary Brock, an Oland neighbour in Rothesay and a wealth advisor with Canada National Bank

Financial, with whom Oland had invested more than one million dollars.

Oland took his female companions travelling, skiing and even out sailing on his yacht, much to the irritation of his crew. He also enjoyed couples' massages in a room at the Chipman Hill Suites — nicely decorated hotel rooms in several renovated heritage buildings in uptown Saint John. Union Club members such as Oland enjoy a special discount.

Oland and Sedlacek texted during the day of his death about a trip to Maine. Though they mainly communicated through texts, Diana invariably phoned Richard at approximately 6:30 each evening to talk about their day. Whether she was so intimate with her husband, Jiri Sedlacek, who had retired in 1988 at age 60 as director of corporate planning for Bata Shoes, we don't know. Tall with a strong build and a full head of white hair, the eighty-seven-year-old testified in court in 2015 that he first learned of his wife's affair with Oland about fifteen months after the murder when his lawyer shared a media report about it with him.

Jiri Sedlacek was questioned twice by Saint John police and was ruled out as a suspect in Oland's murder. But the police never asked to see his bank or phone records, or the GPS for his car. It was hard to believe that Sedlacek, a worldly frequent traveller, who described himself in court not as a Canadian but as an "international citizen," didn't know about his wife's eight-year affair. Undeniably, it could be a strong motive for murder.

Sedlacek told the court he met Oland around 2003 and had socialized with him and his wife, Connie, eight to ten times over the years. Sedlacek said he liked talking to Oland, describing him as "well-travelled and interesting." Sedlacek admitted he "probably" would have been "very upset" if he had known his wife was cheating but insisted that he didn't even suspect — all those long weekends away without him and frequent nights when she came in late or sometimes just didn't come home notwithstanding. It would be enough to make any husband suspicious, maybe even angry enough to kill.

When Oland didn't answer his iPhone on July 6, 2011, Diana Sedlacek called repeatedly and threatened to call his home. No answer. The next morning, on her way to a hair appointment, she drove past 52 Canterbury, saw the commotion, and called Connie to ask if she knew why there were so many police cars outside her husband's office. Connie called Richard's long-time employee and friend, Robert McFadden, who delivered the shocking news that her husband was dead, and the search was on for his killer.

That afternoon, the Saint John police came to Richard Oland's home on Almon Lane to speak to the family. They asked Connie and the three adult children, Lisa, Jacqueline and Dennis, to think about why Richard might have been killed and who might wish him ill. They did not provide any details about how he died or the death scene. Later in the day, the family went to the Saint John police station to give their statements and answer police questions. In their efforts to be helpful, they naively set the stage for what ensued and created a distorted and misleading image of Richard Oland they could never repair.

Dennis was kept late for questioning while his mother and sister Lisa waited. They were asked by the police to go home without him but refused. He was bullied, hectored and badgered in an interrogation room alone for hours on end. It's not illegal for police to do this, but under Canadian criminal law he was not required to say a thing, nor could police hold him without charge.

Halfway into the interrogation, Constable Stephen Davidson pointed out the inconsistencies in Oland's answers, read him his rights, and informed him that he was the primary suspect in his father's murder. At this point Oland could — and knowing that police had already concluded he was guilty, one might say should — have refused to speak to police further, as Bill Teed, the family's lawyer, advised him in a telephone call. He could have stormed out (such an action could not have been used against him in court). But he chose to stay. By being deferential and helpful, as is his nature, in his efforts to cooperate, thinking that this would show he was innocent, Oland made a series of moves and comments the police considered incriminating.

For example, information he readily volunteered about his after-work visit to his father's office the previous day was interpreted by police and later prosecutors as revealing a confused state of mind. He helped his interrogators construct a motive by recounting anecdotes and sharing information about Richard's difficult, sometimes demanding and critical nature. He provided Davidson with a detailed written and verbal account of his activities for the previous day.

He said he believed his father had high expectations of him that he wasn't meeting. In a tactic aimed to trigger a confession, police concocted a lie that Oland's office had video surveillance cameras. Davidson told Dennis the cameras could verify whether he was telling the truth about his presence at Far End Corporation and asked Dennis what clothing he had worn the day before.

Instead of shooting back that the video would show what he was wearing and more importantly would show not only that he hadn't killed his father, but the guilty party in the act, Dennis said he was wearing "these pants, these shoes," indicating the clothes he had on. He also said he had worn a blue shirt and navy jacket. Despite Davidson's aggressive questions, he was steadfast in maintaining his innocence. When it turned out that Dennis had worn his summer weight brown Hugo Boss jacket to his father's office, police attacked Dennis's credibility. They said that it was not an honest mistake or an unforced error, but rather a deliberate and purposeful lie to mislead police. Regardless, it was a costly mistake.

Although plenty of people did not get along with Richard Oland — daughter Lisa who had once worked in the office with him at Brookfield Transport described him as a hard-nosed businessman who could have had "anyone for an enemy," and an acquaintance noted that "to know him was not to love him" — it didn't take police more than a few hours to begin directing their most pointed questions to Richard's relationship with his forty-five-year-old son Dennis. While Connie was quick to tell police she didn't believe Dennis would ever hurt his father, Diana Sedlacek described what she saw as a "strained relationship," in part, she said, because Richard considered Dennis "lazy."

When Dennis's first marriage broke up in 2008, he faced the potential loss of the family home, SevenAcres — willed to him by his grandparents. SevenAcres, situated on one of the toniest roads in Rothesay, is an impressive older home with spacious grounds.

Many members of the Oland family have owned property in Rothesay for decades. His parents' splendid, wooded estate on Almon Lane, which had belonged to Connie's family, borders the SevenAcres property and connects to it by a pathway through the woods, although a "No Trespassing" sign sits at the head of the laneway. It is screened from the road by a double barrier of log fencing and box hedges, further buffered by spacious paddocks and a barn that once served as stables for the Rothesay Pony Club, an organization that taught riding skills to generations of Saint John's elite. Indeed, Jacqueline had operated the club until Richard decided to cut off funding as it was losing money, and it went out of business.

SevenAcres, originally purchased by New Brunswick Oland patriarch George Bauld, has been in the family since the 1930s. Dennis's cousin Andrew Oland lives down the street, and Oland family lawyer Bill Teed is within walking distance.

Situated on the Kennebecasis River, Rothesay is about a twenty minute drive northeast of Saint John. The name Kennebecasis is derived from the Mi'kmaq "Kenepekachiachk," meaning little, long bay place. The river runs for about ninety-five kilometres, draining an area in the Caledonia Highlands, an extension of the Appalachian Mountains, into the Bay of Fundy.

The Canadian National Railway secondary mainline still runs through town, although it no longer offers passenger service. The Rothesay station, built between 1858 and 1860, has been named a National Historic site — one of the oldest railway stations in Canada, made in the two-storey architectural style common to railway stations from that era.

Richard, quick to step in and help Dennis through his divorce, loaned Dennis more than $500,000 to buy out his wife's share in SevenAcres. Monthly child support payments left Dennis perpetually strapped, such that he was repaying only the interest on the loan — he would pay the principal with his eventual inheritance from his parents. With Sedlacek's encouragement, Saint John police speculated that money had become a source of friction between the two men.

The loan and Dennis's precarious financial situation were not the only red flags leading police to suspect Dennis might have been involved with his father's death. As investigators began to piece together the events leading up to the murder, they zeroed in on the early evening hours of July 6. Dennis Oland readily volunteered to police that he had visited his father at the office after work that day to discuss family genealogy, one of several passions the two men shared. According to Dennis, it had been a pleasant but uneventful visit, and he left for home at about 6:30 p.m.

Two men working at the print shop below Far End Corporation told police they heard six or seven "exceptionally loud, quick pounding thumps" lasting about ten seconds coming from the office on the floor above them between 7:30 p.m. and 8:00 p.m.

John Ainsworth, the building's owner, operator of the ground floor print shop and Oland's landlord was one of the two men who heard the loud thumps on July 6. Curiously, he did not go up to investigate the noises at the time, nor did he go up the next morning to assist Maureen Adamson when she sought help after finding the body.

At about the same time the noises were heard at 52 Canterbury, time-marked video showed Dennis Oland shopping at two different stores in Rothesay. Nonetheless, police clung to their fraying theory that Dennis committed the murder an hour and a half earlier. They were keenly curious about discrepancies between what Dennis said he was wearing when he visited his father — a navy blazer, khaki dress pants, dark brown dress shoes and a blue, white-collared dress shirt — and other evidence they had gathered. Security cameras at Dennis's Wood Gundy office showed him leaving the building that day wearing a brown sports jacket and beige pants.

Police showed less interest in the fact that he was not even in the building at the time of the murder. Nor did they allow that in the trauma and grief of suddenly learning of his father's death, Dennis might easily have forgotten which jacket he was wearing — particularly considering he had two that he wore on alternate days, one brown and one navy. Although Dennis stated during his police interrogation that he was wearing the same pants and shoes, the clothing was not immediately seized for DNA testing as one would expect.

The police had a witness, Bill Adamson, who had been waiting in his car outside the office for his wife Maureen to finish work. Adamson reported seeing a man enter 52 Canterbury wearing a dark brown sports jacket and light-coloured pants carrying a red, reusable grocery bag. He said he did not see the man's face so could not positively identify him. Maureen, still at the office when Dennis arrived, noticed Dennis's brown jacket. It was such a sweltering day, she wondered why he was wearing a coat.

A short time after Dennis left Oland's office, a woman saw a man at Renforth Wharf just outside Rothesay "dressed very nice." According to the woman, the man walked onto the pier, picked something up, then walked to the far end where he briefly sat down, opened a bag and took something out. He then wrapped the red object he had picked up, put it in the bag and walked briskly back toward the parking lot.

"I knew it wasn't right," the woman told police investigators. "There was a purpose to what he was doing, a real purpose." Police snapped up this overreach as a clue: a well-dressed man walks to the end of a pier, does something such as picking up a bit of litter and walks back to his car. When police later showed her video from Richard Oland's funeral, she identified the man she had seen as one of the pallbearers, Dennis Oland.

On July 9, 2011, scuba divers searched the waters around Renfrew Wharf but found nothing. By then police had already fingered Dennis as their prime and only suspect. But they only told reporters they believed Richard Oland knew his killer and that the motive for his killing might have been financial. They called it a homicide, although among themselves they referred to it as a murder.

Derek Oland, Moosehead's executive chairman, was fishing in a remote part of Labrador when his younger brother's body was discovered and could not get home until two days later, arriving late afternoon on July 9. By then, the initial shock of the gruesome killing was wearing off, and family and the community had begun adjusting.

In the days following, the flags at Saint John's municipal buildings and at the Rothesay Yacht Club were lowered to half-mast. Saint John's daily newspaper, the *Telegraph-Journal*, ran the story on its front page, "Dick Oland Dead," along with a detailed obituary.

John Ainsworth created a memorial in front of 52 Canterbury with a large photograph of a smiling Richard Oland, flanked by fresh flowers and the message: "Richard, you will be sorely missed. Thank you for all that you've done! God speed, friend." Saint Johners were invited to sign the poster.

CHAPTER SEVEN

The Funeral

JULY 12, 2011

It had rained overnight, and the morning of Richard Oland's funeral dawned with showers and fog. By noon, as the service began, the skies had cleared, and the sun shone through the stained glass windows and skylight of Our Lady of Perpetual Help Roman Catholic Church in Rothesay. Oland's casket, covered with a pall of white and gold, was bathed in glittering light.

Close to five hundred mourners packed the church, just across the road from Dennis and Richard Oland's homes. They filled the pews and rows of extra chairs. Some stood along the back wall. The church is new, but designed to honour the parish heritage. Richard Oland had helped raise funds to build the church a few years earlier. Designated by the province as a Local Historic Place, the architecture of Our Lady of Perpetual Help echoes the Gothic Revival design of the former church it replaced. The hanging lights of pure copper, the High Altar, the wainscoting under the choir loft, the pews and the brass altar candles all came from the old church.

The Letourneau pipe organ, one of only three copies of El Greco's "The Death of the Count", and the Madonna painting by Toronto artist John Young grace the new space. The kneeler, or prie-dieu, belonged to William Dollard, the first Roman Catholic Bishop of the Diocese of Saint John, the Baptismal comes from the 1770s Saint Paul's Valley Church and the ambry once belonged to Bishop Medley, the first Anglican Bishop of Saint John.

Numerous dignitaries, politicians and business leaders rearranged their schedules to attend Oland's funeral, including New Brunswick Premier David Alward and Lieutenant Governor Graydon Nicholas. Said Nicholas,

> *I think it's difficult in the best of circumstances for a life to be lost. And when you stop and think of all the good that this man has done for this community and all of New Brunswick, this is a beautiful celebration of life for him.*

Premier Alward issued a statement:

> *Mr. Oland's contributions to his community of Greater Saint John and to New Brunswick were as generous as they were significant. He was a great businessman with an equally great regard for his fellow New Brunswickers.*

Reverend Michael LeBlanc began the mass, "God loves us all and receives us all in His own way. Let's always be thankful for all of the good things Dick did for us."

Richard Oland, it turned out, had been doing good almost up until his last breath. Two days before he was murdered, he had met with Pat Darrah, executive director of the Saint John Construction Association; Robert Harris, the Bishop of Saint John; plus a few others to discuss preliminary plans to raise ten million dollars to replace the roof and repair stonework at the historic Cathedral of the Immaculate Conception on Waterloo Street in Saint John. Darrah was one of Oland's closest friends and would deliver his eulogy.

Family members, including Dennis, read from scripture during the hour-long service. The Saint John String Quartet accompanied several vocalists. Darrah, fighting back tears, paid homage to a "dear friend" of thirty-five years and described Oland's many achievements and contributions to his community. Darrah recalled how he enjoyed challenging Oland on any subject that arose during their discussions.

> *I would get a lecture of how that situation or institution worked. And be brought up to speed on the fine points. [If Oland] didn't know the fine details, I could guarantee that within twenty-four hours my phone would ring, and I would have a full description.*

Darrah paid tribute to Oland's widow sitting in the front row with one of her grandchildren in her lap.

> *Connie, Dick may have been the skipper, but you controlled the rudder. We all knew that he could*

be impatient, but one of your hands on his shoulder and things turned calm, kind, and considerate of others.

Among the forty-seven messages of condolence left on the funeral home's website several spoke to his character. At the end of the service, people filed out to a recording of Frank Sinatra singing "My Way." It was *the* farewell and sendoff song for Richard Oland those who knew him well agreed as they shook hands and shared hugs. But aside from a few such as Darrah, there were few outward signs of sorrow. The media and police presence caused some observers to compare the event to a mafia-style funeral.

The casket was lifted into the hearse and taken away for interment; a modest memorial stone was erected in the Our Lady of Perpetual Help cemetery.

CHAPTER EIGHT
An Accomplished
Yet Ornery Man

Sailing was Oland's greatest passion. He started sailing at nine and remained active in ocean racing throughout his life, winning many international competitions. Of his myriad achievements, he felt most satisfied at being acclaimed the 2010 winner of the Canadian Yachting Association's Gerry Roufs Trophy. It is "awarded annually to the sailor whose achievement in international offshore racing has had significant impact on the recognition of sailing in Canada."

He won the 2010 US-IRC National Championship in his crewed New Zealand-built, fifty-two-foot yacht, the Vela Veloce, bought two years earlier. Oland won his inaugural race in that boat, the annual Easter Ocean Race from Auckland to Tauranga, New Zealand. After that, Oland had raced along the East Coast of North America and in the

Caribbean, winning major international competitions, often as the only Canadian entry. He'd recently put that vessel on the market for $850,000 because he was having an even fancier, faster, sleeker boat built in Spain.

"He loved sailing. Every time I talked to him, it was always about the boats and the sailing," said Gerry Hoeksema, a close friend of Oland's who spent a great deal of time on the water with him, as quoted in the Rothesay Yacht club online newsletter two days after Oland's murder. *The Challenge and Adventure* issued a lengthy and laudable tribute July 8 under the headline, "Richard Oland, owner of Vela Veloce, has Died. "

> *To me, he was just a great guy and he was a good friend who did open up a lot of people's eyes that sailed with us, to show us that there was so much more than what was just around here. It's going to leave a big hole. A lot of people are going to miss him.*

Most people with fond memories of Dick Oland were listed among the members of the Rothesay Yacht Club and shared Oland's love of sailing. Mcgregor Grant, a lifelong friend who grew up next door, was one. Grant said in an interview for the online newsletter that he was "shocked" when he heard the news of his friend's death.

Grant, who sailed many times with Oland, said his friend was "larger than life," a thought echoed by other club members. "It's just awful news. It shakes me a little bit. It just blew me away; I can't believe it."

Another old friend, Bruce Tennant, was walking into the RYC clubhouse when he was interviewed for the newsletter.

He said he was stunned when he heard about Oland's death. Tennant recalled fondly how when Oland and his wife Connie were first dating in their teens and early twenties, they would sail over to Long Island, New Brunswick, near St. Andrews-by-the-Sea, where Tennant had property. The gang had picnics together, spending the afternoon on the beach.

Clark Sancton, a frequent lunch companion of Oland's at the Union Club on Germain Street in Saint John, described the man he had known for more than thirty years as "intense but brilliant," saying, "Always had his mind on what was good for the community and always worked for the community good." Sancton, president of the Sancton Group of Companies, said "he'll be sorely missed by the city."

"He has been a great promoter of the city of Saint John," Mayor Ivan Court said. "He never gave up on the city." Oland "loved" the city of Saint John and the surrounding communities. Court called him a "doer," saying, "He wanted to get things done. You need more people like Dick Oland."

That Richard Oland was a big fish in a small pond is readily apparent. Robert McFadden said that his boss always "went by Dick — a common guy," but he enjoyed receiving business awards, yacht racing trophies and adding to his fortune.

Appointed an Officer of the Order of Canada in 1998, Oland was following in his father's footsteps and those of other civic-minded Olands who put community and country first. The Order of Canada, established on July 1, 1967, on the 100th anniversary of Confederation is the second highest honour for merit in the system of Canadian orders, decorations and medals, after the Order of Merit. The businessman, sportsman and philanthropist had a high profile as a director of several major Atlantic regional companies, including Eastern Provincial Airways, Newfoundland Capital Corporation and Ganong Bros. Limited.

Dick was probably best known among Saint John residents as president and chief organizer of the 1985 Canada Games, held in Saint John. The games, which take place every two years and alternate between winter and summer, were first held in Quebec City in 1967 as part of Canada's Centennial. It was largely due to these efforts that Oland received his Order of Canada.

Richard Henry Oland was born in 1941, the second son to Philip Warburton Oland and Mary Frink Oland, following the birth of his brother, Derek, two years earlier. An abundance of anecdotal evidence documents Richard Oland's insistence on having his own way — in his home and in community — and provincially-funded projects he took great satisfaction in bringing to fruition. He was usually right, people said, but his family, friends and fellow volunteers didn't appreciate his high-handed style.

In 1996, Richard Oland shared a stage with King Charles when the then-heir to the throne opened the new home for the provincial museum in the heart of the city. As president of the museum board, Oland had pushed to create the facility. According to Shirley McAlary,

> *Richard was very generous with his time and his money. He wasn't the person to just have a meeting and then leave it at that. He wanted to get the job done and get it done right. He was very strongly opinionated. He was a person anxious to do good things.*

In a statement issued after the murder, Derek and sister Jane recalled their brother's many contributions to Saint John and New Brunswick. Derek noted that in recent years he and Dick would sometimes meet for lunch, slowly mending the longstanding rift caused by Dick's ousting from Moosehead in 1981.

The family has generally avoided publicity since the murder. Much of the information about Dick Oland's life comes from his obituary and magazine articles. In recent years, he had divested himself of day-to-day work responsibilities and was travelling the world and spending his time enjoying life. On Sundays in winter, he skied at Poley Mountain, the best-known ski resort in southern New Brunswick. In summer, he rode horseback through Kingshurst, a scenic riverside area in Rothesay with stunning views of Kennebecasis Bay. On the day of his murder, he had returned relaxed and "mellow" from a fishing trip with friends. McFadden recalled, "He was in a great mood."

Oland attended Rothesay Collegiate Private School for Boys, but in Grade 10 — apparently for behavioural rather than academic reasons — he was shipped off to Regiopolis College, a Kingston, Ontario Roman Catholic boarding school run by Jesuits. Years later, a friend of Connie Oland, a clinical psychologist, would diagnose him with what was then called Asperger's Syndrome, an autism spectrum disorder characterized by difficulties in social interaction and nonverbal communication. Such a personality disorder might explain his tendency for unpredictable, arbitrary and capricious behaviour. However, Connie in a letter she wrote for the court, said "Dick's personality was the norm for our family, and we all knew how to work around that norm." She said her late husband "just did not always

seem to understand how his words might offend someone."
She would sit him down at the kitchen table and explain
it to him. "Accordingly, Dick would then make amends
and peace would be restored between them." While his
immediate family and friends were often exasperated by his
controlling, sometimes bullying ways, they had long ago
learned to deal with them.

As a teenager, Dick worked summers at Moosehead
Breweries and went sailing on the Kennebecasis River. After
high school, Oland earned his Bachelor of Arts Degree
from the University of New Brunswick in 1966, followed
by a Certificate of Brewing Technology at Wallerstein
Laboratories in New York. Wallerstein provides consultation services to the brewing industry, including research
into fermentation, as well as enzymes used in manufacturing and food industries. He was well grounded in the
brewing business.

Despite his reputation as a prickly character who was not
universally liked by his peers, Oland was active and respected
as someone who got things done in the community yet
remained modest about his achievements. He and Connie
went to Christmas parties at a local inn, which was "no big
show," said former Rothesay Mayor William Bishop. "He
was just an ordinary citizen."

He was an ordinary citizen who was extraordinarily civic
minded, Bishop went on. "He came in about two or three
times a year and made sure I knew how the town should be
run. He's one of those people who gets right in your face to
make sure you're listening."

"New Brunswick's free enterprise system has become a
twentieth-century version of the Family Compact," Oland
once told a reporter in reference to a cabal of families,

fiercely loyal to British Conservatism, who controlled Upper Canada — now Ontario — for much of the nineteenth century.

He had directorships in several charitable organizations, including the YMCA-YWCA, which presented him with a public service award, the Huntsman Marine Science Centre and the United Way of Greater Saint John Inc. A long list of community involvements included chairman of ParticipACTION, a councillor for the Town of Rothesay and past-president of the New Brunswick Museum.

Under his leadership, the museum overcame credibility issues in the wake of a 1990 trashed artifacts scandal and expanded into its major gallery at Market Square. Among his many awards, Dick was Sport New Brunswick Executive of the Year, Transportation Person of the Year and received the Paul Harris Rotary Fellowship Award in appreciation of significant contribution to the community, as well as receiving an Honorary Degree from UNB (D.Litt.). All this is to say that, like his brother Derek, Richard was a man of impeccable credentials and accomplishments despite his personal peccadillos.

Most of his fortune came from selling his thirty-three per cent share of Moosehead Breweries to Derek. While at Moosehead, he was instrumental in designing and building one of the world's most advanced and fastest beer packaging lines at the Saint John Brewery. "My father was a very important part of the huge growth that came to Moosehead during his tenure there . . . just as important as Derek's," Dennis said admiringly. "When he left in 1981, Moosehead was the most modern brewery you could find, with the fastest production line of sixteen hundred bottles per minute."

By 1980, then thirty-eight-year-old Oland was a

vice-president of Moosehead Brewery and vied with his brother, executive vice-president, for the company presidency. In a bitter public feud and series of legal battles, Derek outmaneuvered him, threatening to resign and move his family to New Zealand if he was not made sole president of Moosehead. Forced to choose between his quarrelling sons, their father and then-company president, Philip Warburton (P.W.) Oland, who had originally thought leadership of Moosehead could be shared equally between Dick and Derek, chose Derek as his successor. In choosing Derek, P.W. was following a long-held tradition of selecting just one chief for the family business. He chose Derek because "the younger one wanted to be president and hadn't the experience," as he "rather succinctly if tactlessly" explained to a *Financial Post Magazine* journalist in the 1992 article.

"I couldn't work for Dick because of the nature of the guy," Derek would tell author Harvey Sawler for his book, *Last Canadian Beer: The Moosehead Story* (2009), claiming his brother was prone to "argue with anybody." But the episode also spoke volumes about the ruthless side of the family patriarch, who was prepared to sacrifice family relationships to advance his business interests if necessary.

When Oland left the company in 1981, he started a trucking business that counted Moosehead Breweries as a valued customer and oversaw preparations for the 1985 Canada Games, but the wounds of their rupture never really healed, leading to two decades of frosty relations between Dick and Derek. After their father's death in 1996, Dick, who continued to be a one-third owner of Moosehead, sued Derek on two separate occasions over his management of the business. Both cases were settled out of court, before Derek finally bought Dick out completely in 2007.

Richard Oland explained the family break this way in the *Financial Post* interview; "I was just looking for opportunities and if they weren't present in the existing system, I had to leave. Moosehead was just a career option like any other."

Maybe so, maybe not. Oland's relations with his own family seemed to deteriorate after he left the brewery. "He was never the same [after 1981] with his children," Connie told police the day they came to talk about his death.

The teenage Richard Oland began courting the girl next door, Constance Katherine Connell when she was sixteen. In 1965, Dick and Connie wed. In her inexperience with the criminal element and in her well-meaning effort to explain why her husband might be a murder victim, she inadvertently helped police build the case against Dennis. She told police he was a "strong and controlling" man who could be verbally and emotionally abusive with their two daughters, Elizabeth "Lisa" and Jacqueline "Jackie" Lee, but especially with his only son, Dennis James. The couple had seven grandchildren.

Their children "had issues" with their father, Connie said, but it was Dennis who bore the brunt of her husband's belief that "a father could not be friends with his son." Dennis told police that after his dad left Moosehead, "Things got complicated with [his] father . . . You kept your distance." Dennis's wife Lisa said Dennis had done his best to win his father's respect but could never live up to his standards.

Oland's reputation around Rothesay and Saint John was that of a hard man to get along with, according to a group of local friends and business associates who often gather at Slocum and Ferris, a popular eatery at the Saint John Farmer's Market. S&F is a daily hangout for the city's old boys' network and gossip exchange. It's been around since 1895, founded by George W. Slocum and

John D. Ferris, who left Queens County, New Brunswick, to become produce merchants in Saint John. Both were staunch Loyalists, the Ferris family having come from New York and the Slocums from New England. The partners maintained links with the farmers of the Saint John River Valley, who sent them produce downstream by riverboat. Slocum and Ferris did not buy the goods outright but took a commission. The second-floor office above the shop still contains a folio-size ledger from the 1910s, recording the firm's transactions in fine cursive script. At Slocum and Ferris, even during the inflationary times of the early 2020s, two can enjoy a breakfast bagel all day with coffee for fifteen dollars. Out-of-town journalists covering the Oland case went to the diner to gather background information and colourful quotes.

"Dick was a dick," was a sentiment oft repeated at S & F after his murder — and one that no one disputed. "A very capable guy," as one put it, "but there would be a few people, after he got through with them, with footmarks on their backs."

Slocum and Ferris's unofficial greeter is Ralph Willett, who hands out his business card labelled "The Red Ball Kid" to journalists interested in the Olands. Red Ball was the name of the first brewery that the Olands bought in New Brunswick when they expanded operations after the 1917 Halifax explosion that levelled the city and their brewery. A trader in beer-related memorabilia, Willett is a long-time acquaintance of the Oland family, including Dennis and Richard. He explained that the Oland story connects back to Richard's grandfather George Bauld and his great grandfather George W.C. Oland. "When W.C. died, he favoured his younger son Sydney over George B. Everything that went wrong with the Olands started with W.C.'s will."

Though Richard Oland's marriage had survived, ostensibly intact, for forty-six years, the reality was that Dick and Connie led separate lives, according to daughter Lisa. It was not unusual for Dick not to return at night to the recently refurbished family home on Almon Lane, a tree-lined side road in old Rothesay. Oland had unearthed the original plans of the 1930s house and had completed renovations just before his death. He spent enormous amounts on restoring the house, deco style in pale green stucco, to its past glory. He and Connie had moved temporarily into the carriage house on the property while the work was being done.

There is no doubt his eight-year affair with Diana Sedlacek exacerbated family tensions. As the relationship became more public, Diana began fueling talk of marriage. She spoke openly about her weekends with Dick to her fellow real estate agents at RE/MAX, recalled Shirley McAlary. On Tuesdays, the women realtors toured new listings together. McAlary drove. Sedlacek rode shotgun, with Leslie Oland in the back seat. "It was a work-hard-play-hard" mentality, McAlary said.

Dennis was increasingly feeling guilty for not telling his mother about his father's mistress. His sisters were also concerned. Unwilling to broach the topic directly, he talked to McFadden about passing on a message to his father to cool things off with her. McFadden did not carry out the task. Of course, Connie was aware of Sedlacek, whom she described to police in a very anodyne manner as "Dick's friend." The Olands had socialized with the Sedlaceks to the extent of dinners at their respective homes several times over the years. After the murder, Connie had to tolerate a panicked phone call from Sedlacek about the police cars gathered outside his office.

Starting from scratch after leaving Moosehead, Oland established three major enterprises — property developer Kinghurst Estates Limited; Brookville Transport Limited, with as many as seven hundred drivers at times; and an investment firm, Far End Corporation. He was the president and CEO of Far End and Kingshurst Estates, president of Brookville Transport and general manager of Brookville Manufacturing Co. Dennis worked as night dispatcher for the trucking company during summer break while in university. Oland's daughter Lisa worked for a time in the Brookville office.

The last time Derek would see his estranged brother alive was in the spring of 2011 at the Union Club, "an old-fashioned gentleman's club established in 1884 and housed in a Victorian building around the corner from Dick's office." The brothers were usually part of a larger group gathered around a table for lunch. After his murder, some regulars admitted they had always been wary of Dick's presence. One told a friend he did not enjoy meals with Dick because of Oland's habit of "stirring things up."

At its current location since 1890, the Union Club is a showplace and an integral part of Saint John's business and social community of. The Club provides the business elite of the city with a private place to discuss and share new ideas, "certain of a high level of discretion." Club management prides itself that "it is often our members who are the ones shaping and directing the future of Saint John."

CHAPTER NINE

The Investigation

Two days after the funeral, twenty police officers with dogs acting on a warrant arrived at Dennis Oland's stately home. Police spent eight hours searching the house and grounds and left after 8 p.m. with four large garbage bags, several cardboard boxes and some paper bags. They seized a total of fifty-seven different items: legal papers, bank statements, a purple purse with a note inside, bedding, Dennis Oland's clothing and shoes — even a clothes dryer lint collector. They dug holes in the yard searching for the murder weapon.

A week after the search at Oland's home, several Saint John police cars arrived with search warrants at the Royal Kennebecasis Yacht Club to which the Oland family — and much of Saint John and Rothesay's elite — belonged. The police searched the *Loki*, a yacht belonging to Dennis Oland's wife Lisa and a friend of hers. Divers looked for a murder weapon beneath the water around the wharf and marina. Later, they executed search warrants at Dennis's Wood Gundy office. Despite the extensive searches, police found nothing to advance their case and link him to the murder.

In the months following, police refused to say how Richard Oland was killed but word got out they were looking for a drywall hammer, a two-headed construction tool with a round head and an axe-like blade. Tom Oland, one of the Saint John Oland clan, told a reporter he was asked by the police whether he owned a drywall hammer.

"The only weapon they mentioned was a drywall hammer." said Oland. "That's what must have killed Dick."

Tightly knit, socially interconnected Saint John was riveted by the murder and rife with rumour: *Dick Oland had been bludgeoned to death with a double-headed hammer . . . Police are about to make an arrest . . . They'll never catch the killer . . . The reason no one has been charged is . . .*

For four hours on November 9, 2011, and a further hour on November 17, Constable David MacDonald visually inspected Dennis's coarsely woven brown linen jacket for blood but found nothing. On November 25 — months after the warrant for police seizure of the jacket had expired, so illegally — the jacket was sent to the RCMP forensics lab in Nova Scotia for further examination. The lab eventually identified five "reddish" spots, invisible to the naked eye. Four microscopic specks on the jacket were confirmed to be blood that matched Richard Oland's DNA — two spots on the outside right sleeve, one spot on the outside upper left chest, and one spot on the outside back bottom hem near the centre.

The police and the Crown bragged to insiders that they built a chargeable case against Dennis around those inconclusive findings. However, the police did not make public that Dennis Oland was the only suspect in the case until May 2013. New Brunswick Provincial Court Judge Ronald LeBlanc, who conducted the preliminary hearing in 2014, said this accusation was premature. LeBlanc wrote,

> *With respect, this conclusion on their part was totally unjustified and indeed irrational. The explanations given by Dennis Oland could not have formed the basis for a reasonable belief that he had murdered his father.*

The police built their case on Oland's voluntary statements the day after the murder. Davidson read Dennis his rights and he phoned the family lawyer Bill Teed, who told him to stop talking to the police — good advice that Dennis failed to follow. When the interrogation resumed, Davidson said, "there is absolutely no question in my mind that you did this, and I want to know why," and then he told Dennis that his opportunity to speak with a lawyer had passed. It was a lie aimed at intimidating and isolating Dennis, who repeated that he did not murder his father. Police finally "allowed" Dennis to leave just after 11 p.m. — as if he couldn't leave whenever he wished but instead didn't because he wanted to help — wearing the pants and shoes he said he had worn the previous day.

The police probe into Richard Oland's murder was problematic from day one. Veteran officer Glen McCloskey, who was not officially part of the investigation, had seemingly taken charge. McCloskey informed the team's lead investigator Rick Russell that he had put Dennis Oland under police surveillance as he left the station to go home after his interrogation. McCloskey was an inspector in charge of the Criminal Investigations Department at the time.

Earlier in the day, McCloskey had appeared at Richard Oland's Canterbury Street office. At 10:52 a.m., he was the eighth police officer to climb the stairs and pass through the office doors without any protective clothing since Adamson and Chiasson had reported a body. All told, as many as sixteen officers and a handful of other people would enter the crime scene that day without any shoe covers or gloves.

McCloskey toured the office in street clothes twice on that day and likely touched the back door, although he couldn't recall it in court. He admitted to having gone outside and walked around the alley that the killer or killers could have used as an escape route before the forensics officer had completed his work. He was on his second visit, this time accompanied by Constable Greg Oram, another police officer who also wasn't needed at the murder scene, when they were told to leave.

In 2015, Constable Mike King testified that his former supervisor McCloskey had taken him into his office prior to Dennis Oland's preliminary hearing and urged him not to reveal that he (McCloskey) had entered the crime scene. McCloskey was a top-ranking officer as the inspector in charge of the criminal investigations division, overseeing the major crime unit and forensic identification unit. He was not an investigator. His desk job involved human and financial resources and reviewing case files, or as he explained in court, he oversaw "how we made out; where we're going."

In his testimony at Dennis Oland's 2015 trial, McCloskey recounted that on the morning of July 7, 2011, he got a call from King about a "dead body." McCloskey walked over to 52 Canterbury Street with David Brooker, head of the

Major Crime Unit, who opted to wait outside. McCloskey was there only briefly, but then he came back. On his second visit, which he marked out for the court on an office floor plan, he had returned "just to look around" and went out the exit door into the alley. He testified that he couldn't remember if he touched the door. McCloskey made a third visit to Far End Corporation on Saturday, July 9 to assist police investigators in case any additional resources were needed, he said.

King retired from the Saint John Police Force in April 2015 around the time McCloskey, now deputy chief, took on the role of acting chief for about six months when Bill Reid retired. On September 8, 2015, shortly before Dennis Oland's trial was to start, King told the Oland case lead investigator Constable Stephen Davidson that McCloskey wanted him to alter his testimony. Davidson corroborated their conversation in his testimony and said he did not pass the revelation on to his superiors. King said he told the Crown prosecutors on September 29, shortly before he was scheduled to testify, that McCloskey had asked him to lie. Court was adjourned early that day and did not sit the following day.

When King took the stand, Dennis Oland's defence lawyer, Alan Gold, questioned him about whether he made the allegation against McCloskey "because you got turned down for inspector, and you're bitter?" "False," said King. The process hadn't started when he withdrew his application for health reasons, he said, adamant that he was not disgruntled, nor did he have an issue with McCloskey.

"There was no misunderstanding for me," King told the court. He said he told McCloskey in no uncertain terms, "I never lied on the stand in thirty-two years," and he "wasn't about to start" — whether "a murder or a traffic ticket, I was telling the truth."

Sergeant Mark Smith, head of the forensics unit of the Saint John Police Force, spent three days following the search of Dennis's home doing a "very thorough search" of Dennis's car. Ten different areas of the car were swabbed, including the driver's door inside latch and handle, the trunk release button, the headlight switch, the signal light switch, the steering wheel, the emergency brake, and the car seats. In other words, anything Dennis would have touched when driving home. No blood evidence was found. The swabs were sent away on July 21, 2011, for forensic testing at the RCMP crime lab in Nova Scotia, but no blood or DNA was detected through these tests either.

Further, tests for blood and DNA in the laces, stitching and tread of the six pairs of shoes seized from Dennis's home yielded no results. The bag Dennis used to carry genealogy papers to his father's office and to bring the camp logbook home was likewise clean. Smith didn't find any blood in the keys of Dennis's Blackberry cellphone, and Richard's DNA was not found anywhere on the phone.

Problems with the investigation and breaches of proper police procedures were so numerous that Judge John Walsh instructed the jurors mid-trial:

> *At the end of the trial, it will be for you to determine whether evidence about the inadequacy of the police investigation alone, or along with other evidence, causes you to have a reasonable doubt about whether Dennis Oland committed the offence charged.*

CHAPTER TEN

Dennis Oland's Arrest

Diana Sedlacek and Oland got together about three times a week, including "fairly frequently" at his uptown office and, "often after church on Sunday." She commented, "He was very interested in wanting to share his week with me, show me what he had done . . . ask me questions about what he should do." They also travelled together "many times," and were planning a trip to Portland, Maine later that month. Sedlacek typically ended her messages with the affectionate sign-off, "Kisses."

A text she sent to Oland from her Darlings Island home at 6:44 p.m. went directly to voice mail. This was the controversial call to his cellphone that pinged off the Rothesay tower. Sedlacek said she believed Dick had turned off his cellphone, which was missing from the crime scene and was never recovered. Police contended that Dennis took the phone from his father's office after killing him to Renforth Wharf, near his home to dispose of it. Their theory proved groundless because their divers couldn't find the phone in the water and technicians couldn't prove Diana's last text pinged off the nearby cell tower to Richard's cell. A battery of tests carried out by the police and by Dennis Oland's defence team were inconclusive and the cellphone remains unlocated.

Police believed Dennis's motive for murder was financial. He was hundreds of thousands of dollars in debt and spent approximately fourteen thousand dollars per month more than he earned on items such as trips to Hungary, Italy, England, and Florida. As has been noted, he still owed his father more than $500,000 on the loan that bankrolled his divorce. With Richard's death, Dennis became either co-director or president of his father's three companies. He also received a payout of $150,000 as the co-executor of his father's will and trustee of an additional fund. Good financial news, at least, in a time of tragedy — but also, some said, a fiscal motive for murder.

Asked in his initial police interrogation who might have killed his father, Dennis ventured that it could have been someone looking for money for drugs, or it could have been Richard's "vindictive girlfriend." His willingness to speculate led police to conclude he was just trying to throw off suspicion against himself — lack of physical evidence was not suspicious; trying to help the police investigation was suspicious. Police tunnel vision was increasingly apparent in their determination to shape the evidence to fit their preconceived theories of Dennis Oland's guilt.

It didn't help public perception that police not only didn't arrest anyone for the crime, but they also refused to release any of the information they'd filed with the courts to justify their various search warrants. The police wouldn't tell reporters what they were looking for or if those searches were even related to the Oland homicide investigation. That police cone of silence, suggested Halifax media lawyer David Coles, "raised suspicions of the man-in-the-street there may be some miscarriage of justice."

Coles, on behalf of the CBC and the Saint John *Telegraph-Journal*, launched a legal challenge to the sealed search warrants in December 2011 — six months after the murder. Coles argued that a 1982 Supreme Court ruling required police to disclose any information they'd used to convince the courts to grant them a search warrant once the warrant itself was executed. The only exception to such blanket disclosure is for the kind of "hallmark" evidence only the killer could know, and which therefore might prove critical to winning a conviction. But as chief investigator Constable Stephen Davidson said later at Dennis's trial in a disingenuous attempt to keep the public out of the loop, "Basically, everything that we seized could be hallmark evidence." Police only wanted to make public those things that supported their theory that Dennis killed his father.

Davidson worried too that if the names of witnesses who'd provided information to police were unsealed, some of them would clam up or unnamed others might pressure them. Anthony Shaw, who worked in the building where the murder took place and had spoken to police early on, did change his mind and told the judge, he was now "done co-operating."

Davidson wasn't the only one who argued that the details in the search warrants should remain a secret — but for very different reasons. Gary Miller, a prominent New Brunswick criminal defence lawyer representing Dennis Oland, complained about the "media frenzy" and the already "poisoned atmosphere" in the city against his client. Bill Teed, who represented other members of the Oland family, warned that his clients' right to privacy had not only been invaded,

> *it's been run over by a truck . . . What this family has had to put up with and deal with as a result of this murder, as a result of the investigation, as a result of this media attention . . . the innocent rights that we try to protect for them has been just about drowned.*

In the end, Provincial Court Judge R. Leslie Jackson sided with the media and slowly unsealed warrant by un-redacted affidavit by unmasked name. The salacious details, incriminating tidbits and family secrets tumbled out — about the state of the Oland marriage, about Richard's mistress, about his relationship with his son.

Finally, on November 12, 2013 — two years, four months and five days after Richard Oland died in his office following "repeated blows" to his body, and after having interviewed more than sixty witnesses, seized 378 pieces of evidence and sent 243 items for forensic testing — Saint John police charged Dennis Oland with second-degree murder in the death of his father.

In Canada, murder is classified as either first or second degree. First-degree murder includes a great many categories that have no relevance here, but first and foremost includes "any killing that was planned and deliberate." Second-degree murder is defined as any murder that is not first-degree murder — so not planned and deliberate.

According to the Crown, Richard Oland's murder represented an act of spontaneous rage committed when the "bank of daddy" (as Alan Gold, lead counsel for the defence, indiscreetly labelled it) refused to cover his son's financial losses — making it second-degree murder. The maximum sentence for second-degree murder is twenty-five years without chance of parole; the minimum sentence is twenty-five years with eligibility for parole after ten years.

In laying the second-degree murder charge, police said they didn't have enough evidence to lay a charge of first-degree murder, which requires proof of "planning and deliberation." If it was indeed a spontaneous act of rage, where did the drywall hammer come from? There was no hammer in the office, so the murder weapon had to be brought in by the killer. Do you change into a Tyvek suit to avoid getting blood on your clothes, as some contend, in front of your intended victim? That might raise suspicions about what you were doing.

Or maybe you change into a coverall in the bathroom and then race back across the hall into the office and whale away into the victim with the hammer you had tucked into your pants before he sees you coming. Plausible. But not a very spontaneous act of rage. Kind of sounds planned and deliberate. And what was the motive for a planned and deliberate murder conceived and executed by a man who stood to gain little that would help his financial situation? So, the Crown mixed a spontaneous motive with a planned and deliberate execution to come up with a second-degree murder charge.

Nonetheless, the Crown and Police certainly went all out to convict Dennis Oland, guilt be damned. So why wasn't Dennis charged with first degree-murder, given the planned and deliberate nature of the crime? Careers are not built on unsolved murders of prominent citizens. The Crown needed a conviction so justice could be seen to be done, and who better to carry the can than a disgruntled family member who had conveniently visited the murder scene just an hour or so before the crime was committed by a person or persons unknown.

The year before laying charges, in November 2012, investigators had met with the Crown to lay out what they thought at the time was a beyond-reasonable-doubt case against Dennis Oland, but Saint John police chief Bill Reid said prosecutors asked for a "multitude" of additional information and forensics evidence before finally agreeing to proceed. Which was fine with Chief Reid. "We were in no hurry to make a mistake," he told reporters the day after the arrest.

Uncle Derek Oland was convinced they already had. He quickly issued a statement on behalf of the family declaring, "Dennis is, in fact, innocent, and we will support him and his family through the course of whatever legal actions unfold." Refusing to be drawn into the questions and gossip that had bubbled just below the surface of everyday life in Saint John for more than two years, Oland urged the community to "allow the evidence to be examined and the rule of law to unfold as it will."

In general terms, the mistakes made in focusing on Dennis Oland could be attributed to police inexperience, as Oland's defence team and other Canadian criminal lawyers observing the case suggested. As Toronto lawyer David Butt put it,

> *While most Canadian cities are blessed with miniscule numbers of homicides each year, the flip side is that homicide detectives there do not*

gain real-world experience very quickly. Take for example a city like Toronto, where best practices are constantly refined in the heat and light of dozens of cases per year, fought with vigour by defence counsel experienced in homicides. The reservoir of knowledge, skill and institutional memory inside a homicide squad like that is built on hundreds of tough-fought cases. This cumulative experiential advantage can quickly become worlds removed from a police department and court system lucky enough to deal with only the occasional homicide.

With one of the lowest homicide rates in Canada, Saint John police have few cases to solve, and most are drug or gang related. Butt goes on to say,

Even if evidence is mishandled in the way described, the typical response by the judge is to allow the jury to hear the evidence anyway and give it whatever weight they think it deserves in light of the errors in handling it. This avoids the binary admissible/inadmissible dichotomy, which can be extreme in some cases, and allows the jury to act in a more nuanced way as they see fit.

So, a year after police received the required additional direction from prosecutors on the further interviews and forensic work needed to make an arrest, the Saint John police did indeed lay charges against Dennis Oland. Although he had agreed to come in voluntarily on police request, police wanted a public show. With sirens howling and in front of media cameras, he was arrested at a car wash near Rothesay without incident and appeared in a Saint John courtroom a day later. His family — including his mother, wife, two sisters and uncle — were also in court and issued statements proclaiming his innocence.

Upon Oland's arrest, Chief Reid told reporters the Crown had approved the charge three weeks earlier. Reid said at the time no one else would be charged as a result of the police investigation. "It's very complicated. Unlike most serious crimes, we had very little evidence in terms of witnesses, people directing us, those types of things so it was always process driven." Reid described the investigation as a complex one that was like "putting together a mosaic."

> *Our members did a fantastic job, but it was a process-driven investigation, as opposed to someone saw something and they are our eyewitness, or here is where you are going to find this or here is where you are going to find that. We did not have anything like that in the case. We built a case from nothing, essentially.*

No one appeared to notice that Dennis is left-handed while the killer was clearly right-handed, having delivered a lethal blow to the left side of Richard Oland's head.

CHAPTER ELEVEN
The Quiet Man

Those who know him well say Dennis Oland is quiet, unassuming, pleasant and down-to-earth — and not given to sudden outbursts of temper, as those who might wish him ill would have it.

He was born on Valentine's Day in 1968 into the same affluent milieu as his father. Sixty-six reference letters were submitted to the court by family, friends, neighbours, businesses acquaintances and clergy, testifying to Dennis Oland's exemplary character. In his reference letter, his uncle Derek described him as "one of the most decent and kindest of men." Oland's lawyer, Alan Gold, told reporters Dennis was "overwhelmed" by the show of support.

Dennis Oland's mother, Connie, in her character letter to Justice John Walsh after her son's first trial, noted that her late husband had thought their son's personality was like that of her uncle, Gordon Fairweather. A Progressive Conservative Member of Parliament for the New Brunswick riding of Royal from 1962 to 1974, Fairweather was named the first head of the Canadian Human Rights Commission in 1977 by a Liberal government and from 1989 to 1992 served as founding chair of the Immigration and Refugee Board of Canada. "Dennis has always had a caring personality and 'stood up' for the underdog," she wrote.

She noted that when her mother-in-law died in 1995, it was Dennis to whom Richard turned for help in planning his mother's funeral. As their children grew up, Connie and Richard maintained close family ties, she explained. For example, even when Dennis was living and working in Toronto, he would come home for their annual family ski trip. He, in turn, taught his own children to ski and sail and canoe, she wrote, describing him as a "caring father," with "great patience." He has been more of a father to his stepson Andrew than was the boy's biological father.

"He doesn't have his father's aggressive style," said Robert McFadden, Richard Oland's accountant, who now plays the same role with Dennis at investment firm Far End Corporation — still in the Canterbury Street premises where Richard was murdered. In his opinion, Dennis Oland was not a man prone to irrational and murderous outbursts of rage, McFadden said.

For a time, Dennis headed the local YMCA; as a teenager, Dennis had worked as a YMCA canoe instructor before graduating to become a canoeing director. At eighteen, he served as interim camp director for a few weeks until the position was filled by someone with more experience, Connie said.

Dennis and Lisa were active in the provincial Progressive Conservative Party. In an official gazette from April 2004, he is listed as the representative of the Saint John-Kings Progressive Conservative Party District Association. Connie noted that in 2010, Lisa Oland ran Conservative candidate Dorothy Shephard's winning campaign to become MLA for Saint John-Lancaster, while Dennis worked in the background. Re-elected in every subsequent election, she has served as Minister of Health and in 2022 she was reappointed Minister of Social Development.

Like his father, Dennis Oland was committed to community volunteer work, helping with local schools or as a member of the YMCA board. Gary Howard, a friend and business associate, shared the occasional coffee or beer with Dennis. He said in a 2011 interview that Oland devoted himself to his volunteer role, adding, "It wasn't just taking a seat (on the board); he did it for the right reasons."

Both Dennis and Richard Oland were involved with the Greater Saint John Economic Development Agency — Enterprise Saint John — established in 1994 and renamed Develop Saint John in 2017. Dennis Oland was about to become chairman in 2008 when newly divorced, he withdrew, citing family reasons. Develop Saint John is a not-for-profit agency with an annual budget of two million plus dollars, funded by the city, several surrounding municipalities, the province and the Atlantic Canada Opportunities Agency. Dennis had to drop most projects to focus on his children after the marriage breakdown, according to Connie Oland.

Dennis attended Rothesay Collegiate, the same private school as his father and several other family members. He was born with a 45 per cent hearing deficit. He later went to Bishop's College School in Sherbrooke, Quebec, where he was a cadet officer and head of a unit. In both schools, he participated in sports and leadership training. Missing friends and family, he returned to Saint John High School for Grade 12. In 1990, he graduated with a Bachelor of Arts degree with a major in political science from the University of New Brunswick. After graduation, he worked in the investment industry in Toronto for a few years before moving back to Saint John. The New Brunswick Securities Commission listed him in 2011 as an investment dealer with CIBC World Markets Inc.

Dennis got his first job at the age of nine. He delivered newspapers and used some of his earnings to buy a small motorcycle. From that bike he learned the basics of fixing motors, often assisted by his father. "Together, over the years, they worked on boat motors, cars, stoves and washing machines," Connie said. These days in his spare time, Dennis is a hobbyist who enjoys restoring vintage cars, including a much-admired mint-condition, dark green 1967 Volvo Amazon 123 GT. In a June 2014 article he published on the website of IPD, a company that provides parts and accessories for restoring old cars, he explained how he became a lover of Volvos, particularly the 123 Amazon GT, a model that his grandfather P.W. Oland had once owned. In 2010, Dennis set out to find and restore one. However, finding another green 1967 Volvo 123 GT with tan interior proved easier said than done.

"Finally, in the winter of 2012, I spotted an ad on Kijiji that there was a car in Kitchener, Ontario, a 1967 Volvo 123 GT, 43,000 miles, runs, needs work . . . green." Dennis went to look at it. He bought the car for $2,500 and paid five hundred dollars for a second Volvo — a 122 — for extra parts and panels. He then arranged to have both cars shipped home to New Brunswick.

His love of all things mechanical, particularly cars, is reflected in his being elected chairman of the Maritimes branch of the Canadian Automobile Association at age thirty, a position he held from 2002 to 2006. In a November 2015 article on the case in *VICE* entitled "Blood, Beer, and the Maritime Rumour Mill," journalist Julia Wright commented after spotting Dennis and Lisa leaving Port City Royal restaurant, a trendy Saint John eatery, in the Volvo: "In a town of 12-year-old Toyota Corollas and brand-new Ford F-150s, a ride like that stands out: I'd often spotted it parked on Charlotte Street. I'd even tweeted a picture of it, once: 'My ride's here.' I had no idea, then, who it belonged to. I sure did now."

The car "is a real head turner and I am enjoying it a lot," Dennis wrote in his article.

A slender, youthful, quite bland-looking man neither tall nor short, with close-cropped sandy gray hair and a penchant for smart-casual clothes, his general demeanor was captured by a news photographer at Richard Oland's funeral and commented on by his detractors who accused him of having an inappropriate smile when he should have looked distraught. In fact, the corners of his lips curl upward naturally in good times and bad. To the delight of political cartoonists, Andrew Scheer, former leader of the Conservative Party of Canada (2017-2020), has a similar demeanor.

Many would describe Dennis as nondescript, just the kind of person who would not stand out in a crowd or be easily remembered. He'd make a good spy, unlike his larger-than-life, taller and heavier father. This laid-back outlook was observed by many during his father's funeral on July

12, 2011, where Dennis delivered one of the readings from Scripture. "He was calm and collected; I could see no agitation at all," cousin Tom Oland said.

The police combed through his prior life after his arrest, trying to find proof of his poor judgement and weak character. The worst they could come up with was that in 1988, a twenty-year-old Dennis fatally injured his father's $25,000 show-jumping horse after losing control of his Jeep Cherokee and horse trailer when he swerved to avoid a cat on a highway outside Brockville, Ontario. Whether that demonstrates a positive empathetic character in trying to save a cat or someone prone to panic in a crisis depends on your perspective. It does show how deep police had to dig to find even innocuous incidents suggesting Dennis Oland was a flawed man. Whenever he was reached by members of the media after his father's murder, Dennis declined comment, saying only, "I don't think this is a good time to talk."

Until March 2020, Dennis and Lisa lived in SevenAcres, the Rothesay home where his grandparents, P.W. and Mary Oland, had raised his father, his Uncle Derek and his Aunt Jane. Dennis and Lisa were married in the Rothesay United Church in 2009 and were raising a blended family of four children in the wealthy enclave.

"What is Rothesay?" the novelist Mordecai Richler once asked a Saint John cabbie. "It is a very good neighbourhood," the cabbie told him. "The Irvings live there." Dennis would just say it was home, the place where he has lived for all but a few years of his life. "Welcome to the feudal Maritimes," Richler wrote in the late 1990s in a travel piece for a Canadian publication. "Whatever isn't owned by the Irvings in the Maritimes belongs to the McCains or has no redeeming value."

Rothesay would argue Richler needed to do further

research. By their standards, the Irvings are newcomers. "The Irvings are new money," said former and long-time Rothesay mayor William Bishop. "The Olands are old money." Perhaps, but in a Google search of Rothesay notables over the last one hundred years, the Olands do not even get a mention. Bishop is quoted in a *Maclean's* magazine feature by Meagan Campbell on the Oland case in the December 30, 2015 edition, published just after the guilty verdict: "I think you find that with Maritime families — the Irvings, the McCains, the Olands — they don't try to dominate or take over. They play their role, and they fit in. It seems embedded in us."

Like his father, Dennis is an expert sailor. Connie shared an anecdote in her letter to the court about father and son competing against one another in a 2007 sailing race. The boat on which Dennis Oland was crewing passed the finish line before his father's. "They both got a chuckle out of this."

> *While he was no doubt suffering some financial stress after an expensive divorce in 2007-2008, 'suffering' is a relative term. His father loaned him the money — in fact, as noted earlier, more than $500,000 — to buy out his first wife's share of their property as part of the divorce settlement. But full repayment waits until he and his sisters receive their inheritance when their mother dies. Dennis's debt will be deducted from his share. Meanwhile he makes monthly interest payments when he can.*

In 2008, Dennis finalized his divorce from Lesley Phinney, whom he met at Dalhousie University. The Truro, Nova Scotia native proceeded to carry on an extended affair with her ex-father-in-law. The affair has been cited by some in Saint John as a more plausible motive for Dennis to murder his father in 2011 than the feeble circumstantial motives upon which the Crown based its case. Like Diana Sedlacek, Lesley is a fashion-conscious petite blonde and a real estate agent with the same RE/MAX office in Saint John. Remarkably, neither the Crown nor the defence made any reference to the affair in court, although lead defence lawyer Alan Gold in an unguarded moment later admitted that would have been one hell of a motive.

In Rothesay, the Olands blend in — but almost everyone in that town is well off. The average household net worth is $2.6 million, average annual income almost $300,000. House prices in the Maritimes are the lowest in Canada. In 2023, the average house price in New Brunswick was $185,200 according to Statistics Canada. In Rothesay, however, it was $305,269 — still far below the national average of $713,700.

The Oland clan was known to hand out free beer around the yacht club. Lisa Oland opened an upscale, quirky designer clothing consignment shop around the time of the murder. The Exchange on Germain sold items such as a Burberry blouse, on sale for ninety-six dollars. A chart on the wall outlined how to dress for the Kentucky Derby. When he was awaiting trial, Dennis helped her selling clothes occasionally. The shop has since closed.

"They (the Olands) seem to be just good, regular people in the community," Mayor Bishop was quoted in the *Maclean's* article.

Dennis was not involved in Oland brewery concerns except for a job one summer when he was a teenager. Richard discouraged his son from a career working for the brewery, even though Dennis was close with his cousin Andrew, who would ultimately become Moosehead's president. Andrew and Dennis Oland are neighbours. Instead, Dennis became an investment advisor, working for several years in Toronto before returning to Saint John in 1994. As an investment advisor at CIBC Wood Gundy, one of his clients was his father but, as even Dennis admitted to police, he was more his father's order-taker than his investment advisor. Dick kept one million dollars on account at his son's firm.

On Tuesday, October 21, 2008, Dennis's most tangible connection to his father — a boat — burned to the water-line due to an electrical fire while docked at a marina in St. Petersburg, Florida. The *Aloma II*, an eighteen-metre motorboat with a distinctive canoe stern built in Sydney, Nova Scotia in 1910, had been part of the Oland family since 1947, when Dennis's great-grandfather, George Bauld Oland, who originated the Moosehead brand that very same year, bought it as a beat-up military vessel.

Boating has been part of the Oland family since at least the time when George B. learned to ply the harbour waters from Dartmouth to Halifax on the *Gambrinus*, a barge used to transport beer kegs. Perhaps that's why Richard felt so comfortable on the boat. "Dad was completely at peace on the *Aloma*," Dennis records in a written history of the *Aloma* he wrote for the Royal Kennebecasis Yacht Club newsletter that he compiled post-fire.

"As a child growing up in the 1970s and 1980s, it was truly the good old days. The best of times was with that boat," the *Telegraph-Journal* quoted Dennis as saying in a news story about the *Aloma's* loss. "My sisters and I grew up on this boat and with my father as the captain you could always count on a big adventure for every trip and he never let us down,"

Dennis Oland wrote in the *Aloma's* history. He wrote about his fond childhood memories as a Royal Yacht Club "Club Rat," a junior sailor and "a great lover" of the family's boat, where he and his sisters would get some quality time with their dad. He recalled landing the boat on his own, on his first try — "the proudest 12-year-old in the world."

"Dammit!" his grandmother Mary said at the time, "you drive just like your father."

"I didn't get to see him a lot, and when we got on the boat that all changed," he added of his father, describing him then as "relaxed, a huge smile on his face . . . If there was water, we went there, and if there wasn't, we sometimes tried anyway."

At the time of the fire, the *Aloma* belonged to William Cory and Betty Sattler, Americans who purchased it from the Olands in 2002 and who were trained at the helm by Dennis. He was "a delightful young man," Sattler wrote in an email to *Maclean's*, describing how she watched him maneuver the *Aloma* through difficult waters expertly, "with two fingers on the wheel."

Rothesay locals relate that Dennis is spotted walking from time to time through the grounds of the yacht club where he did so much of his growing up, engaged in the pursuit — boating — that of all things brought him closest to his father.

CHAPTER TWELVE
Theory of the Case

Like an NHL hockey team that finishes the regular season at the top of the standings by a mile, scores the most goals and allows the fewest, but then gets knocked out in the first round of the playoffs, the Oland defence team was complacent. The defence called only three witnesses, including Dennis himself, in the belief the jury would not convict on inconclusive and circumstantial evidence. They were wrong. They forgot the wisdom of never taking anything for granted. Even if you have the best team and should be winning, you can lose.

"Never did I expect the jury to come back and say, guilty," Oland said in the fall of 2015 in reflecting on his conviction after a trial stretching over four months — the longest and most expensive in Saint John's history. As recommended by the jury, in February 2016, he was sentenced to life in prison (twenty-five years) with a possibility of parole in ten years.

"There's no evidence," said an exasperated Gary Miller, one of Dennis Oland's team of lawyers.

Three years of legal wrangling ensued.

As noted earlier, Dennis Oland was in the crosshairs from the moment his father's body was found by a police force that typically investigated just two or three homicides a year. Police searched the uptown, picking through garbage cans. The canine unit searched the alley and surrounding streets. A constant police presence remained outside Oland's office for several weeks. At least fifteen police officers worked on the case, but two years passed before Dennis was charged with second-degree murder in the fall of 2013. The police took an inordinate amount of time to lay charges, although they did not consider anyone else a suspect.

"It was very clear from the beginning who the perpetrator was," Chief Reid told reporters at the time of Oland's arrest.

Everybody knows the first thing to do when assessing a potential suspect in a crime is to determine whether the accused has an alibi. A murder case requires two pieces of information: When did the victim die, and where was the suspect at this estimated time of death? In this case, plenty of video footage showed Dennis Oland arriving and leaving his father's office.

But it wasn't the police who found the video evidence of Dennis Oland's activities on July 6, 2011. The CCTV footage of his movements in Saint John and later in Rothesay was obtained and provided to the police by a team of private investigators hired by the Oland family, according to Dennis Oland. Evidence was emerging that Dennis had an alibi, but the police pressed on.

Inexplicably, the pathologist never pinpointed the exact time of Richard Oland's death. The office air conditioning was cranked up, which could have slowed decomposition. However, there were three witnesses, two who heard a noisy scuffle and another who heard voices raised in a dispute coming from Oland's office across an alley an hour or more after Dennis Oland left Canterbury Street. He was seen, again on video, shopping in Rothesay at a drug store and a grocery store. This was at about the same time his father was overheard arguing with someone and loud thumps that lasted ten seconds were heard by two workers in the print shop below his office.

Further, plenty of people did not have a good relationship with Richard Oland. For one thing, it was no secret that he had affairs with any number of women, most of them married. Possibly a jealous husband or an angry ex decided to act.

As discussed earlier, Oland had a reputation around Rothesay and Saint John as being tough. Even his own daughter Lisa described him as hard-nosed. So, it is conceivable he pushed a business associate too far. And as has been noted, there were those who said Richard had had business dealings with organized crime. The controversy surrounding the failure of the Can Sugar Refinery was never probed by Saint John police.

It's also not clear why Richard Oland's long-time mistress Diana Sedlacek or her husband, Jiri Sedlacek, were quickly ruled out by police as suspects in his murder. Dennis Oland's defence team originally contended that Sedlacek or her now-estranged husband were credible alternative suspects in his death. The Sedlaceks were each others' alibi that they were at home on Darlings Island that evening. The alibi doesn't rule out one of them conceivably hiring someone to do the job.

Jiri insisted he had nothing to do with the death of Richard Oland, and police believed him. He testified at Oland's first trial in 2015 and faced a rigorous cross-examination by the defence, arguing that the Saint John Police Force's investigation into Jiri Sedlacek was inadequate.

Later, the defence dropped that line of attack and did not call the cuckolded husband to the stand in Dennis Oland's second trial. In a complete reversal of tactics, Dennis Oland's defence argued successfully against bringing Sedlacek back to the stand at the retrial as a witness. "It is our position that his evidence is not relevant . . . and has no probative value," Michael Lacy told Justice Terrence Morrison. The Canadian judiciary system utilizes the term "probative," which also signifies "prove to be worthy." The judge deliberated for about an hour before agreeing and ruling Sedlacek's evidence inadmissible. Either he was lying at the first trial about when he knew about Dick and Diana, or at age eighty-seven was not able to recall events clearly. No charges were brought against Jiri Sedlacek for his testimony.

Diana Sedlacek, now separated from Jiri, moved to Victoria, B.C. in early 2013. In March 2013, she posted a comment on Facebook, "Living true to myself from my heart – 2 years of breaking away – emerging into a world of possibilities." She returned to testify at Dennis's first trial. Her video evidence was used at the retrial. Meanwhile, Jiri moved to Hampton, a town of 4,300 people on the Kennebecasis River midway between Moncton and Saint John.

Robert McFadden was aware of his employer's numerous relationships with women over the years because he recorded all of Oland's expenses. But they never talked about it, he said, even though Dennis had asked him to at one point. His sister Lisa, who had found Viagra in her parents' medicine cabinet, was concerned that the affair with Sedlacek had become too public and hoped her father would end it. The siblings thought McFadden might help with that.

McFadden concurred with Dennis's view that certain reports suggested the relationship was cooling, at least as far as his father was concerned, which might have worried Sedlacek. "The matter had been festering for some time," McFadden said. As noted, Connie disingenuously referred to Diana Sedlacek as "Dick's friend," as if she did not know her.

CHAPTER THIRTEEN
Plenty of Suspects

Alan D. Gold, one of Canada's best criminal lawyers with a sterling reputation and an old hand in the courtroom, is not easily startled into spontaneous speech. But news that Richard Oland had had an extra-marital affair with his son's first wife came as a shock to the stocky, greying barrister.

Gold had stepped out of a Toronto courtroom to take a phone call from me in September 2016. From his startled reaction to my question, it was obvious that this was the first he had heard about Richard Oland's affair with Lesley Oland.

"That's a powerful motive!" he exclaimed in surprise. *"How is it I wasn't informed?"*

Following the surprise and dismay of a guilty verdict, he and co-counsel Gary Miller had cheered themselves up by flying to Boston to watch a Bruins hockey game. Gold believed he had the complete confidence of his team of New Brunswick lawyers. However, there was still crucial information not shared with the Torontonian if for no other reason than his fellow defence counsellors just did not think to mention something that happened well before the murder. Miller no doubt figured if it came up in court, he could handle it. The matter never materialized, and it was forgotten.

Gold ended the call by explaining his need to get back into the courtroom; he promised to resume the interview by telephone the following day. When he did so, he was far more circumspect and used a voice-altering device to avoid being recorded. The question I had posed to him the previous day had been, "Did you know about the affair with Lesley Oland and, if not, would knowing that have changed how you presented Dennis Oland's defence?"

The theory among some in Saint John goes that the jury might have based its decision to render a guilty verdict on common knowledge of that affair, even though it was not admitted in court as evidence. Jury members could have unanimously concluded it was a revenge killing with Dennis, as the last known person to see Oland alive, the most likely candidate.

It was reported in the *National Post* that after Richard Oland's death the court quickly sealed the divorce records of Dennis and Lesley Oland. Lesley Oland has declined to comment about her relationship with the elder Oland.

"Oh yes, we were aware of the rumours of affairs," Dennis Oland acknowledged in an email. He continued,

They were started by Diana Sedlacek. You can see from texts and emails produced in court that

Diana was a very jealous type. She sent regular emails to the police about various things, even saying that my son Henry is not my son. He most certainly is my son . . . what silliness.

We did learn [through a private investigator hired by the Olands] there was another woman named Hilary Brock that dad had a relationship with. Diana would mention her in angry emails to Dad. Apparently, there was some relationship overlap where Dad was seeing them both at the same time.

We investigated this, but we were not able to find out when that relationship ended or if it did. We found photos of dad and Hilary on trips together, so this confirmed it. Also, a friend of Hilary's came forward to tell us and gave info to prove it. We informed the police about this other woman because we (and the police) had also received an anonymous tip about her. The police interviewed her after the first trial, but she denied everything and that was the end of it for the police. The police never properly investigated this.

Oland's investigator found that Brock, a striking woman with long red hair, had trysts with Oland at the Chipman Hill Suites and booked couple's massages or went on ski trips to Sugar Loaf and sailing excursions on his yacht. Brock is a wealth advisor with National Bank Financial, working out of its Saint John office; Oland was a client. A life-long Rothesay resident who lives near the Oland homes, Brock has declined to comment about her relationship with Oland.

Drawn to the Oland case "by the *Peyton Place* drama," Rothesay resident Martin Fineberg, himself a criminal lawyer, was a regular courtroom spectator at Dennis's first trial and remains among those who still believe Dennis is guilty. *Peyton Place*, for those younger than 65, was an American television soap opera that aired from 1964 to 1969 inspired by a steamy 1956 novel of the same name by Grace Metalious, about infidelity and murder in small-town New England. It was the top selling book in the United States for more than a year, surpassed only by the Bible. It was banned in Canada, but its popularity led to it being widely bootlegged.

Fineberg's theory, which he readily shared with fellow courtroom regulars, held that Dennis brought a protective garment called a Tyvek (similar to those house painters wear) to his father's office on July 6, 2011. On his third visit when he returned for the logbook, he donned the coverall, battered his father to death, and then buried the evidence in a nearby roadbed that was under construction and was paved over the next day. Fineberg was acquainted with the prosecutors on the Oland case from other case files and "attended out of personal interest." Fineberg had known about Oland's relationship with Dennis's ex-wife. "Everybody knows."

A glaring lack of hard evidence against Dennis Oland — no smoking gun as it were — didn't prevent Fineberg or the pool of reporters covering the trials from confidently believing Dennis Oland guilty of the murder.

CHAPTER FOURTEEN

Six Generations of Brewers

Susannah Culverwell Oland, who founded the Oland brewing dynasty in 1867, was inducted into the Nova Scotia Business Hall of Fame in 1993, the only woman entrepreneur so honoured as of 2023, and seven years ahead of her legendary grandson, Colonel Sidney Oland, in 2000.

Even in death Susannah Oland controlled the enterprise she spent her life building. She stipulated in her will in 1886 that her youngest son George Woodhouse Culverwell, known as W.C., would be the chief officer of Oland breweries. She bequeathed her one-quarter share in the company to him (two-thirds) and his sister Huldah (one-third). W.C. quickly bought out his sister's share, giving him 50 per cent ownership, with older brothers John and Conrad each having a 25 per cent share.

Susannah's will indicated that she was "anxious they should succeed me and take my place and partnership interest in the business." Logically, John and Conrad would be next in line to acquire controlling interest in the brewery. However, there did not seem to be any resentment that the youngest brother was put charge.

When the Dartmouth brewery was destroyed in the Halifax explosion in 1917, W.C. and his oldest son, George Bauld Oland, moved brewing operations to Saint John, New Brunswick with the purchase of the Red Ball Brewery. Everyone called George B. "the Major" when he came home after the First World War, because of his rank and war record. With this move to Saint John, the family was divided into two branches. His younger brother Sidney, called "the Colonel" for *his* war exploits, remained in Halifax and continued to build the brewery business there, purchasing the Alexander Keith brewery in 1928.

W.C. expanded in New Brunswick, buying the James Ready brewery in Lancaster, a suburb of Saint John. The Major handled the day-to-day operations under the name New Brunswick Breweries.

The struggle between The Major in Saint John and the Colonel in Halifax for control of the Oland brewing empire, which had begun in W.C.'s lifetime, ended with the assets divided between them after his death. W.C. died in 1933, leaving control of his two Halifax breweries, Red Ball in Saint John and 20 per cent of the Lancaster breweries to Sidney.

George B., who was very accomplished in his own right, felt that as the oldest son he deserved better than he got from his father in life and in death. There appears to have been an antipathy between father and son that is reflected in the former's will — W.C. made a point of returning a watch with gold face that

George B. had given him. Dividing up his considerable assets, W.C. left his wife Ella, 35 per cent and his children 10 per cent each, with the exception of George, who only received 5 per cent. He gifted shares in his five corporations to George — conditional on him repaying his outstanding debts to Olands Brewery Limited within a five-year period.

Sidney seems to have taken his status as the golden child for granted. In the end, George B. controlled most of the less valuable New Brunswick operation, and Sidney ran things in Nova Scotia. George B. never got over his resentment of his younger brother for getting the lion's share.

When W.C. divided the Oland brewing assets unequally between his sons, he was sowing the seeds of a discord that lasted through the subsequent generations. The rift within the Oland family branches, followed by the breakdown between Derek and Richard over control of Moosehead fed the narrative that Dennis had an acrimonious relationship with his father and killed him.

Of George B.'s seven children, one showed particular interest in the family business. Throughout his career, Philip Warburton (P.W.), father to Derek and Richard, tried to turn family competition to his advantage and sought to outsell his rival Halifax cousins. He started in the brewing industry at fourteen, working summers at the Red Ball Brewery.

Tall and ruggedly built, P.W. graduated with a Bachelor of Science degree in chemistry in 1932 from the University of New Brunswick. Then he went to brewing school overseas. He studied brewing and malting at the University of Birmingham in England. During his time abroad, he worked in Copenhagen in some of Europe's oldest breweries, Carlsberg and Tuborg, learning even more about brewing and recipe building.

On his return to New Brunswick, P.W. went to work for his father, managing the existing production line of Oland beers. But he also brought with him a new idea: P.W. wanted to brew a European-style lager. His father, however, was not interested, and he quickly shut down the idea when P.W. asked if he could put it into production.

Being his father's son, P.W. decided it was better to ask for forgiveness than permission. In 1937, with his father away in Boston for medical treatment, it seemed like a good time to break with tradition. By the time his father found out, he had already put his recipe into production, calling it Alpine Lager. Inspired by a Christmas card illustration, the original label featured the world-famous Matterhorn Mountain in the Swiss Alps. It was the Maritimes' first lager and quickly became its most popular beer.

George B.'s reluctance to incorporate P.W.'s ideas was perhaps ironic given his own penchant for innovation and change. One day browsing through the James Ready company files, George B. had come across the unused registered tradename name "Moosehead." The name Moosehead brought to mind the majesty of the animal so plentiful in the Canadian Shield wilderness — tough, proud and truly Canadian. He had found the perfect symbol with which to turn the Oland family brewery into a Canadian icon. In 1933, the Major introduced Moosehead Pale Ale to the public, the first beer to bear the Moosehead brand. In 1947, the brewery changed its name to Moosehead Breweries from New Brunswick Breweries.

P.W. made personal forays into New Brunswick beer parlours and hotels to chat with beer drinkers and find out face-to-face how Oland beers were being received. To introduce new customers to their brands and increase sales, the Olands joined the retailers and trades that supplied welcome-wagon baskets of their goods and coupons given to new home buyers who took up residence in Saint John, Halifax and Dartmouth. In that way they received lists of newcomers and sought to make them loyal Oland customers.

During the Second World War, P.W. served with the Canadian artillery and remained involved with the militia after the war, retiring as a brigadier in 1961. Hardworking and industrious, P.W. married a local girl, Mary Frink, and cut a conservative figure. He would opt for economy class air tickets rather than upgrade and shunned overt displays of extravagance. It is all in the eye of the beholder. A young Paul Zed, son of an immigrant dentist, who grew up to become a Saint John lawyer and a prominent Liberal Member of Parliament for Saint John Harbour, remembers being impressed seeing P.W. driving around in "a Rolls or maybe it was a Bentley." It was in fact a late model Volvo but to Zed it was "a very fine car."

P.W. and Mary stayed close to home, limiting recreational pleasures to Rothesay and Saint John — playing local golf courses, curling in winter and cruising the Kennebecasis and Saint John Rivers in the summertime. P.W. dressed in off-the-rack suits. He was last of the Olands to be a certified brew master.

While P.W. lived a generally frugal life for such a wealthy man, he did take residence in an expansive Rothesay home, SevenAcres. A young Zed would see Richard Oland ride past on his horse on Sunday afternoons and wish it was him.

It hasn't always been an easy path for the Oland brewery, which has endured two fires, Prohibition, the Halifax Explosion, the Great Depression and two World Wars as it expanded beer sales across Canada, into the United States and eventually, around the world. The Nova Scotia branch of the Oland family sold out to Labatt Breweries of Canada in 1971. Labatt is part of the multinational giant Anheuser-Busch InBev group of companies.

"It's fitting that we share our anniversary with the country we call home," explained Andrew Oland, president of Moosehead Breweries, in a 2017 interview on the company's 150th anniversary. "Like Canada, we've faced challenges along our path, but — like Canada — we've risen to the challenge time and time again to not only endure but thrive. And through it all, we've been able to remain fiercely independent and stay true to our own ideals."

Although Richard Oland had resigned from Moosehead Breweries, he was still often viewed through the lens of the family business; he also owned a third of the company until 2007. When reporting on the murder, national media often referred to him as "Dick Oland, former vice-president of Moosehead, an internationally known brand," rather than as "Dick Oland, president of his investment company, Far End Corporation."

How has his murder affected the family business? Derek, now the chairman of the Moosehead board of directors, represented the public face of the Oland family throughout the investigation and trials. Although Moosehead is a small company in the global brewing universe, it is an essential pillar of the New Brunswick economy, providing about three hundred fifty jobs.

In 2018, market researchers estimated Moosehead held as much as 3.8 per cent of the Canadian beer market and that year generated $247.1 million in revenue. While current Moosehead production numbers are hard to obtain, as of 2014, the Moosehead brewery had the capacity to produce

600 million bottles of beer annually. Gordon Pitts, author of *Codfathers: Lessons from the Atlantic Business Elite*, notes the Oland family is among the few to have successfully navigated the times. "They are one of the oldest families in the Maritimes in terms of being in the same business for 150 years or so . . . and they have survived in an industry that has seen huge change."

The Olands rank with the McCains, Crosbys, Ganongs, Irvings and Sobeys as the cohort of Maritime family business dynasties. They are pillars of the community, providing life-long employment for thousands of people and goods for a global market. The McCains produce potatoes and frozen foods; the Crosbys built a fortune in molasses; the Ganongs put the community of St. Stephens on the map with their chocolate and candy factory. Everybody knows the oil-rich Irvings, and "there are few of us who haven't filled a grocery cart at Sobeys." The Olands brew beer.

P.W. Oland was the last in the line of hands-on Oland family brewers who developed new products. Today, the Oland brewers are administrators. The independently owned Oland brewing dynasty is today a shadow of what it once was when it controlled the Maritime market. Despite the shrinkage, Moosehead remains the fourth-largest brewing company in Canada after Molson, Labatt and Sleeman.

In Market Square on the waterfront in downtown Saint John, a life-size bronze statue of a moose is accompanied by signs mounted on a fence along the Boardwalk. These include a timeline, photos, graphics and text telling the story of Moosehead Breweries. It's an acknowledgement of the contribution the Oland family has made to the city's prosperity and the province. The company has been family owned and controlled for six generations. Derek Oland is executive chairman of the board, and his three sons, the great-great-great grandsons of company founders Susannah and John James Dunn Oland, hold executive positions. Andrew is president and chief executive officer, and Patrick is chief financial officer. Matthew is vice president supply chain. Day-to-day operations are handled by a non-family member, Patrick Parent, vice president operations.

Dennis Oland likes to point out the company's success is due in no small part to the modernizations that Richard Oland introduced before he and Moosehead parted company. As vice president of operations, he embraced new technologies that resulted in Moosehead having one of the fastest beer bottling lines in the world at the time.

The family brand has had its share of notoriety even before the murder. At the beginning of the 21st century, Moosehead was so popular, thieves took to hijacking tractor trailers full of its product. In August 2004, a shipment of more than 50,000 cans of Moosehead bound for Mexico went missing. The driver responsible for the shipment was arrested in Ontario and later sentenced to nineteen months in jail. Most of the beer, easily identified by its Spanish-language labeling, was recovered. Also, according to an RCMP news release, "Six of the cans were discovered with bite marks in them indicating a bear had, at one point, been into the beer."

Given the quirky nature of the event, the story made international headlines. Seizing on the free publicity, Moosehead sold T-shirts that read "Beer Heist Tour '04" and made opportune statements to the media saying, "If someone offers you a cold Moosehead in a can that has Spanish on it, the beer is hot." Then again in September 2007, an even larger shipment of Moosehead — 77,000 cans and 44,000 bottles — was stolen in Mississauga, Ontario. A company spokesman urged Moosehead drinkers to "stock up," and told a reporter that, "It strikes us the thieves obviously know what the consumers want."

CHAPTER FIFTEEN

Dennis Oland's Preliminary Hearing

On May 12, 2014, three years after Richard Oland's grisly murder, the preliminary inquiry of his son Dennis finally began. The proceedings continued sporadically until mid-December. Dozens of witnesses were subpoenaed to testify, including fifty-two Saint John police officers. Provincial Court Judge Ronald LeBlanc, who presided over the proceedings, expressed some concern and many reservations in his findings about the quality of the evidence, the way it had been collected and the rush to judgement by law enforcement.

Justice LeBlanc placed a publication ban over the proceedings, but *The Canadian Press* had a reporter there for most of the hearings, and other media outlets sent reporters from time to time to take notes to be used in post-trial coverage. Curious members of the public, other lawyers, and Oland family and friends also attended. The evidence police had against Dennis Oland spread by word of mouth — the talk of the town in the summer of 2014.

Courts use preliminary hearings to decide whether there is enough evidence to send a case to trial. They also protect the accused from needless, and indeed, improper, exposure to public scrutiny when prosecutors don't have enough evidence to warrant continuing the process. The Canadian system of justice is rooted in the principle that an accused is innocent until proven guilty. The onus is on the prosecution to provide the proof. Sadly, however, once accused and the charges made public, defendants are presumed guilty by society at large and must prove their innocence. Even when a "not guilty" verdict is rendered, in the public mind, the accused probably just got off on a technicality.

At the preliminary hearing, the prosecutor presents the most important parts of the evidence. If this is judged insufficient to convict, the court will dismiss the charge. But that almost never happens. If, as is far more likely, the Court determines there is enough evidence, the accused is committed to trial. This test of the Crown's evidence often leads to a plea deal, but this did not happen in Dennis Oland's preliminary hearing. Although the evidence against him was entirely circumstantial, details of his dire finances and the police's contention that he was the last one to see Richard Oland alive gave the Crown confidence their case was sufficiently strong.

But it wasn't a "slam dunk" for the Crown — not by any means. In fact, much of the evidence cast doubt upon the theory that Dennis Oland was a murderer. The defence, led by eminent Toronto lawyer Alan Gold, raised many doubts about the conduct of the Saint John police and its investigation. Gold's reputation is well-earned. He practices criminal law at the trial and appellate levels. He has appeared as counsel before all court levels in Ontario as well as in other provinces and argued more than fifty cases at the Supreme Court of Canada.

Justice LeBlanc is a former Crown attorney from Bathurst, a small seaport 364 kilometres, a three and a half hour drive northeast of Saint John on New Brunswick's Atlantic coast at the mouth of the Nepisiguit River on Chaleur Bay. At one time a Mi'kmaw summer camp, it was settled by the Acadians in the late 1600s and is now mainly a tourism and sports fishing centre. However, the town of 5,400 has unusually high crime rates — 58 per cent higher than the national average. Violent crime rates in Bathurst are even worse, 94 per cent higher than the national average, with illicit drug trafficking figuring prominently in the mix. This made LeBlanc qualified to handle a high-profile case such as this one.

By intriguing coincidence, the judge at Dennis Oland's first trial, John Walsh, and lead prosecutor, P. J. Veniot in the Oland case came from the town of Miramichi — also in the same far northeast corner of the province, just 74 kilometres south of Bathurst — and were accustomed to the same legal challenges. They too would have had plenty of experience handling serious crime cases. Miramichi crime rates are 36 per cent higher than the national average, and violent crimes are 68 per cent higher. Both Miramichi and Bathurst are among the top eight most dangerous places to live in the province.

The biggest city in northern New Brunswick at 17,500, Miramichi and the surrounding area are popular tourist draws, notwithstanding the high crime rates. It is home to the Miramichi Fish and Game Club on the Miramichi River, of which Richard Oland and friends were longstanding members. The Miramichi River is famous as the spawning ground for Atlantic Salmon, the king of game fish, producing nearly half the rod-caught salmon in North America. For more than a century, the Miramichi has attracted elite sport fishermen from all over the world. Oland spent eight days there just before his murder.

If the New Brunswick Justice Department, in assigning judges and prosecutors from as far away from Saint John as possible, hoped for more objective jurists, it probably failed. The fact that Oland was a member of the Miramichi Fish and Game Club and a regular high-profile visitor to the city was no secret, and locals would have had more interest in the case than most alternatives to Saint John.

In his fifty-page ruling, delivered on December 12, 2014, LeBlanc opined that the police were too quick to conclude that Dennis Oland killed his father because there remained many unanswered questions about the case. LeBlanc noted that the Crown had failed to prove that Oland even had a motive to kill the multi-millionaire; there was no evidence showing Oland had rebuffed his son when he asked for money or that Dennis had even asked for money. That ruling called into question the vital issue of motive and punched a huge hole in the Crown's case.

LeBlanc also said the Crown had no evidence that being denied money would cause Dennis to attack his father. He placed great weight on "the very friendly reception given to Dennis Oland by his father at their meeting in his office," which was witnessed by Maureen Adamson, Oland's long-time personal assistant. That could prompt a jury to conclude there was no animosity between father and son.

Further, two men working in the print shop below Far End Corporation, Anthony Shaw and the building's owner John Ainsworth, had not heard quarrelling or shouting at the time that Dennis was on the premises. The judge told prosecutors they had "failed to establish a reason for Dennis Oland to kill his father" — as Richard's wife Connie received the $37 million inheritance.

"For these reasons, at least at the preliminary inquiry stage, there does not appear to be any motive proven that would establish that Dennis Oland had a reason to kill his father," LeBlanc wrote.

So weak was the case the Crown presented that it is not immediately apparent why it was not dismissed at this level. A decision to do so would have saved the province of New Brunswick almost two million dollars and the Oland family the estimated ten million dollars in court costs and legal fees incurred to conduct the trials.

Dismissing the case for lack of evidence would have represented a repudiation of years of work by the police and prosecution to assemble a case in the most high-profile murder in New Brunswick judicial history. The violent murder of a prominent member of the community required closure to ease the minds of citizens that justice can and will be meted out, even to a member of one of the province's wealthiest families.

The Crown emphasized at the preliminary inquiry that the victim's phone was missing from the crime scene. However, no one would ever say with any clarity why this was significant, except that it was the only thing determined by police to be missing from his office. It later evolved that a letter from Diana Sedlacek was also missing from Oland's desk, but police made no reference to it. "The disappearance of Richard Oland's iPhone continues to be a mystery. No explanation was given as to why Dennis Oland would want to take it," LeBlanc wrote.

Much was made by the prosecution about the last phone call Oland received on the evening of the murder. LeBlanc noted cellphone records were submitted showing a call to Oland's iPhone had pinged off a Rothesay tower at 6:44 p.m. on July 6, 2011, near the Renforth Wharf. The wharf is where Dennis stopped on the way home after visiting his father.

The Crown theorized Dennis took the iPhone and then disposed of it somewhere. Police divers had searched the waters around the Renforth Wharf where Dennis and Lisa moored their boat but found nothing.

About a dozen officers from the Saint John police major crime unit also used dogs to search for the missing iPhone on the grounds around Dennis Oland's home on Gondola Point Road and a wooded area near a local ball field at the Bill McGuire Community Centre on Shore Road. They searched his home and outbuildings and even dug up his yard. After many hours searching, police had no iPhone, but they did have boxes and bags of Oland's belongings — more than fifty items. Tests for traces of blood found nothing.

An analyst from Rogers, Oland's cell service provider, testified at the preliminary hearing that the ping at 6:44 p.m. on July 6, 2011, was not the last time Richard's cellphone accessed the Rogers network. On July 9, 2011, the Rogers Communications computer system received a "roaming error," showing the phone was turned on but was outside the network's jurisdiction. When the cell provider pinged the phone three times in the test for police, it registered as functioning. LeBlanc said that "quite surprisingly" Oland's cellphone company had proved that his phone was functioning three days after his murder. But where was it? The judge said the "voluminous amount of cellphone information, the records, and test calls done by police did not provide sufficient evidence that the phone was "anywhere near that (Rothesay) tower." Based on that evidence, he added, "a jury could conclude Richard Oland's cellphone was outside Canada on July 9."

Dennis Oland was not outside Canada on that date. But it's easy to imagine a foreign contract killer taking the top-of-the line iPhone as a trophy. After leaving Canada, he could have tried to use the phone or turned it on to download its data. Overseas travellers who try to call home encounter the same roaming error message if they haven't updated their service.

LeBlanc also pointed to unanswered questions about the handling of another key piece of evidence: Dennis Oland's brown jacket. It had been drycleaned just ten hours after police accused Oland of the murder and told him they would be executing search warrants. The Crown contended that drycleaning the Hugo Boss sports jacket Oland wore on the day of the murder was an effort to wipe away blood evidence.

But LeBlanc questioned why Dennis Oland would keep the cleaning tag on the jacket, along with the dry-cleaning receipt, after being told he was a suspect in the case. Police forensic experts found no traces of blood on the shirt, pants, or shoes Dennis was wearing. The judge noted the blood spatter forensic evidence given by RCMP Sgt. Brian Wentzell, a bloodstain analyst from Nova Scotia, was "unchallenged." In his cross examination by the defence, Wentzell had conceded that if Dennis Oland was the killer, he would expect to have found traces of blood in his car, on his clothing, and on a reusable grocery bag that contained the family camp visitors' logbook Oland carried home from his father's office that day. Wentzell found no evidence of a cleanup at the murder scene and no trace of bloody footprints leading away from there.

The defence explained that Lisa Oland took Dennis's jacket to the cleaners because Richard Oland's visitation and funeral were pending, and she expected Dennis would want to wear the jacket. The judge said he found it hard to believe that even though Oland informed police during his interrogation at the police station that he was wearing the same pants and shoes he had on the day before, police did not seize the garments for tests. LeBlanc questioned why Dennis Oland would keep a blood-stained jacket while disposing of the murder weapon and his father's iPhone.

LeBlanc indicated in his decision that the police presumed Dennis Oland's guilt too quickly. "This conclusion on their part was totally unjustified and indeed irrational. The police merely had a hunch, and an unsubstantiated one at that." He said Oland's routine behaviour that night — shopping, watching a film, making a quick run for milk, and reading a book in bed before going to sleep "appears to be inconsistent with the behaviour expected from someone who (has just) committed a crime of extreme violence."

In the end, LeBlanc said he had to decide whether a properly instructed jury could conclude Oland had killed his father. There were certain facts, when combined with the rest of the evidence, that could allow a jury to conclude Oland's guilt, his ruling noted.

True, Dennis had the opportunity to kill his father. True, his father's DNA was found on the brown Hugo Boss jacket he was wearing; and it's true that a jury could conclude the jacket was dry-cleaned to "destroy evidence." Dennis

Oland may have intentionally lied when he told the police he was wearing a navy blazer when he had been wearing a brown jacket. What's more, there were no signs the murder resulted from a robbery or a break-in. Richard Oland's violent death and the state of the crime scene pointed to a crime of passion; and finally, a jury might conclude that the end of all e-communication from Richard Oland following his son's visit could be incriminating. For these reasons, LeBlanc committed Dennis Oland to stand trial. The publication ban over all the contents of the preliminary inquiry would not be lifted until after the trial verdict was rendered.

In the months leading up to Dennis Oland's trial, scheduled to start in September 2015, a series of *voir dire* hearings were held on the admissibility of certain pieces of evidence. Dennis Oland attended each day of the four "trial within a trial" pretrial hearings, which started in March and were held intermittently throughout the summer. The public was unaware of this since the hearings and the judge's rulings fell under the publication ban.

The Crown sought to enter some additional evidence related to Richard Oland's cellphone and petitioned the court to have some exhibits released for more DNA testing.

Dennis Oland's lawyer Alan Gold argued that police search-and-seizure warrants had expired, violating Dennis's Charter rights, and tried to have the brown jacket excluded from evidence. Gold and his co-counsel Gary Miller argued that testing of the jacket occurred after an unreasonable search and seizure. The jacket had been seized during a house search on a warrant dated July 13, 2011, due to expire on November 2, 2011. By the end of 2011, the Saint John police had received two lab reports from the RCMP forensics laboratory finding no link to Dennis Oland at the crime scene.

In March 2012, the Halifax police forensic lab — using a new test on the brown jacket — found two spots of Richard Oland's DNA. Then, a further report dated June 26, 2012, cited three more areas of the jacket matching the victim's DNA, but with a lower rate of probability. The testing of the microscopic specks was so extensive, continuing after Dennis Oland's arrest and even after the preliminary hearing, that observers wondered how there was any fabric left to test on the spots in question. Nonetheless, Justice John Walsh, New Brunswick Court of Queens Bench, who was presiding at the *voir dires* in an April 7, 2015 ruling, granted the Crown's request for the tests as "contributing reliably probative evidence."

At the end of April 2015, Saint John police chief Bill Reid retired after thirty-seven years with the force. Deputy Chief Glen McCloskey was appointed acting chief for the summer and first two months of the Oland trial. It was not public knowledge that McCloskey had walked through the murder scene and then asked the officer in charge to keep his presence there a secret.

At the pretrial hearings, the defence claimed Saint John police made many errors in their Information to Obtain (ITO) documents. Police officers routinely file ITOs to a Judge seeking authorization to obtain a search warrant that will allow them to look for evidence. This document is accompanied by an affidavit (a statement of facts) from the officer.

Each ITO issue was addressed by Justice Walsh in a written decision, citing case law since that is what determines the evidence that is presented to the jury, and the cases relied upon often are the basis for appeals. Walsh agreed the ITO drafted to search Oland's house was poorly worded and misleading in parts, but he upheld the decision to issue the warrant and concluded that common law practice offered sufficient authority for further testing of entered exhibits outside Saint John.

Walsh refused an attempt by Saint John police to enter more evidence in the form of pay stubs and two letters from Dennis to his father from 2003 that had been obtained from Oland's CIBC Wood Gundy office after the ITO warrant had expired. The judge pointed out this police action had violated the search and seizure provisions of the Charter of Rights.

"Police, seemingly without pause or concern for the limits of the authority given to them, went ahead and retrieved additional evidence, ostensibly seen at the time as very personal information related to Dennis Oland," Walsh wrote in his June 10, 2015 pretrial hearing decision. It was the second time during the murder investigation that police "failed to respect a court order," the court document revealed. Some of the applications used to obtain the warrants also had "errors and omissions," Walsh found, noting,

> The police applied for and obtained a general warrant to forensically examine the assorted items seized under the house warrant [including the brown sports jacket] and then, inexplicably, allowed [the warrant] to lapse before conducting the examinations contemplated.

Police did not pay sufficient attention to the requirements of the judicial orders; "whether one characterizes it as carelessness or negligence," was open to debate, he said. However, Walsh ruled there was "lawful authority for the forensic examinations of the things seized under the house warrant." And while there were errors and omissions in the applications police had used to obtain both warrants, they weren't enough "in their nature and number" to invalidate either document, he said. Still, Walsh took the opportunity to underscore the importance of the search warrant applications in the administration of justice, writing,

> *It is upon these front-line documents that judges must rely to assess, weigh and maintain the sensitive balance between the public's right to have crime investigated and citizens' rights to have their privacy protected.*

The third pretrial hearing concerned efforts by the Saint John police to prove that Richard Oland's iPhone and Dennis's Blackberry were in Rothesay after 6:30 p.m. on the day of the murder. That could convince a jury to conclude the younger Oland had taken his father's cellphone after killing him. The Crown sought to have radio-frequency engineer Joseph Sadoun testify as to the location of the victim's iPhone based on a text message from Richard's lover Diana Sedlacek to his cell at 6:44 p.m. Call detail records show the cell towers with which a cellphone connects to receive calls and text messages was a new area of law in 2011, Walsh noted in his decision.

The defence objected to an engineer's ability to advise the court on the location of the iPhone based on one text message. Nonetheless, the judge admitted the police field tests and allowed Sadoun as an expert witness while limiting what questions the Crown counsel could ask him. Gold argued that the location of the iPhone was immaterial given there was no evidence Richard Oland did not leave his office for a period before his death.

However, the lawyer did not delve further into any evidence that this did or didn't happen. Toxicology tests on Oland's body showed alcohol in his urine. Oland's staff said no alcohol was kept at the office, and he had eaten lunch at his desk on the day of his murder. Alcohol in his system suggested that he left 52 Canterbury after Dennis's departure. Who knows where he might have gone? No one came forward to say. But it could be that Richard Oland attended an after-hours business meeting at his private club where alcohol is available. The Union Club at 125 Germain Street is just around the corner from Oland's office. Unfortunately, there were no witnesses or video cameras either at his office street door or the door to the club to confirm this speculation. Occupied with proving a murder case against Dennis Oland, the Crown engineered a timeline that obscured as much as ninety minutes leading up to the attack on Richard Oland.

Dennis Oland left his father's office at 6:12 p.m. At 6:30 p.m., he swung back to 52 Canterbury Street to retrieve the camp logbook he'd promised to pick up for his Uncle Jack Connell. He tucked it into a grocery bag and was seen on CCTV placing the bag into the trunk of his car.

The Crown's case argued that Dennis committed the murder on this return visit, catching his father unawares from behind and bludgeoning him to death with a hammer because he refused to loan him money. This didn't happen. Forensic tests on both the logbook and the reusable plastic bag showed they were clean, a clear indication the logbook was removed from the office before the murder. Blood and other matter covered every surface of the room after the killing.

As mentioned above, toxicology tests revealed traces

of alcohol in Oland's urine, proof that he had a drink an hour or so before his death. As it was off the books, Bob McFadden said that he had no idea where his employer went when he left the office on the evening of July 6, 2011, after his meeting with Dennis. But he was certain Oland didn't step out to a nearby public bar or restaurant for a meeting and to share a drink. "Not his style," he said in an interview in March 2019.

He must have gone out because he did not keep alcohol at his office. Dennis recalled his father was wearing a thin navy sweater over a dress shirt when he left him at 6:30 p.m. However, when his body was found, he was formally dressed in his suit jacket as he would be if he had gone out and had just returned.

Where did he go? What happened in the time elapsed between Dennis leaving and when John Ainsworth and Anthony Shaw at work in the print shop on the floor below Richard's office heard loud thumping sounds that lasted ten seconds or longer? They described the noise they heard shortly before 8:12 p.m. as being like someone moving a heavy piece of furniture. The time was confirmed by a time stamp on a customer's fax. Cheryl Johnson, working late at her law office across the alley from Oland's office, also reported hearing two men engaged in a loud argument around the same time, between 7:40 and 8 p.m.

That was about the same time Dennis was video-taped shopping with his wife at Cochran's Country Market on Hampton Road in Rothesay, where the couple bumped into his Aunt Jane Toward, Richard Oland's only sister.

One possibility — Richard Oland's nearby club. The Union Club at 125 Germain Street, around the corner from Oland's Far End Corporation, is a private member-run club and an integral part of the business and social community exclusive to Saint John. Founded in 1884, and operating from the same uptown location since 1890, the starchy atmosphere carefully maintains the proportions and customs of another century.

It's a club rule that members live within a fifty-kilometre radius of Saint John. New members must be sponsored by a current member. "It is the members shaping and directing Saint John," the club's website says, and membership guarantees valuable contacts, both professionally and socially, as well as a high level of discretion (while enjoying the amenities). The Whistlestop Bar is a speakeasy, allowing club members to keep a locker of alcoholic beverages.

Not the kind of place that welcomes the average citizen of Saint John. An elderly woman stopping for a rest on the cool marble steps of the ornate red brick Victorian building, a Saint John landmark, one afternoon when I visited the city in 2019 was well aware of the exclusive nature of the club. "I am sitting with the rich," she quipped to me, her shopping bag beside her as she waited for the bus.

Did Oland pop around to the Union Club for an after-hours meeting and a drink? General Manager Charlene Roy says it isn't likely. "Members can only access the Union Club during business hours." she said, responding in part to questions I asked her by email. Notwithstanding that, the club's website states its members can book after-hours meetings.

"Richard was a frequent patron to the Union Club for lunches," Roy said. Richard usually presided at a group table of friends and business acquaintances. He and brother Derek, both longtime members, had lunch there together on occasion, despite the cool relations between them.

Old-school club rules require that members and their

guests put their cellphone ringers on silent mode and not make or answer calls in the Lounge or Dining Room. It's possible that Richard left his cellphone in the office for this reason, where it was perhaps stolen by his killer(s), who may have taken advantage of his absence to do a reconnaissance visit ahead of the murder.

The Union Club is a relic of another era, when men conducted business over brandy and cigars at their private club. Personal electronic devices may be used in all areas of the building, however conspicuous use of business papers is limited to the P. W. Oland Room and private function rooms. Philip Warburton Oland, Richard's father, and president of Moosehead Breweries was a life member of the Union Club. A life member means membership of more than fifty years.

The Union Club is affiliated with more than fifty other private clubs around the world and being a member is an endorsement of success. Richard Oland could have been at the Union Club, or as Dennis speculated,

> *I can't recall if we asked the Union Club staff if Dad dropped in there. Having said that, had he been there, I believe strongly that we would have found out about it somehow. Dad was on a first-name basis with the staff there, and most of the patrons would have been keen to pass on helpful/key information like that.*
>
> *The investigators were left to speculate on this drink thing and using a bit of logic (based on his drinking habits/social habits) it seemed more likely that a visitor (perhaps the killer) brought a drink in with them. Or that Dad may have stepped out to*

meet someone in their car for a chat. In either case,
the likely drink would have been beer. He loved his
beer and would have enjoyed having a social drink
in the evening if someone were to drop in.

In their car for a chat? If Can Sugar's out-of-pocket East Bloc investors were making a last-minute effort to collect their 17.5 million debt, they plausibly could have asked Oland to take a meeting with them to discuss next steps. Ukrainian/Russian standard protocol is to begin a meeting with a drink.

"[The matter that ended in a bloody murder] had been festering for some time," McFadden said in the March 2019 interview. In this scenario, following a fruitless discussion, Richard Oland was driven back to his office, where his assailants ambushed him a few minutes later. Message delivered: Nobody says no to the Red Mafia.

If this is what transpired, it could also be that the fateful meeting took place in or near Rothesay. This turn of events would explain why Diana Sedlacek's text message urging Oland to pick up (*"U there?"*) pinged off the Fairvale cell tower near Rothesay. This could also be the reason Oland's iPhone was missing from the crime scene. His killers took it because they called him to set up the meeting and needed to wipe any trace of the call.

Saint John police investigators discovered that the iPhone was operating outside the country three days after the murder on July 9. When a technician called the iPhone's number, the message came back "roaming error," indicating it was live and on a foreign network.

McFadden believes that Sedlacek was somehow connected to Oland's murder.

Inexplicably, Saint John police declined to treat Diana

Sedlacek's husband Jiri as a person of interest in the case. As noted, Jiri Sedlacek, an international businessman, claimed under oath he had no knowledge of his wife's affair that had been going on for eight years — a constant relationship she talked openly about with her friends and real estate colleagues and one that involved dozens of trips, including jaunts to Spain, cities in the United States, Toronto and Montreal. Diana also swore in court that Jiri didn't know.

The defence accused the Saint John Police Force of tunnel vision for focusing on Dennis Oland as its sole suspect while not probing other possible suspects. Richard Oland's aggressive personality and reputation for sleeping around meant there could be more than a few people who wanted to see him dead.

CHAPTER SIXTEEN
The First Trial: Setting the Scene

Given the unusually large number of prospective jurors to be vetted, the Crown reserved the Saint John's Harbour Station hockey arena in the city's core for the arraignment and jury selection. Five thousand people from Saint John and Kings counties, ranging in age from nineteen to seventy, received summonses for jury duty. As the first thousand potential jurors queued up, court officials divided them into eight groups. Arena food vendors opened their shops for the proceedings. The event was unprecedented in New Brunswick legal history. The defendant made his plea of "not guilty" over a microphone on September 8 in front of a large crowd.

In anticipation of a lengthy trial, Justice John "Jack" Walsh ordered fourteen jurors be chosen — twelve plus two alternates. Lawyers can only receive names, addresses, and occupations for those in the jury pool. In a case of second-degree murder, each side has peremptory challenges. During the process, 132 prospective jurors were rejected by the judge or lawyers. By September 10, eight men and six women had been selected.

Jurors were paid forty dollars a day for the first nine days and eighty dollars a day thereafter for the length of the trial. They were ordered not to discuss the case, their deliberations on the verdict, or the reasons behind their decision — standard court procedure. The penalty for divulging information? A maximum of six months in jail and a fine of up to five thousand dollars.

Observers compared the arena scene to the kind of spectacle that surrounded prominent criminal trials and public hangings in the nineteenth century.

Oland reflected on how he had enjoyed a great concert by the American rock musician Bob Seger in this same place on the evening that coincided with the last day of his preliminary hearing on November 26, 2014. Spotted having fun with his friends at the event, some local members of the media posted negative comments.

The Oland murder trial was a once-in-a lifetime case for Saint John prosecutors. For the politically motivated trial lawyer, this could be a career booster. For example, Bernard Lord had transitioned from a young Moncton litigator with his own law firm in the 1990s to become a prominent Conservative MLA and then premier in 1999, winning forty-four of fifty-five seats — New Brunswick's first Conservative Premier since Richard Hatfield (1970-1987). Curiously however, when it came to the Oland trial, no one seemed to want the job. Two Crowns begged off in the early stages.

"They've had almost two and a half years with it, with all kinds of Crowns and all kinds of cops." Defence lawyer Gary Miller said in a CBC interview in late 2013, describing the disclosure file in the case as "voluminous." The police continued to investigate for a further two years beyond the preliminary hearing, adding reams more material to the file.

With just weeks to go before the gavel was to drop on the September 16, 2015 start of the trial, Crown John Henheffer, the lead prosecutor for the preliminary hearing and pre-trial hearings, stepped aside for health reasons. The Office of the Attorney General issued an emailed statement to the media late Wednesday afternoon August 13, 2015, that retired Crown prosecutor Paul (P.J.) Veniot had taken over the case.

"We can confirm that P.J. Veniot has joined the prosecution's team for the trial of R v Dennis Oland," the statement said. "The trial will continue as scheduled."

Veniot, who lives in Miramichi, would be joining another "lad from the 'Chi'," Justice Jack Walsh. As a Crown prosecutor in Miramichi, Jack Walsh was among the first to use DNA evidence when Allan Legere was on trial for murder in 1991. Legere had escaped police custody and gone on a seven-month killing spree in 1989. With Walsh as one of the prosecutors, Legere was convicted of four counts of first-degree murder. This brought Walsh to prominence in the legal field both nationally and internationally. He became a recognized authority on DNA and was invited to several countries to speak on the use of DNA evidence in criminal cases.

More than four years passed since the murder of Richard Oland and more than two years since Dennis Oland was arrested and charged with second-degree murder before he had his day in court. In a navy blazer, grey trousers, pale blue shirt, and a navy tie with red-and-white diagonal pinstripes, the slender boyish-looking man, now forty-seven, arrived at the Saint John Courthouse with his mother. It was the same navy blazer (or one like it) that he confused with the brown sports jacket he wore to his father's office on July 6, 2011, the day his father was murdered. Connie carried a blue seat cushion to make the oak wood bench in the front row of the visitors' section of Courtroom 12 more comfortable. The right side of the room's visitor section was reserved for Oland's family and friends. The middle rows of benches seated the general public, and the left side of the room was reserved for the press.

Those spectators who wanted a seat in the smallish courtroom on the fifth floor of the courthouse had to get there well ahead of the 9:30 a.m. start. Security screening in the courthouse atrium resembled that of an international airport. All attending court were obliged to remove their jackets, empty their pockets, and remove belts and shoes. Belongings such as purses, cases and backpacks were put into bins and run through an x-ray machine as their owners passed through the metal detector, and a police constable ran a hand scanner over everyone coming through.

The Saint John Law Courts building, opened in 2013 at a cost of fifty million dollars, is a utilitarian structure of glass, grey stone, and dark brown brick. It has an intentionally cold, dull ambience, with long empty hallways that overpower the casual visitor, suggesting the proverb from Dante's *Divine Comedy*, "abandon hope all ye who enter here."

According to Statistics Canada reports for 2014/15, New Brunswick had Canada's highest criminal conviction rate, with 77 per cent of defendants found guilty. Quebec was close behind with 73 per cent and B.C. with 72 per cent. The Saint John Police Department had a 100 per cent conviction rate in its homicide charges. All three provinces use pretrial conferences, leading to high conviction rates — often resulting in plea bargains after the sides consider the evidence. For comparison, the conviction rate in Ontario in 2014/15 was just 54 per cent; Ontario didn't use pretrial conferences at that time.

The new justice complex consists of thirteen court-rooms, office space for the judiciary, court services, public prosecutions, sheriff services, probation services, the NB Department of Public Safety, policing and a barristers' lounge. Covering 150,000 square feet, the complex is both energy-efficient and spacious and aligns with the provincial government's Green Buildings Program. Located on a hill at the city's centre, it dominates the skyline. The Saint John police station, low-rise but built in a similar architectural style, sits directly across the street.

The justice centre replaces the historic stone Saint John County Courthouse and the Northumberland County Courthouse, both completed in 1829. The Saint John Courthouse, now the Saint John Theatre Company's Courthouse features a free-standing spiral staircase; it was designated a national historic site in 1974 and later honoured with a Saint John Heritage Award. It's hard to imagine its modern replacement ever being turned into a cultural centre or honoured for its grace and beauty.

Judge Walsh ruled against Dennis Oland sitting beside his lawyers at the counsel table but acquiesced with the defence's request for communication purposes that he did not have to sit in a prisoner's box. Oland sat at a table across a narrow aisle from his lawyers, a clear plexiglass partition between his table and the wooden barrier separating the court from the visitors. He was partially concealed from the jurors seated on the other side of the room by a computer monitor on the table before him.

Large black computer monitors like the flat screens in public areas and restaurants hung from the courtroom's low ceiling so viewers could see exhibits. An interactive screen in the witness box allowed witnesses to digitally mark documents or photos. The altered materials could be printed out in the courtroom and entered immediately as exhibits.

The courtroom was a nightmare for spectators. The ten monitors in the courtroom, off most of the time, presented irritating impediments to a clear view of the court, lawyers, and the judge's bench. Other courts bring in or drop down a big screen temporarily when required from time to time. Acoustic tiles and carpeted floors muffled sound to the extent that jurors, spectators and media needed earphones to hear what the judge, lawyers and witnesses were saying. Unfortunately for spectators, these devices were discouragingly scarce. Each day, a lucky few snatched them up, and many people went without, including Oland's family and friends. Even Connie Oland had to beg for headphones on occasion.

No television cameras are allowed in New Brunswick courts, and photographers cannot take pictures. But reporters and others had their laptops and phones and tweeted a steady stream of the judge's observations, lawyers' questions, comments and witnesses' testimony.

"Crown counsel has the job of proving the charge," Judge Walsh explained. If after hearing all the evidence, jurors did not believe Oland was guilty beyond a reasonable doubt of causing the death of his father, he must be found not guilty

134 Who Killed Richard Oland

— even if they believed that Oland was "likely guilty."

Walsh cautioned the jurors to avoid talking about the case or following media reports about the proceedings. He explained that what a lawyer might say in court is not evidence. The monitors were used to display photos of the crime scene and autopsy photos of the victim's body. Richard Oland's family and friends as well as others looked away, but the disturbing images were nearly impossible to avoid. Journalists reported the pathologist's autopsy findings and posted pictures online. Fascinated Saint John residents and Canadians from coast to coast followed the daily proceedings.

Senior Crown prosecutor Paul Veniot, on the case for less than a month, might have asked for a postponement to get better acquainted with the file, but he did not. Instead, he relied on co-Crowns Patrick Wilbur and Derek Weaver to help him get up to speed. A continuance would have created a need for a new jury pool — the significance of which would later become apparent.

In his opening statement, Veniot spoke at length of Richard Oland's difficult and demanding personality and his high expectations of his family — especially Dennis, his only son. Veniot painted a portrait of a stickler and a bean counter, a family head who insisted "you were not given things" but had to earn them. The jury heard that one of New Brunswick's richest men, who had a million-dollar plus sailboat on order in Spain, kept his wife of forty-six years on a two thousand dollars a month household budget. She was required to provide receipts for any expenditures.

The trial of a member of the Oland family, famous because of the international popularity of Moosehead beer and the fact the family-owned brewery was a major employer in Saint John, drew public interest near and far. The revelations of Oland's adventurous life that only very rich people experience added excitement to the drama.

Veniot explained there was no evidence of a break-in at the murder scene at Far End Corporation and nothing was missing from the office except the victim's iPhone. The Crown would show, he claimed, that Dennis Oland was the last person to see his father alive.

In presenting its case, the Crown contended that Dennis Oland was in financial straits and had killed his father for financial gain. The Crown prosecutors made much of microscopic blood stains on Dennis Oland's jacket. They also tried to link the murdered man's missing cellphone to Dennis when all they had to support this contention was innuendo and supposition. A divorced father of three, Dennis was living on overdraft. But in 2011, so were as many as one in six Canadians, judging from the overdraft fees charged by Canada's banks.

Hard up as Dennis Oland was, there was no evidence he asked his father for financial help or that there was tension between the two men over money issues. Robert McFadden, Oland's accountant since the mid-1980s, swore under oath that he never witnessed any animosity between father and son. Richard Oland wanted the $500,000 loan he made to Dennis to pay out his first wife's divorce settlement to be secured on his home's mortgage. He wanted the first right to buy the house, his childhood home, which had been in the family about seventy years, if his son no longer lived there, he said. McFadden handled Richard Oland's personal finances as well as his business dealings, and he testified that his employer hadn't even mentioned his son's loan for at least six months to a year before his death.

Lead defence counsel Alan Gold pointed out that it wasn't the first time Richard Oland had assisted his son financially. He helped Dennis in 1998 when he bought the house, and again in 1999-2000 when he purchased the adjacent farm property. It also wasn't the first time Dennis had fallen behind in payments, the courtroom heard. In 2002, he had difficulty making the eleven annual payment on his mortgage debt; Oland simply added a year to the term, said McFadden. Similarly, when Dennis had defaulted on payments in 2007, 2008, and 2009, his father "cut him some slack," said Gold. "He did," agreed McFadden. "Nice to have a Bank of Daddy, isn't it?" commented Gold, a surprisingly prejudicial remark from the defendant's own lawyer.

Reporters seized on the 'Bank of Daddy' remark from the lawyer quick with a quip. It made headlines across the country. It was a comment to the jury the Crown's Veniot would wish he'd said.

In presenting its case, nothing the Crown said was a fact. The prosecution had no murder weapon, no witnesses to the attack, and no blood transfer evidence on Dennis's car or the bag he carried into and out of his father's office. Had there been fresh blood or fluids on his jacket from such a violent attack on his father, traces would have rubbed off on the car's upholstery. Other than anecdotal evidence and rumours, there was no hard evidence of strain or animosity between the two men or that Dennis asked his father for money on July 6, 2011.

CHAPTER SEVENTEEN
The First Trial: The Pathologist

The New Brunswick pathologist who performed the forensic autopsy on Richard Oland was one of the first witnesses to testify at Dennis Oland's murder trial. Dr. Ather Naseemuddin was also the first to examine in detail the victim's battered and broken body, so vital to the investigative machinery.

Forensic pathology focuses on determining the cause of death by post-mortem examination of the corpse or partial remains. The pathologist is also frequently asked to confirm a corpse's identity. The requirements to become a licensed practitioner of forensic pathology varies from country to country but typically include a medical doctorate with a specialty in general or anatomical pathology and subsequent study in forensic medicine as a minimum requirement.

These are highly qualified professionals able to speak with authority about their findings.

The methods forensic scientists use to determine death include examination of tissue specimens to identify the presence or absence of natural diseases and other microscopic findings, interpretations of toxicology on body tissues and fluids to determine the chemical cause of overdoses, poisonings or other cases involving toxic agents, and, as in this case, examinations of physical trauma. Forensic pathology constitutes a major component in the trans-disciplinary field of forensic science.

The pathologist is one of the more enigmatic characters in this tragic saga. Dr. Naseemuddin and his office were reluctant to provide copies of his official findings, which are supposed to be a public document, or give interviews, despite several requests and without any reason given.

Dr. Naseemuddin obtained his first medical qualifications in India and trained as a pathologist in the United States. He is a cautious man, not given to easy speculation about probabilities. For instance, he declined to comment about the type of weapon used in the attack even though police believed it was a tool like a drywall hammer.

The police never showed Naseemuddin any tools or photographs of tools to seek his opinion on a possible weapon, supporting the defence's argument the investigation was inadequate. The pathologist testified that in some cases, if an alleged weapon is known and brought along to the autopsy, he can compare it to the injuries. In this case, no weapon was ever found, and months passed before police asked him for his opinion.

"It would be conjecture, really, to suggest what caused this," Naseemuddin told the court, avoiding the question why he could not give an informed opinion as to whether a drywall hammer could have caused the injuries inflicted on Richard Oland. Naseemuddin did say forty of the injuries were made by an instrument with a sharp edge, while the five blunt-force ones were caused by either a different tool or a second edge on the same tool. He also noted the blunt-force ones, which were circular and measured between 2.0 and 2.5 centimetres in diametre, also left a cross-hatching pattern in the skin. He had never seen such a pattern before, he said.

The wounds sound exactly like they were made by a drywall hammer. Why couldn't a skilled and trained pathologist give an informed professional opinion on something so basic in a timely manner?

Oland had so many injuries, the pathologist numbered them using pieces of medical tape. Even so, he inadvertently counted one wound twice. He initially thought the wound was a laceration and assigned it No. 26 but later realized, when examining the skull, that it was a fracture and assigned it No. 45, he said. It is likely Oland was facing his attacker before being overwhelmed. The defensive-type wounds to Oland's hands occurred first, suggesting that he was either trying to ward off his attacker and grab the weapon or reacting to a blow to his head and trying to protect himself, Naseemuddin said. His broken fingers on both hands would have caused "excruciating pain and a lot of bleeding."

Seven of the lacerations on Oland's head were parallel and closely spaced together, suggesting they were inflicted in rapid succession, he said. Some of the "chop wounds" fractured Oland's skull, exposing his brain. Another part of his skull was caved in, Naseemuddin said, adding Oland was "incapacitated very quickly." He said the cause of death was a combination of brain trauma and "extensive blood loss."

In all, he suffered forty-five sharp- and blunt-force wounds to his head, neck and hands. He would have survived only "minutes" after being attacked.

"These injuries were rapidly fatal," he said, as graphic autopsy photos of the deep gashes were displayed on a large screen, and Oland family members averted their eyes.

The pattern of blows that killed Oland indicated that the murderer was probably right-handed. Dennis is left-handed. He is clearly seen in the video of his police interrogation writing his statement with his left hand. The Crown questioned Naseemuddin about the most severe injuries being on the left side of Oland's head, but the defence failed to raise the crucial fact their client was a southpaw. Arguments never materialized about whether the killer was left- or right-handed.

When I asked Naseemuddin to comment on the probability of a right-handed killer in a telephone interview January 15, 2016, he wouldn't say from which direction, right or left side, the initial blows to Oland's head came to render him helpless. Naseemuddin said he couldn't recall being asked by the Crown prosecutors or the defence whether Oland's attacker was right-handed or to give information about the direction of the fatal blows. He refused to comment further. But the pathologist conceded that the broken fingers and other defensive wounds indicated that Oland was facing his attacker when the assault began, rather than being hit from behind.

He noted the fatal blows creating a fist-sized crater had crushed the left side of Oland's skull. If those blows were delivered by an attacker in front of the victim, he would be right-handed. "Everybody knows about the right-handed killer," Dennis Oland's best friend Val Streeter said in a telephone interview in October 2016. No one knows why the defence didn't raise the matter as his lawyers refused to comment.

Hairs found on Oland's broken fingers were not from Dennis and initially could not be identified. However, under closer examination, the hairs turned out to be Richard's. Naseemuddin carefully chronicled each blow for the court, which was warned that the autopsy photos would be difficult to view. Given the expert conclusion that he was alive throughout the attack, his heart would have been pumping and each blow would generate considerably more blood spatter than if he had been dead. Naseemuddin agreed the defensive wounds to Richard Oland's hands could have been suffered by Oland in defending against his attacker and that Oland appeared healthy and capable of defending himself. The pathologist concluded that six fractures on the left side of Mr. Oland's head were "more rapidly fatal" than the ones to the right.

When a prosecutor asked if Oland could have survived for a while after the attack, Naseemuddin reiterated that he was incapacitated very quickly. There is "no way" if attacked at or before 6:30 p.m. Richard Oland could have lingered for several hours and made the thumping noises heard by workers in the office below an hour or so later. Naseemuddin said police asked him about the "survivability" of Oland's injuries because they were trying to determine if an injured Oland could have made the sounds before he died. He told investigators the notion of Oland moving around or making noises hours after the attack was "beyond a possibility." During cross-examination, Naseemuddin acknowledged he could not say if there was more than one assailant.

Naseemuddin testified that he didn't know if Oland habitually took Aspirin but confirmed it can interfere with blood clotting and stated that he became covered in blood while performing the autopsy. During redirect, however, the prosecutor pointed out that the report by the provincial forensic toxicologist found "no common prescription or drugs of abuse."

Still, given the amount of blood at the crime scene, Gold asked Naseemuddin whether Oland's attacker would have been covered in blood. "Certainly, the weapon. I don't know about the clothing," he allowed. But Gold pointed out that when he asked the pathologist during the preliminary inquiry whether it was likely the attacker would have had a substantial amount of blood on him or her, his answer, under oath, was "yes." Gold repeated the question and Naseemuddin said "I would agree that answer is true." Judge Walsh asked the jury to read the autopsy report.

Naseemuddin was also less than definitive about unexplained traces of alcohol found in Oland's system. The defence's forensic toxicologist testified that it's possible the victim consumed a small amount of alcohol about an hour before his death, based on the low level found in his urine. Like the New Brunswick pathologist, the Crown's expert testified the trace amount was consistent with consumption "several hours" before death but would not narrow it down any further. The defence suggested he met someone for drinks in the time between his son leaving his office and his murder.

Oland consumed some alcohol but how long before the killing is unclear. Robert McFadden and Maureen Adamson were adamant that Oland did not leave the office between arriving in the morning and Maureen leaving at 5:45 p.m. on July 6, 2011. But did he go out after hours? Visiting a bar or someone's home for a drink was "not his style, not what he would do," McFadden said in an interview. Perhaps a business meeting then? McFadden said he didn't know. No one has come forward to confirm a meeting with Oland the night of his death. But then, they wouldn't if they were connected or involved in his murder.

Perhaps evidence Oland went out after Dennis left his office did not fit with the Crown's case, so they did not pursue this line of inquiry. That day he was wearing a navy-blue business suit and a white dress shirt with red and blue stripes under a thin navy sweater. Court photos posted on the internet showed the shirt front, collar to hem, and left sleeve to the elbow were completely soaked in blood indicating a frontal assault to his left. Dennis said his father was seated at his desk in his sweater when they met early in the evening to discuss family genealogy and look at an 1826 family will Dennis had found on a recent trip to England. This was confirmed by Adamson, who also testified that Richard was happy to see Dennis. Adamson was helping with the family history project and asked Dennis to take a logbook home to his mother as she had finished scanning it into the computer.

Forensic toxicologist Dr. Albert Fraser examined urine, blood and eye fluid samples taken from the victim's body during the autopsy, performed at the Saint John Regional Hospital's morgue on July 8, 2011. He found a small amount of alcohol in the urine, but none in the blood or the clear gel in the eyeball that fills the space between the lens and the retina (called vitreous humour).

"The low concentration of ethyl alcohol in post-mortem urine along with negative ethyl alcohol findings in post-mortem blood and vitreous [humour] indicates alcohol consumption several hours prior to death," Fraser stated in his report. Defence lawyers accused the Crown of improperly providing information to a forensic toxicologist that risked "tainting" his expert opinion about the alcohol found in the body.

In 2014 emails to the forensic toxicologist, Crown prosecutor Patrick Wilbur told Fraser there was no evidence Oland had consumed any alcohol on the day of his death and asked him to consider other possible explanations. The emails could be why Fraser testified that cough syrup could produce the same effect. However, there was no witness testimony from his staff or family that Oland was suffering from a cold and taking cough syrup. In any event, no cough syrup container was found at the crime scene.

CHAPTER EIGHTEEN
The First Trial:
The Brown Jacket

The key piece of evidence in the Crown's case against Dennis Oland was his brown Hugo Boss sports jacket, which had microscopic specks of blood. Police seized upon discrepancies between what Oland said in his interrogation and other evidence they'd gathered. Police said that he deliberately misled them.

Prosecutors enlarged upon the argument that Dennis lied about which jacket he was wearing. During the Crown's opening statement at the beginning of the trial, Paul Veniot said the jacket had four areas of bloodstains on it as well as DNA that matched the victim's profile.

Saint John police Constable David MacDonald was the forensics officer in charge of seizing items at Dennis Oland's Rothesay home on July 14, 2011. The defence bolstered its case by showing how careless the searchers had been. Under cross-examination MacDonald testified he asked Constable Rick Russell to identify which items he wanted from the closet in the master bedroom.

"He identified a brown jacket and did so by grabbing the jacket with this hand," MacDonald said. When asked what, if anything, Russell was wearing on his hands, the forensics officer testified, "He had bare hands."

Asked, "Would it be normal to touch an object when you're going to be seizing it in that manner?" MacDonald admitted it would not. MacDonald said he donned a fresh pair of gloves for each item he seized; those items included several of Oland's shirts and pairs of shoes.

The Hugo Boss was the only brown jacket found in the search. The Crown alleged without proof that Lisa Oland laundered the jacket before taking it to the dry cleaners. That suggested Lisa was aware of the blood and gore stains alleged to be on the jacket. If so, that would make her an accomplice to murder-after-the-fact, and if prosecutors really believed she did that, she also should have faced criminal charges. Any suggestion the jacket was washed falls into the realm of impermissible speculation. Yet that is precisely the kind of evidence the Crown asked the court to accept as proof of Oland's guilt.

There is no evidence to support the widespread idea the killer donned painters' coveralls to protect against the spray of blood and gore. Would there be any blood on Oland's jacket if he had been the killer and wore protective gear? Only a few little stains — "invisible to the naked eye," to quote police forensic experts — on one article of clothing in such a vicious attack is highly improbable. Removing the Tyvek suit without transferring trace DNA evidence onto clothing and shoes and car upholstery would be a challenge. Also, for Oland to bring a Tyvek suit with him when he went to visit his father contradicts the Crown's theory of the case.

Taking such precautions would necessarily imply planning and premeditation, which is antithetical to the Crown's theory of the case — a crime of passion born of an enraged mind.

To say Oland lied about the brown jacket constituted overreach by a prosecution team with no evidence to present and keen to find anything to support its case. The defence argued that under the stress of the situation Oland simply made an innocent mistake about which jacket he was wearing. He wore the navy blazer on the next day, the day the body was found and life for Richard Oland's family changed forever.

The Hugo Boss jacket was a dubious piece of evidence from the beginning. After being mishandled by Russell, the lead investigator, MacDonald then rolled it up and placed it inside a brown paper bag measuring about thirty centimetres by thirty centimetres. MacDonald testified that he "folded [the jacket], rolled it into" a paper exhibit bag and stored it in the forensics office at police headquarters. It sat in the Saint John police locker for nearly four months before forensic testing was performed. There were also reports that the jacket was simply stuffed into an unsecured box in the evidence locker. Instead, the box sat on a corner of the desk in Inspector Glen McCloskey's office. He was a senior officer in the city's police force, but he wasn't assigned to the homicide division.

The day after Oland's body was removed from the crime scene, MacDonald was part of the team that spent several hours examining the body prior to the autopsy. The murder victim's blood-stained shirt and other clothing was bagged, as was his Rolex. The police team also extracted bodily fluids, blood, urine and vitreous samples.

On November 9, 2011, after he spent five hours visually inspecting the brown jacket for bloodstains, MacDonald noticed a "red blood-like stain" on one of the elbows. He testified he also found four small red "blood-like" stains on the front of the jacket, "diluted" stains on the inside of both cuffs, and three more stains — two on the right elbow and one on the left shoulder. MacDonald said he circled the stained areas with a white marker, placed a scaled sticker beside each one and then photographed them. The stains were small and difficult to capture in the photos of the dark jacket, so he magnified one of them 500 per cent. This was a technique he was trained to do when dealing with fingerprints. For Oland's preliminary inquiry in 2014, MacDonald brightened the exposure on some of the photos to better represent the "slight discolouration of the threads" he had observed.

The constable's observations required testing by the RCMP forensics lab in Nova Scotia, and so MacDonald drove the jacket to Halifax. There he hand-delivered it to the lab, where technicians confirmed the red stains were indeed minuscule blood stains containing Richard Oland's DNA. MacDonald picked up the jacket eight months later in July 2012. He did not say what it was that prompted him to retrieve the evidence from its paper bag four months after the murder. Curiously, he transported the jacket to the RCMP lab again on October 26, 2012 for further testing and retrieved it on February 14, 2013. Cuttings of the jacket were also subsequently sent for analysis. No reason was given for the retesting.

The defence gave little credence to MacDonald's "weak positive" as a result of his re-examination of the jacket. A weak positive means it took fifteen seconds for the spots to materialize when tested. According to Gold, the RCMP protocols suggest any reaction taking more than ten seconds should be considered negative. RCMP Sgt. Brian Wentzell testified the drops were so small that he missed one of them on his initial examination of the jacket. He said it would be impossible to determine if they belonged to Richard Oland or indeed if the blood was human or animal.

Gold argued that if Dennis Oland was wearing the jacket at the time he allegedly committed murder, there would have been significant amounts of blood stain rather than a few hard-to-detect specks. Police forensic experts agreed that Oland and his attacker were near each other and there would have been some spatter, but they declined to speculate on how much. Wentzell testified that forty of the forty-five killing blows were sharp force trauma, which would mean less blood spatter, unlike blunt force trauma.

Patrick Laturnus, a retired RCMP blood specialist who testified for the defence, said Oland's jacket would have been visibly blood stained after such a fight. Gold argued that blood spatter from the attack covered the walls, furnishings, and floor of the crime scene. Yet no blood was found in the defendant's car, home, on a bag that he carried from the meeting or on his cellphone, which he used in the car to make calls to his sister and wife. With the crime scene spattered with copious amounts of blood in a 360-degree pattern, how could Dennis, his jacket and his other clothes have stayed so clean? As Laturnus had taken pains in his testimony to explain, if Dennis Oland had committed the crime, he could not avoid having blood trace evidence on his person, his belongings or his car.

The lack of a blood trail from the office and no evidence of any cleanup at the scene suggests the killer(s) walked away with little blood on their person, the Crown argued. It is more plausible the killer took a large plastic bag from his pocket which he laid out and stepped on, stripped down, bagged the weapon and left. Any specks or droplets landing in the hall or on the back door weren't found because that area wasn't tested with luminol. Rumours of a bloody tee-shirt found at the scene never materialized, although Oland's detectives spent time looking for it.

If, as Laturnus said, the brown sports jacket had been worn during the murder, it would have had significant and visible blood spatter on it. The Crown suggested the lack of blood could have been caused by washing and then dry-cleaning the jacket. In fact, washing a designer linen jacket in a washing machine would have destroyed it; certainly a dry cleaner would be shocked by that kind of cleaning. However, the dry cleaners testified they examine clothing items for stains before they clean them, and in this case, they did not see any bloodstains on the jacket.

Maureen Adamson testified that her boss had a skin condition that would make his scalp bleed, and that he was "touchy-feely" when he talked to people. Oland had moved into his father's home for a few months while his own house was undergoing renovations, and while he was there, he hung his clothes in his father's closet, the trial heard. Gold contended in his final address to the jury that the spots of blood on his client's jacket could have been months or even years old at the time of Richard's death and were so subtle that the dry cleaner hadn't noticed them.

In his examination of John Travis, Dennis's manager at CIBC Wood Gundy, Gold attempted to show how Richard Oland's DNA could have been innocently transferred to his son's jacket. He determined that Richard Oland was a mentor to Travis and was therefore able to confirm that the elder Oland had a habit of standing close to people while talking to them. Like Adamson, Travis said Oland would "invade your space when he spoke to people — get in close, touch your back, grab your shoulder." A few photos submitted to court show Oland clasping a person by the elbow when talking to him or holding their shoulder and leaning in.

Another possibility is that the jacket and other items kept in the evidence box was tampered with in the months of investigation. Some criminal lawyers analyzing the Dennis Oland trials observed that as the jacket wasn't locked up in a secure place, it could be reasonably argued that it was rendered not relevant and never should have been admitted into evidence. Yet it became the most tangible evidence the Crown had in the case against Dennis Oland.

CHAPTER NINETEEN
The First Trial:
The Money

Prosecutors set out to create a portrait of a free-spending underachiever, theorizing that money — or lack of it — created a motive for Dennis to kill his father. Dennis did not stand to gain anything financially by killing his father. His ability to pay off his debts would not have improved by one iota. As the terms of Richard's will made clear, no one in the family except Connie, the sole beneficiary, gained by his death.

McFadden testified that upon Connie's death, the trust Oland established would be dissolved, and the remaining assets would be distributed to the three children, Dennis Oland, Jacqueline Walsh and Lisa Bustin. He said that after Connie's death, Dennis's portion of his inheritance would be reduced by $538,000, with $269,000 going to each of Dennis's sisters. This covered the expenses of his divorce paid for by his father.

Keep in mind that Richard Oland's net worth at his death was $37 million, which with inflation and return on investment of a modest 4.5 per cent would be worth about $63 million in 2022 and more with higher inflation. With a bolder 10 per cent return it would be worth (deep breath) $116 million plus. When asked about the current value of Oland's estate, McFadden simply gave a broad smile.

Even at only a 2 per cent rate return, the original $37 million would be worth $47 million in 2022; even more by the time of Connie's death. That divided equally among the three siblings would mean at the very least more than fifteen million dollars each. Deducting $538,000 from Dennis's portion would not be terribly consequential for him in the overall inheritance scheme of things. So why worry, let alone commit murder, for such a (relatively) piddling amount?

The Crown focused on Oland's debt load, a heavy burden to be sure for most people. He was "on the edge financially," overspending by an average of fourteen thousand dollars a month in the months leading up to his father's death. His credit card and line of credit were both over limit, and his latest $1,666.67 interest-only payment on the $500,000 mortgage loan had bounced.

The Crown alleged Dennis's motive for murder stemmed from being financially desperate and having a penny-pinching father who refused to open the vault. However, the investigators had limited their analysis to the months immediately preceding the murder. They also failed to create a balance sheet, thereby overlooking Oland's true net worth. Forensic accountant Eric Johnson, testifying for the Crown, focused primarily on the six-month period from January 1,

2011 to the day the body was discovered — July 7, 2011. Johnson read from a binder several inches thick, condensed from an even larger volume.

A total of $102,835.93 was deposited into the account during those six months and $102,171.58 was withdrawn. Oland's bank account and credit card activity showed combined spending of $120,972.16, including about sixteen thousand dollars on trips to Florida and England during that period. His pay was only $34,124.02, resulting in a deficit of $86,848.14. Between November 2010 and May 2011, Johnson found foreign currency transactions on Oland's Visa totalling about $20,000, apparently for trips to Hungary (twenty-three days), Florida (twelve days) and England (eighteen days). Dennis Oland's secured line of credit remained near its $163,000 limit, and on July 7, 2011, the day his father's body was discovered, he owed $163,939.68 on the line of credit, according to a Court exhibit.

Oland had increased his Visa limit by seven thousand dollars to $27,000 in February 2011, but by July 7, the balance stood at $32,928.53 — more than $5,500 over the limit. However, Oland's credit card still worked, and he continued to draw money from it. There were one hundred dollar cash advances on July 1, July 2 and July 3 and then eight hundred dollars on July 6, the day of the murder, bank records show. Similarly, Oland had increased his line of credit by $88,000 to $163,000 in March 2011, but it too was overdrawn by more than nine hundred dollars in July. Meanwhile, his investment account had been cleaned out and his RRSP account had only $20.13 left.

However, limiting Oland's financial review to a six-month period would prove problematic for the Crown's case. Oland's second bi-weekly loan payment for the month of July 2011 cleared. So did the previously bounced cheque. A defence-ordered wider review of Oland's finances showed his overspending was even greater during the same six-month period the year before — approximately twenty thousand dollars per month in 2010. Reviews of Oland's finances for 2009 proved Oland faced a similar cash crunch in that year too. The defence therefore contended Oland's cash flow problems were nothing new and nothing unusual for a financial advisor. Living on overdraft is a common lifestyle for a divorced dad. Dennis was no exception.

A list of all Oland's $1,666.67 interest payments to his father shows the post-dated cheque on July 5, 2011 (the day before his father was killed) bounced due to insufficient funds. But the next cheque, dated July 19, 2011, went through and before month's end so did the bounced payment. It makes an objective observer wonder why a recurring problem like this, which Dennis was used to dealing with year after year, would suddenly become a motive for murder, as the Crown contended. Who would kill a golden goose like Richard Oland, whose fortune was growing larger every day?

In 2011, Oland's Visa credit card revealed about sixteen thousand dollars was spent in "discretionary travel." Forensic accountant Johnson agreed with defence lawyers that if those expenses weren't incurred, it would bring down the balance on the credit card. Travis provided evidence that Oland might live in the red day-to-day, but he was financially stable. He went to work for Travis at CBIC Wood Gundy in 1996 and had been with the firm for fifteen years at the time of his father's murder.

The big reveal through the media's trial reports of how the other half lives had Saint John mesmerized. Johnson looked at Oland's main chequing account, his Visa, line of

credit, investment account and RRSP account. He found the
chequing account rarely had a positive balance that lasted
more than a month. The balance spiked upward when his
pay was deposited but declined as funds were used to pay
bills and other living costs.

Johnson confirmed he was not asked to do a net worth
analysis of Oland by police or the Crown. As a result,
his review of Oland's finances did not consider any of
his assets. Johnson found evidence of at least two different sources of rental income, with cheques for $850 and
$650 regularly deposited into his account. He suggested
it would be reasonable to infer there was a corresponding
asset. Johnson also agreed with the defence that an analysis
doesn't give a "true sense of a person's financial position
unless you do a balance sheet."

His analysis didn't look beyond July 7, 2011, so while
Johnson found Oland bounced a cheque on July 5, the
forensic accountant missed that the payment did eventually
go through on July 19. In fact, the full month of July proved
slightly better than the previous months, ending with a
positive balance of $572.68. Oland's finances for 2009 and
2010 showed similar "peaks and valleys" and again showed
him maxing out or exceeding his credit limits. A colour-
coded chart demonstrated that the spikes and dips seen in
Dennis Oland's main CIBC chequing account in 2011 had
also occurred in 2009 and 2010, highlighting consistency
in his spending habits. Between January 1, 2010 and July 7,
2010, Dennis Oland's spending outstripped his income by
$128,659.58 — about forty thousand dollars more than in
the six months in 2011 before his father was killed.

Dennis also travelled to the Caribbean Island of St.
Maarten during the period under review, spending about nine

thousand dollars on the trip, which implied he wasn't worried about money. Comparing Oland's debt load between 2009 and 2011, Johnson acknowledged that "it was increasing as time passed." However, Travis testified Oland's book of business, valued at $200,000 to $300,000, was an asset that could be sold to another broker if need be. So, what does all this prove? Essentially that money problems amounted to a lifestyle and not a reason for Dennis Oland to murder his father.

CHAPTER TWENTY

The First Trial: An Incredible Verdict

Judge Walsh's address to the jury began on December 15, 2015, and he took more than a day to instruct the jury. The Crown had needed to prove Oland's guilt beyond a reasonable doubt, and Walsh reminded the jury of myriad possible doubts, including the weakness of the blood and other DNA evidence on the jacket.

As Gold put it, "We shed our DNA as we go through life. We cough, we spit, we get nosebleeds, we pick scabs." And some people in particular are DNA "shedders." Other questions centred around the lack of evidence concerning a financial or emotional motive; a computer forensic expert hired by the family had found no antagonistic emails or other messages between Dennis and his father, even after mining an electronic history the size of "the Library of Congress ten times over."

After just two days deliberating, the jury decided. "It's verdict time," said Greg Marquis, a law historian at the University of New Brunswick and author of a book about the case. In response to an email alert from the court communications officer, Marquis and reporters flocked to court. Courtroom regular Judith Meinert was driving to Halifax to visit her family; another regular, Patty Dow, was in Moncton, and almost none of the other regulars arrived before the judge entered and the sheriff instructed the courtroom to rise. The audience — mostly the defendant's friends and family from Rothesay, expecting to celebrate an acquittal — sat back down and stayed rigid, as if posing for the sketch artist.

It was a freezing Saturday morning at 11:10 a.m., six days before Christmas and ninety-four days after the start of the trial, when the judge announced the guilty verdict. Shock ensued. Oland collapsed, weeping and crying, "Oh, no!" and "Oh, God! My children." His mother bent forward in grief and his sister, in tears, moved to stroke her back. Wife Lisa turned to the jurors and said, "How could you do this?" The family put out a statement, with Connie as spokesperson, "We are shocked and saddened. Our faith in Dennis's innocence has never wavered. All Oland members are certain Dennis had nothing to do with the death of his father."

Meinert was in the car, listening to CBC Radio as her husband drove, when she heard the news. "It's a good thing I wasn't driving," she said. "I probably would've put the car off the road. I thought he was going to be found not guilty by reasonable doubt." Meinert was equally shocked by Dennis's outburst. "I think it just bushwhacked everybody because he had been so self-contained throughout the trial."

CHAPTER TWENTY-ONE
The Appeal and the Beating

From the day Dennis Oland was sentenced — February 11, 2016 — and led away in handcuffs, he faced a long and arduous road. Friends and family refused to accept the guilty verdict. Hundreds of supporters mounted a sustained letter-writing and Facebook campaign to free him. Dozens of supporters showed up at the sentencing. Friends and family became regular visitors to the Atlantic Institution maximum security prison at Renous, thirty kilometres west of Miramichi, a two a half hour drive from Saint John. Oland's best friend Val Streeter kept an eye on his children and checked in on Dennis twice a month.

Immediately after sentencing, the defence launched an appeal to overturn the guilty verdict, order a new trial, or enter a full acquittal and have Dennis released from custody.

They also asked that he be released on bail as he was no threat to the community. However, New Brunswick Court of Appeal Justice Marc Richard denied bail on the grounds it would undermine the public's faith in the justice system; at this juncture no convicted murderer in New Brunswick had ever been released on bail pending appeal. The defence appealed that decision too. The application for bail went to the Supreme Court and was challenged by Ontario, Alberta and British Columbia as precedent-setting, but the appeal was successful.

When news of a life sentence with eligibility for parole after ten years for Dennis Oland first broke, Toronto criminal lawyer Christopher Hicks said publicly what scores of other Canadian criminal lawyers were thinking. Hicks commented that the sentence not only represented the minimum period of parole ineligibility, but it was also "disproportionately low" for an offence that involved forty-five bludgeoning and stabbing blows to an older and innocent man. The jury unanimously recommended ten years. Crown lawyer Patrick Wilbur had called for two to five years beyond the ten years due to the brutal nature of the elder Oland's death. He wanted Dennis to serve between twelve and fifteen years in jail before parole eligibility.

"This was a brutal crime of rage and hatred," he said in an interview with Canada's online legal newspaper *AdvocateDaily.com*. The Crown's position of twelve to fifteen years was more in the proper range given the allegations, even for a first offender, said Hicks, a partner at Hicks Adams LLP.

I would venture that the sentence imposed by Justice Walsh was a signal that he believed the conviction of Dennis Oland for the murder of his father Richard was a wrongful conviction.

The sentence also increased the probability that Dennis Oland would be released on bail pending his appeal to the Court of Appeal of New Brunswick, and sure enough, he was. However, notwithstanding these signals to the legal community that the case was far from over, Oland served ten uneasy and difficult months in jail awaiting the outcome of his bail application. In the visitors' room in Renous on July 31, 2016, all visitors had left except for two people visiting with Oland. Two fellow inmates, both from Halifax, walked over and without provocation attacked him. They viciously punched and kicked him, knocking him to the floor, and continued to punch and kick him until his visitors and guards intervened. Cody Alexander Muise and Aaron Marriott also faced charges for assaults on other inmates.

A legal cat and mouse game began. Even though the attack was recorded on surveillance cameras, the case was adjourned repeatedly to accommodate the two prisoners' lawyer's requests for more time to prepare. At the *fifth* court appearance in May 2017, both lawyers said their clients had received a copy of their files and a DVD of the alleged assault but were unable to view the DVD. They wanted more time to allow them to watch the DVD.

Another month and a half passed. On June 22, 2017, convicted murderer Muise, 28, serving a life sentence for first-degree murder in a 2010 shooting death in Spryfield, Nova Scotia, and Marriott, 27, serving time for attempted murder in connection with a shooting outside the IWK children's hospital in Halifax in 2008, elected trial by a New Brunswick court judge.

Judge Denis Lordon set a trial date for both men for September 26 at 9:30 a.m. in Miramichi provincial court. When that date arrived, the two entered new guilty pleas. Consequently, the video of the attack on Dennis Oland in the visitor's room fifteen months earlier was not entered into evidence and not made public. In November 2017, Muise and Marriott were each sentenced to four months, via video conference from prison in Renous.

No trial meant that no reasons were ever given for the attack on a man they did not even know in front of his family, but it can't be ruled out that it was initiated by organized crime — as a warning to the family that there was nowhere either Dennis or they were safe. One person close to the family said they were warned not to talk publicly about the case. The Maritimes business community speculated that Richard Oland had business dealings that involved organized crime that had gone wrong, and his death was a mafia hit.

In the most important break for the defence, Dennis Oland's conviction was overturned by the New Brunswick Court of Appeal on October 24, 2016 and a new trial ordered. The tribunal concluded that Justice Walsh had misdirected the jury in his instructions concerning an inaccurate voluntary statement by Oland to police during interrogation the day after the murder. Oland told police he was wearing a navy blazer when he visited his father's office instead of the brown jacket. The trial judge told the jurors if they found Oland's statement about which jacket he had worn was "an intentional lie," they could "consider this evidence" of guilt along with all the other evidence. Walsh failed to instruct jurors the Crown had not provided proof that Oland had lied deliberately. In other words, without evidence of a lie

164 Who Killed Richard Oland

it could not be considered. New Brunswick's highest court released a written statement detailing the legal reasoning behind the court's decision to quash Oland's conviction and order a new trial.

Chief Justice Ernest Drapeau wrote, "With respect, that instruction was prejudicial to the defence and is erroneous in law." Drapeau called the evidence "a puzzle." He wrote that a legal framework must be applied when it comes to questions about lies, and jurors must have independent evidence that the lie is fabricated or concocted to conceal involvement in a crime.

> The jury must be told that it cannot rely on a deliberately false statement as a piece of circumstantial evidence on the Crown's side of the scales unless there is independent evidence that the statement was concocted. If the record did not reveal any "independent" evidence from which concoction might be inferred, the judge would have had to instruct the jury the appellant's "lie" about the jacket could not be used as inculpatory evidence. He did not.

He said further that Dennis's behaviour after Richard's murder "appears to be inconsistent with the behaviour expected from someone who committed a crime of extreme violence." Under the law, jurors are prevented from discussing their findings, so we will never know what they were thinking.

Toronto lawyer David Butt says the New Brunswick Court of Appeal's decision to overturn Oland's murder conviction because of an error in the trial judge's instructions to the jury illustrates a problem with the system that should be changed.

As Dennis's lawyer Alan Gold explained, the judge's error

> *had to do with Dennis's statement about what jacket he was wearing. To use it as evidence of guilt, the jury had to be instructed to be satisfied it was a fabricated statement, i.e., intentional lie to throw police off the track. The jury was not told this.*

Chief Justice Drapeau's decision was parsed by Canadian criminal lawyers. In a CBC television interview, Butt argued there's no way of knowing if that error had any influence on the jury's decision to find Oland guilty of second-degree murder. Butt, who researches jury comprehension, said,

> *We don't actually spend any time asking ourselves and finding out if the jury actually made a mistake in their reasoning process. We don't make any inquiry into what the jury did in the jury room. So really, despite the correctness or otherwise of the instructions, we're actually in the dark as to whether they reached the correct verdict.*

Butt suggested that jurors could be provided with a form to give reasons for their verdict. Legislative changes could also see jurors reveal information about the reasons for their verdict — similar to the current requirement for judge-alone trials.

"I think it would be an important step forward. Once you have those reasons, then you can assess whether they thought the case through properly."

His suggestion fell on deaf ears.

> *As far as I can tell, my suggestion that juries give reasons for their decisions has no traction whatsoever. This does not surprise me, because the rationale for the status quo is deeply entrenched, and is as follows: Judges are legal technicians, while juries are the common-sense conscience of the community. These are different but equally important ways of making legal decisions, and in our justice system there should be room for both.*
>
> "*So, we should not conflate the two by trying to make juries act more like amateur judges. Instead, we should protect the privacy of jury deliberations and rely on jury unanimity to weed out misapprehensions of the evidence by individual jurors, and to also weed out suspect paths of reasoning. However, the darker subtext of the status quo that juries need not give reasons for their decisions may be that we implicitly invite sympathy and prejudice to play too big a role.*

Without proper instructions, jurors could have leapt from "bare lie to guilt," wrote Drapeau, on behalf of the three-justice panel. He noted the "bare lie" may well have provided the argument that brought to the Crown's side one or more of the wavering jurors. Oland's circumstantial case is not one "where the evidence pointing to guilt is so overwhelming that the outcome would necessarily have been the same, with or without the [trial judge's] error," Drapeau wrote in the decision.

A judge's instructions are meant to guide jurors on how

they should apply the law to the evidence in a case. When an appeal court finds errors in a trial judge's instructions, it says, "We're going to have to do this all over again because the jury might have been misled by that error in the instructions. It's always 'might.' Nobody ever asks whether they actually were," said Butt, noting,

> *We may have a jury who completely misunderstood the instructions and frankly doesn't have the first idea whether they're applying them correctly. Or we may have a very intelligent and sophisticated jury who understands those instructions well and applies them perfectly. The difficulty is we never know in any given case because we never ask the jury, "How did you reach your conclusion?" We simply ask for the conclusion itself.*

As a result, appeal courts are left to err on the side of caution and order a new trial because a judge's flawed instructions might have led jurors to their verdict, said Butt. He continued:

> *My thesis is, instead of guessing that they might have erred, why don't we have a process that asks a little bit more of the jury, that they reveal their thinking a little bit more? If they did make that mistake, fine, we need a new trial to be fair to everybody. But if they didn't make that mistake, there's no sense in putting the public to the expense of a brand-new trial if no mistake was made at the first one.*

It is illegal for jurors to discuss how or why they reached
a verdict — partly to protect those on trial who are ultimately found not guilty, and partly to allow jurors to speak
freely during deliberations without fear their discussions will
later be subject to scrutiny and criticism. Butt contends that
jurors should be asked to provide, "briefly," their reasons for
their verdict, possibly by filling out a form.

> *When you sit with a judge alone without a jury,
> the judge is required to give reasons, and we
> assess whether through those reasons the judge
> demonstrates that they understood the evidence
> properly. It makes perfect sense that you'd ask the
> same thing of a jury, which is doing the exact same
> task of deciding an important criminal case.*

CHAPTER TWENTY-TWO:

The Retrial: A Tainted Jury

Two years passed before the new trial began. On November 6, 2018, Oland again entered a not-guilty plea, and the family released a statement of support through family lawyer Bill Teed that their faith in his innocence has "never wavered."

"We wish to restate our steadfast support for Dennis and our faith that the judicial process will prove his innocence," Connie, wife Lisa, Uncle Derek and Aunt Jacqueline (Derek's wife) said in the joint statement. The family has endured an "unimaginable ordeal" since Richard Oland's death in 2011, compounded by the arrest and conviction of his only son. To the "innumerable friends and strangers" who have expressed their "unfailing belief in Dennis's innocence, we cannot adequately express how much this continuing support means to us," the statement said.

After all that had gone before, perhaps it should have surprised no one that Dennis Oland's retrial got off to a bumpy start. Although he successfully appealed his conviction in October 2016, his second trial, this time by Judge alone, without a jury, did not begin until November 2018. The retrial was originally slated to be heard by judge and jury, and jury selection began in October 2018. However, the retrial was delayed by two weeks as an unexpected legal issue arose. That issue turned out to be jury tampering.

New Brunswick Court of Queen's Bench Justice Terrence Morrison declared a mistrial on November 20, 2018, after it was discovered that Saint John police officer Sean Rocca had conducted "improper" background checks on jurors, both prospective and even those who had been selected. His illegal activity came to light when he informed the Crown what he was doing. Rocca was working to ensure that the jury would be inclined to support the Crown's case because they had no previous history with law enforcement.

The Crown advised the defence lawyers, and they brought it to Justice Morrison's attention. In 2012, "in no uncertain terms the Supreme Court of Canada condemned the practice of using police databases to conduct inquiries of potential jurors outside legitimate permissible checks for criminal records to determine juror eligibility," Morrison said in his written decision. Rocca testified his sole purpose was to check for criminal records.

Justice Morrison dismissed the sixteen jurors who had been selected in late October 2018 over concerns the jury selection process was tainted. He then presided over the retrial alone, which is what the defence had initially requested. They believed that a judge would decide the case more fairly — strictly on its legal merits rather than any extraneous personal or emotional considerations that might influence a jury.

The shocking jury tampering incident may lead to far-reaching changes in the jury selection process as it also came to light that Saint John Police had conducted the same illegal background checks on prospective jurors in the first trial. However, no one apparently took note of it at the time.

The New Brunswick Police Commission immediately announced it would review the force's involvement in the jury selection process for Oland's retrial after all criminal proceedings were completed. The Saint John Board of Police Commissioners requested an independent investigation of Rocca's actions, especially given that Rocca and many officers on the force saw nothing wrong with what he had done. Just business as usual.

Rocca was an investigator in the Oland case from the beginning, and he became the file co-ordinator in October 2011, three months after the murder. Rocca suffered no disciplinary action for what was clearly a breach of proper procedure. In fact, Rocca was promoted to staff sergeant two months later — one of three officers promoted at the time.

"I am pleased to be part of a progressive leadership team and looking forward to serving the members of the Saint John Police Force and our community in my new role," Rocca said in an emailed statement to the media. Constable Duane Squires, president of the Saint John Police Association, added in a separate media communication, "The Saint John Police Association wishes these officers the best in their new management roles." He declined further comment.

The incident and its aftermath warrant a closer look to better understand the situation. What is and is not permissible when vetting prospective jurors? The Crown and police are allowed to conduct limited background checks to determine if a potential juror has a criminal record. But the judge found some of Rocca's searches in relation to Oland's retrial "went beyond looking for 'arrest flags' which might shed light on a criminal record."

"You think all of this was permissible to this day, right, what you did?" defence lawyer Michael Lacy asked Rocca during cross-examination at the closed hearing.

"Yes," replied Rocca, indicating that his training did not suggest otherwise. Rocca, who sat with the Crown during jury selection October 29-31, 2018 said he used his laptop in the courtroom to search the names of potential jurors on the Case Management System (CMS), "software that facilitates the secure, timely, and cost-effective exchange of information between the police and prosecution." The internal database tracks any contact a person has had with Saint John police — whether as a complainant, victim, witness, suspect or an accused — but if someone has been arrested, a flag pops up on the top left side of the screen, while information about any dealings with police appears at the bottom, he said.

If an arrest flag popped up, Rocca said, he would "prompt" Crown prosecutor Derek Weaver, so he could check the provincial Justice Information System, or JIS, database on his own laptop to see if the person had a criminal record. Rocca, who was also running a PowerPoint presentation of questions for prospective jurors during the challenge-for-cause process, said he missed checking some of the names and noticed "a few" prospective jurors didn't initially disclose they had a criminal record. So, on November 1, after jury selection was complete, Rocca said he decided to run the names of the fourteen sworn-in jurors and two alternates "out of an abundance of caution" to verify none had a record.

The challenge-for-cause process is designed to screen out potential biases in juries — not to check if they have a record that might colour how they view the police. There is a presumption that jurors are capable of setting aside their views and biases in favour of impartiality between Crown and the accused and compliance with the trial judge's instructions. Nonplussed defence lawyers immediately demanded to know under whose instruction he had performed the detailed CMS searches.

"Nobody asked me to do it. I did it on my own," Rocca said when questioned in court.

Neither the Crown nor the defence were aware Rocca was doing the CMS searches, according to court documents. They found out later when Rocca advised the Crown of what he had discovered about two of the sworn jurors and then testified about his previous searches of prospective jurors. The details of what Rocca discovered have been blacked out of the transcript, but it involved "prior contact with members of the Saint John Police Force" and prompted the Crown to file an application to have one of the two jurors excused and replaced by an alternate.

"The first thing that I saw was in relation to juror [redacted] and I saw that [redacted]. So, I checked that matter," Rocca testified, the transcript shows.

> I didn't read the file in, you know, in its entirety but I did see that [redacted] was one of the entries in this particular file and so I just checked, and I confirmed that [redacted] had, in fact [redacted] and that the juror was [redacted].

When he checked the other juror, there was no arrest flag at the top of the screen, but he "glanced down" and saw there was one entry for the person.

"The nature of the entry caught my eye," he said. "So, I opened that file and ... I immediately saw my name on the file, but I also saw [redacted] name."

Rocca said he didn't recall the file and hadn't recognized the juror in court, so he opened another entry "and saw that he had [redacted]. And so, this, to me, would have been much lengthier contact with [redacted] at the time, and so my concern was that he was one of the names read aloud by Justice Morrison" to prospective jurors as possible witnesses in the trial and possible conflicts of interest.

That's when he notified the Crown, he said. The Crown immediately instructed him to stop conducting searches and disclosed his searches to the defence, according to court records. With CMS, the only way to determine if an arrest flag ultimately resulted in a criminal record is to go into the next "layer" of the system and check the details, Rocca told the court. And just because someone doesn't have an arrest flag associated with their name doesn't necessarily mean they don't have a conviction, he said. CMS is only as reliable as the input information.

"There's been a lot of situations that I've been involved in where there isn't an arrest screen for people that have been charged and have been convicted," said Rocca.

Defence counsel Michael Lacy argued the most appropriate source for criminal record searches would have been either the Canadian Police Information Centre (CPIC), which requires police to log in using their credentials and creates an audit trail or the provincial system — not the Saint John police database, which contains "all kinds of extraneous information."

Rocca testified he didn't have access to either of the other systems when he searched prospective jurors in the courtroom, or when he searched the sworn jurors at the Crown's office. He agreed he could have walked across the street to police headquarters after jury selection was complete and logged into a computer that did have access to the national or provincial systems, but he said they also have their limitations. The CPIC, for example, only lists convictions when an offender has been fingerprinted, said Rocca.

"So, there's all kinds of people that when you run them on CPIC have criminal records, but they can come back as not having any criminal record," said Rocca, adding it took him "several years" on the job to realize this.

For a conviction to be registered on CPIC, fingerprints must be obtained under the Identification of Criminals Act, which only allows for fingerprints to be taken in cases of indictable or hybrid offences, RCMP spokeswoman Michelle Schmidt confirmed. Less serious summary conviction offences are only included in the national repository if they are part of an occurrence involving an indictable or hybrid offence. In other words, a person arrested and then released without charge would not register on CPIC. However, they might have had a bad experience with the police.

JIS only lists convictions that originated within New Brunswick, said Rocca, which New Brunswick Department of Justice spokesman Robert Duguay confirmed. Rocca said Saint John police routinely checked all three systems to confirm whether a prospective juror has a criminal record; they would commonly start with CMS because it may reveal a conviction not captured by the other two databases.

"You were checking for contacts that would give rise to a concern on your part that someone might not be a particularly favourable juror for the Crown, isn't that right?" Lacy alleged.

"No, I was checking for criminal records," Rocca insisted. "I didn't see anything wrong with that whatsoever." He said he had performed similar searches for other jury trials, including Oland's first trial in 2015.

CHAPTER TWENTY-THREE

The Retrial: New Evidence for the Defence

Gerry Lowe, the Liberal MLA who represented Saint John Harbour in the New Brunswick legislature from 2018 to 2020, was the first witness for the defence at Dennis Oland's retrial presided over by Court of Queen's Bench Justice Terrence Morrison. Lowe did not testify at the first trial for reasons unexplained by either the defence or the prosecution. However, when he finally did testify, Lowe presented startling new evidence that caused a stir.

He said he saw a man he could not identify exit the street door of the victim's office building between 7:45 p.m. and 8:15 p.m. on the night of the killing and walk north towards King Street. He told the court he was at his favourite restaurant, Thandi, where he ate several times a week. Thandi, offering an appetizing fusion of Indian and Thai cuisine, is on Canterbury Street across the street from Far End Corporation. Thandi's plate glass windows provide an unimpeded view of the narrow one-way street and the entrance to Oland's second floor office.

Lowe's recollection of the event after eight years was hazy, and he was initially unclear on the witness stand if he was at the restaurant July 5 or July 6, 2011, but a time-stamped video confirmed it was the night of the murder. While Lowe couldn't remember which day he saw the man, he did tell police about seeing a photo shoot the same day while at the restaurant. The Crown and defence entered an agreed statement of facts that a photographer was at Thandi on July 6, starting at 7:46 p.m.

The court saw video from the restaurant security camera that Lowe was at the restaurant that night between 7:40 p.m. and 8:35 p.m. — around the probable time of the murder. The time element is critical. Dennis Oland was alone with his father in the office from about 5:45 p.m. until 6:30 p.m. on July 6. He then headed back to his home in Rothesay, a twenty-minute drive. Between 7:30 p.m. and 8 p.m., he was captured on surveillance cameras in Rothesay shopping with his wife Lisa.

"I know I saw a man come out the door (from Oland's office at 52 Canterbury Street) and walk . . . towards King Street."

Lowe may have seen Richard Oland's killer or if not the killer, then perhaps an accomplice. He testified he had spent a lot of time over the years thinking about what he saw the night of the murder.

"I've thought and thought . . . It has been so long. Eight years is a long time." Lowe told Oland's murder retrial on March 5, 2019. The case against Oland proceeded very much as it had in the first trial, with most of the same witnesses testifying. Some of them, such as Diana Sedlacek who had moved to Victoria, B.C. testified on video. Although the circumstantial facts of the case remain largely unchanged from Oland's 2015 trial, which ended with a jury finding him guilty, the evidence is extensive and complex.

The presentation of oral evidence lasted until March 8, 2019, when the court adjourned to give both defence and prosecution lawyers time to prepare written summations and closing arguments. These were presented in court May 9, after which the Judge adjourned the trial to consider and craft his decision. Also on March 8, the court, including Crown and defence lawyers, Oland himself, and the judge, visited the crime scene at the request of the defence. Justice Morrison, accompanied by the lawyers and the defendant, trekked the short distance to Far End Corporation. They saw first-hand the steep stairs to the second floor, the landing leading to the French doors that opened into the office space, the industrial back door, and the shared washroom facilities. The office had been restored to immaculate order, a legal dispute over the cost of the clean-up between John Ainsworth and Far End Corporation after Richard Oland's murder having been settled out of court.

An old friend of Dennis Oland's from the time they had both served on the YMCA board, was having lunch at Thandi and watching through the window as the action across the street was filmed by local TV news crews. He could see it the same way Gerry Lowe had seen it July 6, 2011. "I wanted to be sure everything went okay today for Dennis," he commented to a reporter who was watching the scene from the same vantage point.

The retrial also heard new evidence about the possible bloody footprint found at the crime scene — that was disregarded for three years. The head of the Saint John Police Force's forensic identification section and an RCMP bloodstain pattern analyst testified for the Crown about what appeared to be a footprint while the defence called its own RCMP footwear impression analyst. Justice Morrison professed "a fair amount of confusion" about exactly when and how the possible partial footwear impression was discovered in the victim's blood-spattered office.

Some other new evidence introduced at the retrial included several mysterious sticky notes. They were found by a local resident in a wooded area on the city's west side more than a month after the killing. They had the victim's nickname, Dick, written on them, as well as the names of other members of the prominent Oland family who founded Moosehead Breweries, and "policemen" Mike, Stephen, and Mark. Although the notes don't specify, officers Mike King, Stephen Davidson and Mark Smith were investigators in the Oland murder case. The four weathered notes turned in by the citizen also included the notations: "alcoholic," "Transfer $429," and "Jon insured."

The defence created an enactment video to illustrate how the "killer or killers" could have escaped using the back door. The defence contended the steel door in the foyer outside Oland's office would have been the logical route because it was the most covert exit to an alleyway almost at ground level. The door was never tested for fingerprints or DNA because it had been opened by police on July 7 and therefore was contaminated before the forensics officer got to it.

Alan Gold had planned to have Gregory Baumeister, a core network specialist with the telecommunications company Ericsson, testify about attempts by Saint John police and Rogers Communications to locate Richard

Oland's missing cellphone. Both trials heard that efforts to ping the phone came back with a "roaming error" message. Gold admitted the defence misunderstood what that meant or its significance at the first trial and wanted Baumeister to clarify for the court the meaning of messages generated by those technologies, including roaming errors.

At Oland's first trial, the Crown and defence submitted an agreed statement that roaming error could mean one of three things — the phone is registered on a foreign network with which Rogers doesn't have a roaming agreement; Rogers can't locate the phone because records of its location have been purged after a period of inactivity, with no calls, texts or data access; and finally, that the location of the phone can't be obtained for "some unspecified reason." In this case, the roaming error happened on July 9, 2011. The cellphone was turned on three days after the murder. This was discovered when Rogers called it and found it was outside the carrier's jurisdiction, thus the message came back "roaming error." However, when the Crown and defence disagreed on technical aspects of Baumeister's testimony, Gold withdrew him as a defence witness.

Gold introduced emails into evidence at the retrial from two Crown prosecutors to forensic toxicologist Dr. Albert Fraser regarding his 2011 report presented in court at the first trial on the urine, blood and eye fluid samples taken from the victim during the autopsy. The defence argued that the jury might not have been properly presented with New Brunswick Pathologist Ather Naseemuddin's findings, which could have influenced their deliberations. Gold wanted to make sure the judge understood that Oland had taken an alcoholic drink like Scotch on July 6, 2011, and not imbibed cough syrup as the Crown insinuated.

"There's no question that Richard Oland was murdered on July 6, 2011. The one major issue to be decided is whether it was Dennis Oland who committed this murder," prosecutor Jill Knee said in her opening statement when the retrial began in November 2018.

The only evidence linking him to one of the bloodiest murders in Canada's history was prosecution evidence from blood and DNA analysts who identified four minuscule bloodstains on the jacket Dennis Oland was wearing when he visited his dad on the day of the murder. After an exhaustive search, as we know, Richard Oland's DNA profile was found within three of the bloodstains. The jacket, seized in a police search of Oland's home, was rolled up and folded into a bag for a considerable length of time and may have been kept outside the police evidence locker.

Alan Gold, while cross examining the forensic experts, pointed out that the blood and DNA evidence was limited — for example, there is no way to know when or how they came to be on the jacket.

"We can't say when DNA was deposited, how it was deposited, the order in which it was deposited or how long it was there," Thomas Suzanski, a forensic specialist from the RCMP crime lab in Ottawa, agreed in his testimony. Suzanski's evidence, like that of several other witnesses, was presented to court at the retrial by replaying video from Oland's first trial.

In his decision to exonerate Dennis Oland, Justice Terrence Morrison dismissed outright that microscopic bloodstains on the brown jacket were conclusive evidence. In fact, he said the bloodstains found on the jacket supported the defence's case rather than the Crown's. The defence had argued the blood and DNA was "innocent transfer" that could have pre-dated the murder. Morrison said the absence of blood spatter on the shoes and other clothing Oland wore when he visited his father "calls into question the inference that the blood on the jacket is blood spatter."

> *In my view, [the jacket] is a piece of circumstantial evidence favouring the accused that can be considered, along with all the other evidence in determining whether the Crown has proven guilt beyond a reasonable doubt.*

Richard Oland's missing cellphone comprised the other key evidence in the prosecution's case — the only item taken from the crime scene. Or was it? Dennis Oland contends an envelope containing a letter from Richard Oland's mistress Diana Sedlacek was also missing. Oland's administrative assistant, Maureen Adamson, who handled the incoming office mail, and accountant Robert McFadden, who also worked in the office full-time, had to be aware of the letter. Their boss was open with them about his personal life, keeping a detailed diary that included his free time scheduling. Adamson frequently made travel arrangements for Sedlacek; McFadden took care of his boss's expenses. One can imagine Adamson slitting open the letter from Sedlacek and unfolding and reading some of it before realizing fully who it was from and that the message was personal.

Cellphone records indicate the missing phone received its last message at 6:44 p.m. on the day of the murder. Experts told the court it pinged off a tower on the outskirts of Saint John near Rothesay. The police theory was that Dennis took the iPhone from his father's desk after killing him and buried it or tossed it off the Renforth Wharf on his way home.

John Ainsworth, owner of the building where Richard Oland was murdered, was grilled by lawyer Gold about the loud thumps and bangs he heard on that evening —likely the sound of Oland being bludgeoned to death. Ainsworth insisted, angrily at times, that he does not know what time he heard the noises, beyond the general range of 6 to 8 p.m. That contrasts with his friend, Anthony Shaw, who was with him that evening and believes the noises were made around 7:30 to 8 p.m.

> *If Shaw is right, Oland could not have been the killer since he was caught on security video shopping in Rothesay at 7:30 p.m. — whereas Ainsworth's testimony leaves open the possibility that the killing happened while Dennis Oland was at his father's office before he left at 6:30 p.m.*

"I do not know what time it was," Ainsworth exclaimed under intense questioning by Gold. "I have been suffering with it for eight years. I do not know."

However, a videotaped statement made under oath by Ainsworth in 2011 for a private investigator working for the Oland family and entered into evidence on February 22, 2019, makes it clear that originally, Ainsworth also thought the sounds were made at 7:30 to 8 p.m.

"It was approximately 7:30, or quarter to 8," he said during the interview.

Despite that, Ainsworth said once he had time to reflect on what had happened, he felt he could not be specific about the time. "I was not paying attention," he said.

Gold accused Ainsworth of wanting Oland to be convicted of the murder and thus backing off his original statement. But Ainsworth disputed that allegation.

"I am not that type of person," he said. "I want to be honourable. That's all. Integrity is everything."

The testy exchanges between Gold and Ainsworth closed the prosecution case. However, the judge placed more weight on his video statement.

In his 146-page decision, the judge focused on motive, which "provides context for the interpretation of the evidence."

"Without motive, the trier of fact is being asked to put the jigsaw puzzle together without the benefit of seeing the picture on the puzzle box."

The Crown suggested three motives: Oland had a troubled relationship with his father; Oland "disapproved" of his father's extra-marital affair with local realtor Diana Sedlacek; and when Oland visited his father at his office on July 6, 2011, he was in dire financial straits and had "nowhere left to turn."

Justice Morrison said he had no doubt Oland and his father had a "difficult relationship," but he could not conclude the relationship was "so dysfunctional" as to be abnormal. "In my view, whatever resentments the relationship may have fostered in Dennis Oland they cannot, on their own, account for Richard Oland's murder."

Morrison rejected the suggestion that Richard Oland's affair with Diana Sedlacek provided an outright motive. The gist of the conversation Oland had with his father's business associate Robert McFadden about the affair "hardly belies a burning resentment, let alone red-eyed rage," he said.

McFadden testified that Oland told him in 2008-09, "Maybe you could mention to him to cool it or be more discreet."

"It was a rather tepid suggestion made in a one-off, unrelated conversation at least a year and a half before the murder," said Morrison.

Thirdly, Morrison dismissed the theory that Oland was in dire financial straits and had "nowhere left to turn."

Crown prosecutors posited Oland had asked his father for financial assistance during the visit, his father had refused, and he then killed him in a state of rage.

Morrison accepted Oland's testimony that he was not overly concerned about his financial situation. There was a no "tipping point" in Oland's financial situation that "drove [him] to desperation" that night.

The evidence did not support the Crown's suggestion that Oland's father knew about his missed interest-only payments or that it concerned him. He also found no evidence of the Crown's suggestion that Oland was at risk of losing the ancestral home, worth an estimated $650,000, to foreclosure, noting he had missed only one payment of $481.

Morrison said, even if he found Oland was in a financial crisis on July 6, the evidence showed that when Oland sought financial help in the past, his father did not refuse him.

In addition, Morrison found no evidence that Oland received any direct financial benefit from his father's death. McFadden testified the elder Oland's will provided for a spousal trust for his wife, Connie Oland, with the remainder divided among his son and two daughters only upon her death, he said.

Besides, said Morrison, financial gain as the motive for murder implies premeditation. "This would fly in the face of the Crown's theory that this was a crime of passion born of an enraged mind and would be inconsistent with the charge of second-degree murder found in the indictment."

The Crown alleged Oland lied to police about which jacket he wore, specifically to mislead them. There is "some merit" to the Crown's contention that Oland "deliberately obfuscated" certain facts during his police interview, Morrison said. He noted that Oland "entirely omitted" mentioning that he made a third trip to his father's office that night. But the judge was not satisfied there was sufficient evidence to conclude Oland's untrue statement about the jacket was a lie fabricated to deceive police.

He also pointed out that Oland was under police surveillance as soon as he left his police interview on July 7, and there was no evidence he attended the dry cleaners on July 8.

In Morrison's view, the bloodstains found on the jacket actually supported the defence's case more than the Crown's. The small number and "very small" size of the bloodstains are inconsistent with the bloody crime scene, he said.

In the days following the removal of Richard Oland's body from his Canterbury Street office, city police gathered witness statements and evidence from the crime scene. On July 9, 2011, Sgt. Mark Smith was at the scene looking for a weapon and documents and collecting several blood swabs. Adamson came by the office to advise the police of possible missing items. She listed Oland's iPhone 4, the family's camp logbook and a will as items that had been in the office at the time of the murder. Apparently, Adamson's list did not include a letter from Diana Sedlacek.

On July 9, police filed an affidavit with the Court of Queen's Bench, requesting a judge grant a production order to Rogers Communications for documentation of incoming and outgoing calls for three numbers as well as cell tower data for these numbers. Three numbers? Why so specific? Why didn't the police ask for the complete phone records and cell tower data for several weeks leading up to July 6 and 7?

Police through Crown Counsel must provide disclosure to defence counsel of evidence they have compiled. Failure to do so constitutes a serious breach. By limiting the production call to a few numbers, the police may have overlooked important evidence. It's not clear that anyone has examined Richard Oland's complete phone records, both cell and landline.

"Rest assured that all relevant evidence was carefully reviewed." Oland family lawyer Bill Teed responded tersely in an email in early 2023 when he was asked about "phone records that might indicate calls from an unknown caller or someone connected to Richard Oland's business dealings, setting up a meeting that ended with his murder."

Alan Gold was blunt. "I cannot assist you. I have no access to any such materials," he replied to an email asking if the defence had obtained Richard Oland's phone records. Gold was also asked if there were "calls from an unknown caller from a burner phone or from (former Can Sugar president) John Cardwell? Robert McFadden, Richard Oland's accountant, said the situation that led to the murder "had been festering for some time." Richard Oland had been out of town on a fishing trip in the week or so before his murder. McFadden's awareness of a tense issue suggests there must have been some evidence of this.

"The murderer most definitely took the phone and the envelope [with letter enclosed from the mistress]," Dennis Oland wrote in a 2023 email.

The RCMP tech-crime officers found the iPhone had been backed up on Oland's computer just after 4:30 p.m. on July 6. They concluded it left with the killer. Sylvie Gill, a Rogers Communications investigator, presented spread sheets to the court showing selected incoming and outgoing calls and texts from Richard Oland's cellphone. The last text it received "You there?" from Sedlacek pinged off the Rothesay cell tower at 6:44 p.m. A flurry of subsequent texts she sent from her Darling's Island home pinged off the Quispamsis tower. But these were never received by Oland's iPhone.

The whereabouts of the missing cellphone and its importance was thoroughly confused by Joseph Sadoun, a radio-frequency engineer, who testified for the Crown as an expert witness. Sadoun produced a twenty-one-page report on cell tower coverage for Saint John and Rothesay. Saint John's central business district has two cell towers. Sadoun confirmed that cellphone calls register with the tower that has the strongest radio signal, and generally that is the one closest to the phone. In the case of the "You there?" text, it was the Rothesay tower.

Under Gold's cross examination, however, Sadoun also confirmed that numerous test calls conducted by the Saint John police had not connected as predicted, bringing the accuracy of the test software into question and indicating that land elevation and time of day affected wireless signal transmission. Sylvie Gill confirmed that Richard Oland's habit was to let calls and texts go to voice mail, so it was not unusual for him to not answer his phone between 6:30 and 7:30 p.m. on July 6.

Time of death evidence formed the other "pillar" of the Crown's case, said Morrison. The Crown argued the victim was killed sometime between 5:45 p.m. and 6:36 p.m., when Dennis Oland was alone with him in his office and would have had exclusive opportunity to kill him.

Richard Oland did not use his computer after 5:39 p.m. Morrison wrote this was "probably because something was amiss." Diana Sedlacek had tried to text and call the victim several times, without success. However, the evidence was not conclusive, he said.

The men who heard "thumping" noises coming from the victim's office on the night he was killed raised a reasonable doubt as to the time of death, said Morrison. The noises were heard sometime after 7:30 p.m.

He also found support for the 7:30-8:00 p.m. timeframe from Saint John Harbour MLA Gerry Lowe's testimony that he saw a man exit the door leading to the victim's second-floor office while he was eating at the restaurant across the street.

Lowe, a regular patron of Thandi restaurant, was uncertain which night he saw the man. But he recalled being with a female companion and seeing a photo shoot that night.

The defence had security video of Oland shopping with his wife in Rothesay by 7:38 p.m. If his father was killed any time after approximately 7 p.m., then Oland "could not have been the killer," the judge said, reading from his decision.

In short, I have a reasonable doubt as to whether Richard Oland was killed prior to 6:44 p.m. . . . In the circumstances of this case, if I have a reasonable doubt as to the time of death, I must acquit the accused.

Dozens of Saint John residents came out to hear the verdict, lining up at the courthouse doors early and filling the courtroom on the morning of July 19, 2019, as they had done on December 20, 2015. There was a collective and audible gasp when Justice Morrison delivered his long-awaited decision to acquit. Many wiped away tears. A flushed Dennis hugged and kissed his lawyer. He hugged and kissed each one of his family and shook hands with all friends and supporters.

The Crown decided not to appeal, so the verdict stands. However, Saint John police have said they will not be re-opening the file to attempt to find Richard Oland's real killer, leaving the impression they believe they had the right man but the wrong verdict in court.

The retrial lasted forty-four days, spanning four months, heard from sixty-one witnesses and featured 309 exhibits.

But the story did not end there.

CHAPTER TWENTY-FOUR
The Retrial:
A Key Witness

Gerry Lowe pulled himself up from humble beginnings to become part of the New Brunswick establishment. With only a Grade Eleven education, Lowe made his name as a cab company owner, firefighter, a union rep for Canada Post, and the owner or part owner of many of the city's bars, restaurants and billiard halls.

Before running for city council, Lowe owned and operated Vet's Taxi for forty-three years, and he worked for Canada Post for thirty-five years, serving for twenty-one years as local union representative with the Canadian Union of Postal workers (CUPW), one of the more militant Canadian unions. Paradoxically, Lowe is quite the entrepreneur — he bought and renovated several of Saint John's historic buildings in the gentrifying uptown area where Richard Oland had his office and constructed a housing development in the Old Rockland Road area of the city.

Saint John is arguably Lowe's city and there isn't much happening there that escapes his notice. Lowe sat on the City of Saint John Planning and Advisory Committee and the Growth Committee, and he spent four years as a member of the Saint John Industrial Park Board, which approved the establishment of the new sugar refinery, replacing the historic 'Lantic Sugar Refinery that had closed down in 2001. As noted earlier, Richard Oland was also involved in the refinery project, which collapsed in bankruptcy shortly after its start in 2003.

Born to working-class parents and raised in Saint John, Lowe served as a Saint John city councillor for five years before entering provincial politics. He was elected to council in a May 2013 byelection and re-elected in May 2016. Then in the 2018 provincial election, Lowe won the riding of Saint John Harbour as a Liberal MLA, which covers much of the same area he had been serving as a Ward 3 councillor.

He was the only Liberal to win a seat in the Saint John area in the fall of 2018, squeaking out a hard-fought ten-vote victory when Blaine Higgs' Progressive Conservatives swept nine of ten seats in the Saint John region.

Lowe's campaign spent $120,000 to preserve the victory in a court challenge by the Conservative candidate; a recount confirmed his win. Then incredibly, after only two years in office, he decided he'd had enough already and did not seek re-election in Saint John Harbour in the September 2020 provincial election.

"It's just not my piece of cake," Lowe said in a media interview. Sitting in the opposition benches did not suit his taste for the real power that comes with a cabinet minister position. On his Facebook page, Lowe posted that he came to that conclusion early on as a member of the Liberal caucus, writing, "After much consideration early in my term, I realized that I had made a gigantic mistake in leaving Saint John council and entering an area where I lacked direct contact with the people." He told reporters that he enjoyed working in his riding on homelessness and better housing, but he didn't like the other part of his job as an MLA.

"Once you get to Fredericton, everything is a different world," he said. "It's such a waste of time up there, and it's so political. You don't get to the problems . . . Problems are solved directly when you're around here."

Ironically, Lowe said much the same in 2018 about the futility of municipal politics. When he decided to leave city council, it was because he thought he could accomplish more "sitting at the table in Fredericton" — but he was referring to the cabinet table.

"I love being a councillor, but I feel that to be able to get the things that have been promised to us [as a city], we have to have people there in Fredericton to fight for it."

While he denied he was promised a cabinet post if he would run by then-Premier Brian Gallant, he could have expected to be in a Liberal government cabinet. And it came as a jolt when the Liberals lost the election. Lowe was relegated to the opposition benches — so no seat at the table for him.

Weighing heavily in his decision not to stand for re-election as an MLA was the fact the Progressive Conservatives were heavily favoured to win the 2020 election, making his prospects for a cabinet seat nil. Lowe always wanted to be where the action was, and four more years as a Liberal back-bencher held no appeal for the then seventy-eight-year-old.

Contacted for more details about what he saw that evening on July 6, 2011 at Richard Oland's office door, he refused to elaborate. "I don't want to be rude; I just don't want to talk about it," he told me in a telephone interview September 14, 2020.

Asked before he hung up if he knew Richard Oland personally, he admitted he knew him but stressed they were not well acquainted. This was surprising given that both men were of a similar age, Saint John natives with common interests and were active in Saint John economic development projects and city politics for many years. Oland too was a Saint John property developer, having established Kinghurst Estates Limited, and was active in real estate for thirty years.

Why might a prominent public figure like Gerry Lowe be uncomfortable talking about what happened to a business colleague a decade earlier? Lowe wasn't inclined to talk about it when offered the opportunity to comment or answer questions about what he saw that July evening in 2011.

Many other Saint John residents involved in the case also prefer not to talk. This includes Derek and Connie, lawyers for Dennis and the family and the police. A lawyer who witnessed a loud argument between two men around the time John Ainsworth and Anthony Shaw heard loud thumping noises from the office above their print shop also won't talk about the case. A family friend, who asked to remain anonymous, said this reluctance to discuss the case could stem from fear of retribution if they don't keep quiet.

CHAPTER TWENTY-FIVE:
Questions about "Red Mafia" Involvement

"It's just dreadful that they're so secretive about what's what, I'm sure if they would come out with some information, it would be much better for everybody. It's very, very sad. There're so many crazy rumours going around." —Margaret Steele, Rothesay neighbour, National Post, July 2011.

"It's a whodunit, but nobody really knows who the suspects are. That doesn't happen every day – and certainly not in this genteel community of the rich and famous." —Paul Zed, lawyer and former Saint John Member of Parliament, The Globe and Mail, October 15, 2011.

With Dennis Oland cleared of his father's murder, the question becomes, Who *did* kill Richard Oland and why? A jealous husband? Business associate? Or was it organized crime? The Red Mafia has been considered a suspect in Oland's murder by some since it happened, though most in Saint John remain convinced Dennis was the killer, despite his exoneration by the court.

In 2003, as already noted, Can Sugar Inc. spent millions of dollars to launch a refinery in the city's McAllister Industrial Park. The Can Sugar refinery, financed in large part by Ukrainian investors, had catastrophic start-up problems and, after only a year, the company went broke.

The assets went to the Brazilian sugar supplier, Coimex, although the New Brunswick government was one of the refinery's biggest creditors. In a last-gasp attempt to save the project, in the summer of 2010, another group of Canadian investors, including Alberta billionaire Murray Edwards, offered to buy the refinery, a proposal the group said would create about thirty jobs in Saint John.

But in January 2011, Coimex accepted a lower bid for the equipment from 'Lantic Sugar, killing the deal for Saint John to save its sugar refining industry. The Edwards group challenged the sale of the equipment used in Can Sugar's failed enterprise before the Court of Queen's Bench. Coimex believed, after meeting with the province, the city and the new investor group, that efforts to restart the refinery operation were "much less realistic than originally anticipated." The rejected investors asked the court to block the sale and to appoint a public receiver to decide which bid should be accepted. The court rejected the motion.

'Lantic Sugar, which ran a huge refinery in Saint John for

nearly a century, bought all the equipment in the former Can Sugar plant and moved it out of the city. Documents submitted to the court suggested the refinery equipment, which hadn't been operating for eight years due to the bankruptcy, wasn't working properly. Dan Lafrance, 'Lantic Sugar's vice-president of finance and procurement, said the company got a good deal on the equipment, which it would use for spare parts in its other operations or sell as scrap metal.

'Lantic, Canada's largest sugar refiner, started out in Saint John in 1912. The company began a program of diversification and rationalization in 1981 that culminated in it purchasing St. Lawrence Sugar in Montreal in 1984. 'Lantic consolidated its refining operations in Montreal in 2000 and closed the Saint John plant. At the same time, the company reinvested in the Montreal facility, with a $120 million expansion and an upgrade that doubled the plant's capacity to serve the national market.

Saint John was devastated. The city lost 180 jobs when the company pulled out. The province loaned Can Sugar $1.5 million for its refinery operation and eventually lost $600,000 in the bankruptcy. The last thing 'Lantic needed was unwelcome competition within four years from newcomer Can Sugar.

The mafia theory in the Oland murder has its roots in the Can Sugar project —financed in large part by a group of Ukrainian/Russian investors. New Brunswick has a history of organized crime activities, particularly drug related, linked to motorcycle gangs and the Red Mafia.

Oland and his accountant Robert McFadden had helped the investors to set up Can Sugar in the city's industrial park. Oland, a leading member of Enterprise Saint John (now Develop Saint John), introduced the investors to local business leaders and government officials, including provincial and federal funding agencies who helped get the project off the ground.

"We were also aware of rumours regarding Russian/ Ukrainian mafia in connection with Can Sugar," admits Dennis Oland.

It's a theory in New Brunswick and among some in Ottawa that Dick rebuffed a shakedown by the Red Mafia — and was murdered in a spectacular way as an example to encourage others to toe the line.

This is not so farfetched as it might seem. The Red (or Russian) "máfiya" has become a player in international criminal circles, according to Mark Galeotti, well-known lecturer and writer on transnational crime and Russian security affairs, based in London. Galeotti says the Red Mafia has built a strong North American "Organizatsiya" that includes five major cartels, comprising two hundred gangs in seventeen cities, most notably in New York, Chicago, Los Angeles, San Francisco, Denver and Miami. Galeotti characterizes the Russian mafia as being highly organized, with "national prefects" in a number of countries, including several in Canada. Port cities like Saint John represent key targets.

In early 2004, Can Sugar came before a bankruptcy judge with a list of 125 creditors owed nearly $25 million. Its two main shareholders, Sergei Ryazanov and Alex Chernyak of Toronto, had sunk $17.5 million into the refinery. John Cardwell, Can Sugar's former president and the man who initiated the project, was owed $366,000.

The three men are now nowhere to be found. The executives of Develop Saint John, since renamed Envision Saint John, say Cardwell moved to Toronto, but no amount of digging finds an address, a phone number, an email — nothing. The Business

Development Bank was out two million dollars and the Royal Bank, $1.8 million. The province guaranteed all but $500,000 of the Royal Bank loan. Atlantic Building Contractors of Saint John were owed $322,000, along with a string of about 100 small creditors, adding up to approximately $5 million. No one connected with the ill-fated project can be found to comment on it, and no one in the Saint John economic development community can remember anything about it.

The federal government was going to invest $500,000 in a repayable contribution through the Atlantic Canada Opportunities Agency (ACOA), a business development program. However, Can Sugar did not meet the terms of its contract, so the agency did not disperse any of the funds, ACOA spokeswoman Ann Kenney said at the 2004 hearing. An affidavit filed with the court by McFadden said the company "had positive communication with the Province of New Brunswick and the Atlantic Canada Opportunities Agency." But spokeswomen for both the provincial government and ACOA did not support that view in court.

Kenney argued that since the company was operating under bankruptcy protection, ACOA did not have a contract with it. The agency had no negotiations with Can Sugar after November 2003, she said. Asked at the time if the agency would advance money if Can Sugar fulfilled the requirements laid out in the previous contract, Kenney said ACOA "would have to review the project in light of the financial difficulties it is facing at this time. ACOA has to be very careful because they have filed for bankruptcy protection." Sarah Ketcheson of Business New Brunswick also declined to commit the government to providing necessary additional assistance.

Before Can Sugar sought protection from creditors under the Companies' Creditors Arrangement Act, it had an annual payroll of two million dollars for fifty-five direct and indirect employees. It also added to the economy by using local trucking and other service companies.

Can Sugar had been given thirty days' protection against creditors to restructure its finances. Justice Peter Glennie extended that period by ninety days in January 2004. Without an extension, a court-appointed monitor said the company would not have been able to pay for power or for natural gas to heat the plant. Court documents list several factors that contributed to the company's predicament, including equipment of questionable quality, cost over-runs and $4.1 million worth of low-quality raw sugar.

The court-appointed monitor, Robert C. Smith, acknowledged that Can Sugar may have made mistakes, but insisted it would be a viable operation if "a source of additional revenue" could be found. Historically, the project met fierce opposition from 'Lantic Sugar in Montreal.

That view wasn't shared by the city or the province, and the last-ditch plan put forward in 2010 by a new group of investors fronted by Calgary billionaire Murray Edwards was coldly rebuffed without a public explanation.

In fact, city and provincial officials took steps to erase any mention of Can Sugar. Three years after the bankruptcy, Saint John hired an environmental consulting firm, Neill and Gunter Ltd. of Fredericton (now Stanton Consulting Ltd.). Its 146-page report, *Closure Report Former Lantic Sugar Refinery Site*, DENV file #6515-04-0318, dated December 2007, makes no mention of the short-lived Can Sugar refinery. (The Saint John *Telegraph Journal* and other media outlets reported Can Sugar's grand opening presided over by then Premier Bernard Lord, Senator Joseph Day, and John Cardwell. Several months later, the media would also report on its failure.)

Lawyer Gary Faloon, who represented Can Sugar through its bankruptcy, says the company's records have been destroyed. Prominent Saint John politician Shirley McAlary is vague on the refinery and its failure and says she doesn't know much about it, even though she was Saint John's mayor at the time it failed and had attended the opening.

Steve Carson, CEO of Develop Saint John, (formerly Enterprise Saint John) has led the city's industrial development agency for almost a quarter century. In a telephone interview regarding Can Sugar and the city's role in it, he claimed he was not involved, saying colleague Brian Irving oversaw the project. Irving, the city's general manager, who has also served as general manager of the City's Industrial Parks, insisted he had no role in Can Sugar. He named a third party, who said the same thing and so on. The cone of silence regarding Can Sugar Inc. covers the whole of the city's administration.

In July 2011, when Richard Oland was found murdered in cold blood, Carson called himself one of Oland's friends and a friend of the family. He described Dick in the media as a "great salesperson" for Saint John and a tireless promoter for the city.

"Dick had a really in-depth knowledge of manufacturing, of logistics and transportation and technology. So, it didn't matter what type of business someone was involved in," Carson told reporters.

> *He was very passionate and very intense, and he had a really phenomenal way of connecting with people. So that combination of knowledge of the community and his passion for business was something that was very genuine, and he was a great salesperson for the community.*

In this world of alternate facts, Can Sugar never existed. Neill and Gunter's report baldly states, "The sugar refinery (referring to 'Lantic) was closed in July 2000 after 85 years of operation and decommissioning of equipment and facilities began immediately thereafter." But we know better.

It goes on to say that a 2004 assessment of the 'Lantic sugar refinery lands began in July 2000, and in 2004, twenty buildings were decommissioned and demolished, including a 222,000-litre fuel oil tank. However, for several months from early 2003 to early 2004, Can Sugar operated its refinery in the same building and using the same equipment as 'Lantic.

The sugar lands, called the South Waterfront, is a 4.5-hectare (11 acres) site at the southern tip of the Central Peninsula. Prime waterfront, it is arguably the nicest spot in Saint John, with spectacular scenic views across the Inner Harbour and the Bay of Fundy to Partridge Island. The South End streets, blocks of small, old, mostly rundown homes and businesses, thins here to large swaths of empty space, including Port lands, the former 'Lantic Sugar Refinery site, and the Barrack Green Armoury lands.

Historically, these lands have been used for military purposes, industrial purposes, and as exhibition grounds. While the Armoury is still operated by the Department of National Defence, the broader area lies vacant, positioned for increased use. At the very tip of the South Waterfront lies Tin Can Beach, a favourite neighbourhood swimming and fishing spot.

Records of Can Sugar's existence have all but vanished. All that remains of John Cardwell is a Saint John cellphone number from 2011. On calling it, a recorded voice says it is disconnected. Cardwell appears to be a disappeared person. Those few who will admit they knew him at all then now say they didn't know him well; several say vaguely that they think he went to Toronto. There is no record of his obituary and no alumni records of his having attended university in the Maritimes, Quebec or Ontario. Nor is there any trace of Cardwell in Toronto.

Of his Ukrainian/Russian partners, a LinkedIn profile for Alex Chernyak lists a company that is no longer in business. There is no record at all of Sergei Ryazanov, although the two men were reported to be successful Toronto businessmen with millions to invest in a Saint John sugar refinery project.

A thorough search for Cardwell, Chernyak and Ryazanov by Mark Fenton, a Vancouver-based retired police investigator who runs a cyber security training firm for police and government security personnel, found nothing. Fenton developed a script that has been used not just across Canada, but also globally, to locate suicidal people, terrorists, pedophiles, and other hard-to-locate suspects.

To the business community, federal, provincial and municipal bureaucrats and politicians and larger Saint John, it's as if the ill-fated Can Sugar enterprise never existed. As for Richard Oland, one of the project's biggest boosters, he is more than ten years in the grave and his murderer remains unknown. One wonders about the fate of Cardwell, Ryazanov and Chernyak. Given the suspicion of Red Mafia involvement, one observer ventured that Cardwell is "either in witness protection or deceased."

McFadden plays down any role by organized crime in the Can Sugar debacle. "Dick did not do dodgy deals," McFadden said emphatically in an interview with me in May 2019 in his Far End Corporation Office, adding that Oland hadn't personally invested any of his own money in the sugar refinery. However, he acknowledged that Oland helped the group negotiate bankruptcy protection when the project failed through a combination of poor management and competitive pressure from 'Lantic Sugar. The Ukrainian expats, Toronto based, were no longer in Saint John, McFadden said. But they took their losses in stride —"Ryazanov told me, 'I can make that much in six months in Ukraine.'"

"I've no idea." McFadden said when asked his view on who might have killed his boss — although he speculated that Diana Sedlacek might know a thing or two.

Canadian experts in organized crime interviewed about the case have no problem with the theory that Richard Oland was the victim of a Red Mafia hit. While he was not an actual investor, he was involved in helping to get it set up. A prominent businessman who was seen to have reneged would be held responsible.

"There's not one place in Canada that's spared (from organized crime)," says Luciano Bentenuto, Director General of Security Services for Courts Administration Service for the federal government. He said that violence and twenty-first-century assassinations are carried out in brutal ways to intimidate. It doesn't come more brutal than Richard Oland's killing. From the lack of willingness in Saint John to talk about it, there can be no doubt about the intimidation.

"It's a generational thing. It used to be done pretty quiet . . . the new generation is more Americanized," says Bentenuto.

According to Matthew Light, an academic who studies organized crime, the business crime operatives "need to make a point" — so the execution is spectacular. In a special issue of *Theoretical Criminology*, April 1995, entitled "Crime and criminal justice after communism: Why study the post-Soviet region?" Light, associate professor of Criminology at the University of Toronto's Centre for Criminology and Sociolegal Studies, and co-author Gavin Slade discuss the rise of crime and organized crime after the collapse of the Soviet Union.

At the end of 1991, the Soviet Union was replaced by fifteen independent republics, ranging over a vast area, from the Baltic states, such as Belarus, Ukraine and Moldova in the west, to the Caucasus states of Georgia, Armenia and Azerbaijan in the south, and the Central Asian "stans" in the east, Kazakhstan, Uzbekistan and Turkmenistan among others. Russia, by far the largest post-Soviet republic, encompasses a multitude of different regions with varying levels of economic development and varying degrees of autonomy from Moscow. The Soviet collapse unleashed both new forms of criminality and new debates about the causation and governance of crime in all these countries.

Free market economics left post-Soviet countries and citizens in a state in which what constituted criminality was no longer clear. Finding legal institutions impractical if not useless, people fell back on informal norms and practices. Property and economic crime were widespread. Organized crime and racketeering took advantage of black markets that resulted from shortages and other economic distortions. Profits were laundered in the West.

Asked about the rather prosaic weapon used to kill Richard Oland, Steven Howard, a Lansing, Michigan lawyer with an expertise in weaponry, who goes by the handle "Steve the gun guru," said a weapon such as a drywall hammer is a hitman's "go-to," especially if he has an international assignment. "A specialty hardware tool, like a club, axe, or tomahawk, is easily transported in checked luggage as axes and hatchets are not restricted, and they're available in any big box hardware store."

Warming enthusiastically to the subject, Howard continued,

> *Guns make a lot of noise; gunshot residue can take a half a million years to break down. A hammer is chosen because it's a viable weapon, cheap, sends a strong aggressive message — not for the faint of heart. It's quiet, can be administered without warning, and because there's no noise, it's easy to use.*

> *A two-edged weapon leaves a signature, sharp and dull. Firearms leave a paper trail. But a hammer? Flip it in a ditch. If it's covered in blood, a rainstorm will take care of that along with a million micro-organisms. DNA is time sensitive.*

But the Saint John police investigation gave the Red Mafia no consideration, nor any other theories — sticking with disgruntled son kills miserly father.

"I've never seen the death of a prominent citizen investigated the way this one has been investigated," said Tom Young, Saint John's best-known radio talk show host until he retired in the spring of 2011 after forty years on air. A beloved fixture of Saint John, Young passed away in 2017. "Basically, they've got a body killed in a certain way, and nobody they can pin it on. I don't think it will be solved," he said a few months after the murder.

Young's theory, which is shared by others, is bang on,

lawyer Steven Howard said. "Police are just stupid," he said bluntly. "The U.S. has a 'speed trial clause,' and police and prosecution are encouraged to catch somebody, build a clean clear case, convict, and it's all good for the next promotion." Canadian police agencies appear to hold the same sentiment.

Several cases provide evidence that organized crime operates actively in New Brunswick. In 2020, the New Brunswick RCMP Federal Serious and Organized Crime Unit arrested four members of outlaw motorcycle clubs in connection with organized crime, drug trafficking and proceeds of crime, or money laundering activities in the province. As part of an ongoing investigation, arrests were made across New Brunswick between February 17 and April 9, 2020, in Edmundston.

Millions of dollars in suspected crime proceeds — money traced to the largest tax fraud in Russian history — was laundered in 2017 through Canadian banks and companies by a powerful Russian Crime syndicate run by Dmitry Klyuev. He secretly owned Universal Savings Bank, the bank that received hundreds of millions of dollars in fraudulent tax refunds from the Russian government. He operates as the head and mastermind of an organized crime group that includes amongst its members: lawyers specializing in fraud and forgery; law enforcement officers who extort property from the innocent and protect the guilty; tax officials who authorize fraudulent refunds; and violent criminals who act as the enforcement arm of the group.

Klyuev specializes in fraudulently obtained court judgments to arrange fraudulent tax refunds with corrupt tax officials, but he is equally willing to engage in other criminal activities that rely on extortion and violence.

   The largest sum in the Russian tax fraud case with a Canadian connection was sent out of Canada by a New Brunswick company with an Estonian bank account and a South African director. There is no evidence that the company has done any legitimate business, and corporate records show the company has since been dissolved.

CHAPTER TWENTY-SIX

The Rich and the Dead

Organized crime is suspected in the perplexing and unsolved murders of other rich and powerful men in Canada, both in the recent and more distant past. The bodies of Canadian Pharmaceuticals billionaire Barry Sherman, seventy-five, and his wife Honey, seventy, were discovered on December 13, 2017, by a real estate agent showing their Toronto mansion to prospective buyers. They had been strangled and their bodies, fully clothed, were arranged side by side on the floor in the pool area, their necks tied with men's leather belts to a metal railing, about a metre high around one end of the pool. Initially treated as a murder-suicide by Toronto Police, investigators later concluded it was a double murder.

There are many curious parallels with Richard Oland's murder. Moosehead is the largest Canadian privately owned brewery; Barry Sherman was the chairman of Apotex Inc., Canada's biggest privately owned pharmaceutical company. With a fortune worth an estimated $3.6 billion, the Shermans were among the country's most generous philanthropists and strong supporters of the Liberal Party. Dick and Connie Oland were also generous philanthropists and community activists. As noted, Dick was made an Order of Canada recipient in 1998 for organizing the 1985 Saint John Canada Summer Games. As with the Oland murder, a dearth of concrete information resulted in friends and colleagues floating many theories about who killed the Shermans, including rival drug makers, disgruntled ex-employees, and Russian-Israeli gangsters.

Police found no evidence of a break-in and considered the way the Shermans were killed as personal, even intimate, just as the Saint John police said about the Oland murder. There is widespread anecdotal suspicion but no conclusive evidence that both murders were the work of professionals. Experts in organized crime say independent businesses are targeted by the Red Mafia. Barry Sherman's murder put his life under a microscope, with some surprising revelations. While he was a well-established and widely respected member of Canada's political and business elite, he also provided a financial link between the boardrooms and balls of high society and the seamier denizens of the street, including the criminal underworld.

Like Oland, Sherman was a ruthless and aggressive businessman who gave no quarter and created many enemies; in private some rivals, including senior executives at Germany's Bayer AG and Pfizer, described Sherman in unprintable terms. Like Oland, Sherman's social graces were limited. He is described in a *Bloomberg Businessweek* article as "virtually incapable of small talk, and he was an unapologetic worka-holic, abstemious to the point of joylessness." According to the article, Sherman's habit of entering into side businesses with characters who would never be welcome in the executive suite at Pfizer Inc. made him unique.

Sherman was linked to convicted fraudster, Shaun Rootenberg, who was working to develop an online trivia game. Sherman agreed to invest, then alleged in court that his money had disappeared. According to legal filings, Sherman had been introduced to Rootenberg by Myron Gottlieb, the co-founder of Livent, a theater production company that collapsed in one of Canada's most spectacular accounting frauds; Gottlieb and Rootenberg had met in prison.

Then there was Sherman's long, intimate friendship and business relationship with Frank D'Angelo, a Toronto restaurateur, energy-drink promoter and maker of B-movies. The two talked almost every day, and D'Angelo was among the last people outside Apotex to speak with Sherman, in a late-evening phone call the Tuesday before the bodies were discovered. Touching base, nothing unusual, D'Angelo recalled. The two were business partners, with Sherman financing many of D'Angelo's business ventures. His endeavors lost a lot of money, and when his company, D'Angelo Brands, filed for bankruptcy in 2007, it owed Sherman more than $100 million. Sherman took control, installing his son to run the company.

D'Angelo said he was as confounded by the Shermans' deaths as anyone else — and that he had nothing to do with them. But like everyone in the Shermans' orbit, he had his theories, which he expressed Godfather-style. "I think somebody came to make Barry an offer he couldn't refuse, and he refused," D'Angelo said, suggesting that someone wanted Sherman's cooperation in the drug business, his money, or both, and that Sherman wouldn't yield.

It looks increasingly unlikely that anyone will be arrested for their murders. There's little sign of momentum in either the police or private investigations; a person close to the family said recent police updates have tended to cover leads that haven't panned out. The broader community of which Barry and Honey were so much a part will probably have to come to terms with never knowing what happened at 50 Old Colony Road in Toronto.

Matthew Campbell wrote in a *Bloomberg Businessweek* cover story, "The Unsolved Murder of an Unusual Billionaire,"

> *The Shermans had every reason to expect that they controlled their future, until the moment they didn't, when the boundaries that surrounded two distinguished lives became suddenly, terrifyingly permeable.*

True crime, compared with crime fiction, is more graphic, grittier and documents inferior police work. The Oland and Sherman cases remind us of two other unsolved murders of twentieth-century Canadian tycoons.

Sir Harry Oakes, gold mine owner, entrepreneur, investor and philanthropist was found dead in his bed, and his mysterious, gruesome murder in 1943 has never been solved — and as in the Oland and Sherman murders, there are whispers of an organized crime connection. Meyer Lansky, a known mobster, who operated casinos in Las Vegas and Cuba, wanted to open casinos in the Bahamas. Oakes, a major investor in the islands but puritanical in nature objected to gambling. Lansky was enormously rich and had the wherewithal to employ skilled assassins. The unanswered question — did he do it?

During the Second World War, Edward, the Duke of Windsor and abdicated King of England, was governor of the Bahamas. He didn't think the local police could investigate the sensational murder properly. He first thought to call in Scotland Yard, but that was not an option in wartime. So, he recruited two detectives from nearby South Florida, who then made hash of it all by tampering with evidence and in general discrediting the police investigation. The main evidence against the defendant, Count Alfred de Marigny, Oakes's son-in-law, was a fingerprint from a Chinese screen in Oakes's bedroom. It was later found that the print was taken from a water glass that the count used during questioning by the Miami detectives and transferred to the bedroom screen.

Some observers questioned the Duke's decision in calling in the Americans, and there were even suggestions he might have been complicit in Oakes's death. The governor also had his own interests in bringing gambling to the Bahamas. So, the theory goes that he ensured the murder was hushed up and employed corrupt detectives. Another suspect was Axel Wenner-Gren, a friend of the Duke. A Swedish industrialist, he was thought to be a Nazi spy. The Duke and his wife were known Nazi sympathizers. Was the Canadian Oakes, nothing if not patriotic, about to expose Wenner-Gren as a spy and murdered for that reason? Significantly, the Duke of Windsor arranged to be away from the Bahamas while Count Alfred de Marigny's trial was in progress, in an apparent effort to avoid being called as a witness.

Some speculated that Sir Stafford Sands, a former finance minister and an architect of Bahamian post-war prosperity (called the father of Bahamian tourism), was the culprit. According to that theory, he could have been involved in the murder for the sake of the local economy as he supported the gambling operation as a tourist magnet to the island. It was suggested that Harry Oakes, who disapproved of gambling and vice, was planning to abandon the Bahamas, potentially provoking a financial disaster had his riches gone elsewhere. Was there a plot to prevent this?

The most likely suspect was Harold Christie, an old friend and business associate. He was staying overnight in the next bedroom the night of the murder. Christie found Oakes's body the following morning. Oakes had moved to the Bahamas and become a British citizen largely because of Christie, a local property developer. The police never considered him a suspect because he was such a prominent, respected citizen. After Oakes's murder was made public, many people said that far from being tucked up in bed, Christie was seen out and about in Nassau in the early hours of the night in question. Christie, large landowner in the Bahamas, was rumoured to have confessed to close friends that he had murdered Harry Oakes. Oakes's objections to opening casinos would have cost him greatly. He was (supposedly) right there in the next bedroom when a brutal murder was committed but said he heard nothing.

Oakes's family was away when he was murdered sometime after midnight on July 8, 1943. He was struck four times behind the left ear with a miner's hand pick that Oakes had kept as souvenir of his gold mining days; these blows were apparently designed to cover up wounds made by a barman's silver ice pick.

It was thought he was caught unaware from behind while having a drink with friends at his home. His body was moved to the bed and burned using insecticide as an accelerant concentrated around the head. Mattress feathers spread over and around the body made it look like an Obeah voodoo ritual. Officially the cause of death and the details around it were never really made public. The world press was enchanted with the story of Oakes's mysterious end and made good use of photos of his daughter, the beautiful and charming Nancy. Canadian author Charlotte Gray's book, *Murdered Midas: A Millionaire, His Gold Mine, and a Strange Death on an Island Paradise* focuses on the murder. As Gray put it, most Canadians, especially history buffs, have heard something about Harry Oakes:

> *The mystery of who had killed him has continued to intrigue people, and his name cropped up in novels by leading Canadian writers and in sensationalist bestsellers about the Duke of Windsor, Mafia crimes and currency smuggling.*

Not unlike the Oland murder investigation, police focused within hours on his son-in-law Count Alfred de Marigny, who was arrested and charged with the murder. As with Dennis Oland, the subsequent trial ended with his acquittal.

Oakes's murder has never been solved, and there were no further police investigations in the case after de Marigny's acquittal. Tall and good looking, De Marigny was at home at many a posh resort living a life of leisure. Like Richard and Dennis Oland, he was an accomplished competitive sailor who won many regattas.

Despite the acquittal, he was deported to Cuba on the recommendation of the trial jury — who wanted him gone because of his roguish reputation and alleged advances towards women and girls in the Bahamas. Nancy stood by him through-out the ordeal. She and de Marigny went to Cuba to stay with their old friend Ernest Hemingway. The couple divorced in 1949. Although he was cleared, suspicion and rumours swirled around de Marigny for the rest of his life.

A second, less well-known though arguably more salacious case involved the mysterious disappearance of Toronto entertainment tycoon, Ambrose Small. Small, fifty-three, disappeared without a trace on December 2, 1919. Suspecting foul play, Toronto police investigated Small's wife and his personal secretary, James Doughty. Theresa Small was angry at her husband for his gambling and womanizing. Doughty resented Small, who paid him a meagre salary despite his longtime loyalty. However, there was no evidence linking either of them to his disappearance.

Small was ruthless and unscrupulous. He enjoyed cheat-ing associates. His business contracts contained clauses he called "jokers" that worked to his financial advantage. Small was part of an illegal bookmaking operation taking bets on horse races. He was also suspected of "fixing" horse races, an activity that led to reports he was kidnapped by New York gangsters. The theory was unprovable but reflected the way he ran his life, filled with danger and excitement. His quar-relsome nature and his business practices made him widely hated by his associates. His reputation was little different from Barry Sherman and Richard Oland.

Hector Charlesworth, a Toronto journalist, knew Small personally, and wrote in his book *More Candid Chronicles*, "If I heard once, I heard a score of times the ominous words: 'Somebody will get Amby someday.'"

December 2, 1919 was the day after Ambrose sold his booking agency and his stake in a chain of live theatres for a

hefty $1.75 million (about $23 million today). Small decided
to sell the business due to the growing popularity of motion
pictures. Live theatre, vaudeville in particular, was waning
in popularity. He thought it was unlikely to come back. He
made a deal to sell his chain of theatres to Trans-Canada
Theatres Limited of Montreal.

Small, Theresa and his attorney E.W.M. Flock met with
Trans-Canada Theatres representative W.J. Shaughnessy
on the morning of December 2, 1919, at Allen Aylesworth's
law office at 65 Yonge Street. The document of sale was
signed. Shaughnessy presented Small with a certified cheque
for the first payment, one million dollars. Small passed the
cheque to Theresa and asked her to take it to their bank.
Theresa made the deposit in the Dominion Bank at the
corner of Yonge and King streets at 11:45 a.m.

Lawyer Flock and the Smalls then went to lunch at the
King Edward Hotel, after which the Smalls went to the
St. Vincent de Paul Orphanage, where Theresa made a
donation. She later stated that when they parted company,
Small said he would be home by six o'clock. That afternoon, Theresa told her sister that she and Small planned to
travel the world. After ordering a Cadillac, jewellery and a
fur coat for Theresa, Small met Flock at his theatre office
to clear up some business matters. He invited Flock to join
him and Theresa for dinner, but Flock had to catch a train
to London. Flock left Small's office at 5:30 p.m. He was the
last person known for certain to have seen Small. After that,
Ambrose Small vanished.

Two weeks passed before the Toronto police became
aware that Small was missing and began seriously looking
for him. Theresa claimed that she hadn't reported it out of
fear of a scandal. "I believe my Amby is in the hands of a

designing woman, somewhere, and will come back," she said. Nonetheless, she offered a five hundred dollar reward, later increasing it to fifty thousand dollars, for information on his whereabouts. Circulars were distributed across Canada and the United States. When Theresa increased the reward for information, the Small story became an international sensation. Small hadn't packed any suitcases and wasn't carrying much cash when he vanished. Police found no evidence of him paying for transportation or accommodation by cheque. The Small case remains one of Canada's most perplexing and legendary unsolved mysteries.

In Kevin Donovan's book called *The Billionaire Murders* about the 2017 murders of Toronto couple Barry and Honey Sherman, the Toronto Police Service does not come off well.

The police investigating the Harry Oakes murder fabricated evidence against the main suspect, Count de Marigny, which led to the dismissal of charges.

The Saint John police were described as the Keystone Cops such was their almost comic blundering in their investigation of Dennis Oland in the murder of his father.

Police incompetence and connections to organized crime appear to be a common theme in the murders of wealthy Canadian businessmen.

CHAPTER TWENTY-SEVEN
Investigation Failings: A Deeper Look

As discussed earlier, Inspector Glen McCloskey was among the mob of police officers crowding the crime scene on the day Richard Oland's body was discovered. He walked twice through the crime scene on July 7, 2011, in his civilian clothes, with another officer. He admitted that he may have touched a door that could have been used as an escape route by the killer(s), and he was observed stepping between visible drops of blood spatter to see into another room.

McCloskey wasn't officially assigned to the case but was among the first to arrive at 52 Canterbury within minutes of the 911 call. He and another officer Sgt. Greg Oram circled twice around the desk area, and Oram went so far as to touch a window blind without protective latex gloves. A veteran of the 140-officer force, McCloskey had no valid reason for being there. Although McCloskey was promoted after this to deputy chief, his actions that day contributed to his sudden retirement in 2018.

McCloskey testified he went into the Far End Corporation office in a support role — in case the investigating officers needed extra resources. He entered Oland's office only a short distance on the first visit. Later he went further, stepping between drops of blood to see into another room because he was curious. "I was wrong, I shouldn't have been in there," McCloskey admitted. Gold said it was a professional disgrace to have the public hear what McCloskey did at the murder scene.

"I was embarrassed, for sure," McCloskey said.

He was called to testify at the Oland trial the day after a subordinate officer alleged that McCloskey told him what to say when he testified at the preliminary hearing. Mike King, Staff Sergeant retired, testified that before or during Dennis Oland's preliminary inquiry, McCloskey, his supervisor at the time, urged King not to reveal that McCloskey had been at the crime scene. King said he was in McCloskey's office when McCloskey referred to another officer as being an "idiot" for having said that he was there.

King said his reaction was, "You *were* in the room." McCloskey's reply, according to King, was, "Well, you don't have to tell them that."

McCloskey, who had been by the time of the trial promoted to deputy chief of police, denied King's allegation. When Gold asked McCloskey if he had asked King to lie about McCloskey being at the Oland murder scene, McCloskey replied, "No."

King also testified that McCloskey kept a box of evidence from the Oland case in his office rather than secured in the evidence room, but when asked by Gold, McCloskey said he didn't recall that.

Sgt. Mark Smith, head of the Saint John Police Force's forensic unit, admitted he kept silent about finding McCloskey and Constable Greg Oram at the homicide scene. But he testified it was never his intention to mislead the court.

"I admit to making mistakes at the crime scene, but I'm not a liar," he said.

Smith made the comments when being cross-examined by defence lawyer Michael Lacy at the retrial about why he had failed in any of his notes or at the first trial to say that he found McCloskey and Oram in the victim's office before he had finished processing the scene for evidence.

When Smith was asked about the matter, he said he knew he was going to testify and expected it would come up then. Lacy challenged Smith's "proposed innocent explanation." He pointed out Smith had testified at Oland's preliminary hearing in 2014 and at his first trial in 2015 but never disclosed in his testimony to finding McCloskey, who was his supervisor, and Oram alone together in the office, with the body still present and without any protective gear.

"And that's because the right question hadn't been asked of you, is that right?" asked Lacy.

"I was waiting for the question, yes," replied Smith, acknowledging he never volunteered the information and "misspoke" on another occasion when he denied he was waiting for the "right question."

"So, your claim . . . that you were going to testify, and it would all come out, that was only if someone happened to ask you a question about it, correct?" Lacy stressed.

"It was discussed . . . " Smith started to say, his voice then trailing off. After a long pause, he said, "You're right."

Earlier in the retrial, Smith testified that he grudg-
ingly gave in to superior officers who "wished to view" the
body before his forensic testing was complete. He said he
instructed McCloskey, now-retired Staff Sgt. Mike King,
Sgt. Dave Brooker, and possibly "somebody else too" on
where they could walk and how far they could go. They
were only inside the office for "a few seconds" before they
retraced their steps without touching anything, he said.

Later, Smith left to retrieve some supplies from his van
and when he returned, he found McCloskey and Oram
deeper in the crime scene than he had previously allowed
and ordered them to "get out." Under cross-examination,
Smith agreed it's "very possible" important evidence could
have been compromised by McCloskey and Oram's movements within the office and their proximity to the body.

Most of the police officers at the crime scene were not
wearing any protective gear, such as footwear coverings or
latex gloves. Even Smith did not don any protective gear
when he first entered the crime scene, even though he knew
it was considered a "suspicious death." However, Smith was
photographed wearing the gear, including booties, on the
street during a break. He agreed under cross-examination
that contaminated crime scenes can destroy important
evidence and increase the chances of a wrongful conviction.

"The way you described it to them, I'm going to suggest
to you, sir, was, '[I] just kept waiting for the hammer to
drop,'" said Lacy at the retrial, referring to when the
McCloskey-Oram issue came up in court. Smith said that
when he was previously cross-examined by the defence and
questioned about people being at the scene, he was only
asked about a specific time period and had testified, "Not
at that time." He said he expected the defence would follow

up on that answer, but they didn't. "I was concerned about that," Smith said, admitting that he should have raised it on his own rather than waiting to be questioned about it.

Oram, testifying for the first time at the retrial, told the court he was in the victim's office with then-inspector McCloskey shortly after the multi-millionaire's body was discovered. Oland's defence team accused the Crown of purposely "hiding" Oram by not calling him to testify at the preliminary inquiry or at the first trial. Oram testified he had understood he was going to testify at the preliminary inquiry and had a meeting with one of the Crown prosecutors to prepare, but he was never called. No explanation was ever given, he said.

McCloskey and Oram gave conflicting accounts of the incident. Oram, who was promoted to sergeant, testified he went into the office first. He said he was crouched about two or three feet away from the body, observing the significant injuries to the head, when McCloskey commented he hoped that it was a suicide, and they would find a gun underneath the body because it "would be easier." That's when he looked up and saw McCloskey "half-sitting" on a table in the homicide scene before forensic testing was complete. McCloskey had one foot on the floor and the other leg dangling. It was opposite to where McCloskey earlier had testified to being. Oram said he then followed McCloskey's lead deeper into the scene than Smith had previously allowed, zigzagging throughout the office.

In his testimony, McCloskey said he entered the office first and showed Oram the spot Smith indicated not to go beyond, but then Oram wandered around, went into a back room and pushed a vertical blind aside to peer outside. McCloskey admitted at the retrial he went farther into the office than he had testified to at the first trial and that it was "100 per cent totally wrong" for him to have been in there at all, but he denied he ever sat down or leaned against anything. He also said Smith had "invited" him into the office the first time. Smith disputed that claim.

"My Lord, it was never any intention of mine to mislead the court — this court, the court at the first trial or the preliminary trial," Smith told Justice Morrison. He said he had discussed the McCloskey-Oram "situation" with the Crown before and after the preliminary inquiry and before the first trial. "My thought was that either the Crown or the defence during their strategy, as they saw fit, would bring that up," Smith said. "As like today, follow-up questions cannot be sometimes brought forward by a witness because you don't have time. I wasn't allowed to provide any of this earlier."

Staff Sgt. Mike King refused to lie for McCloskey, testifying he'd "never lied on the stand in thirty-two years" and "wasn't about to start." McCloskey, who was promoted to deputy chief in January 2015, repeatedly denied King's 2015 testimony. He told the court during Oland's first trial that he had entered the office twice — first under Smith's supervision to observe the body and then farther in with Oram out of "curiosity." An independent investigator hired by the New Brunswick Police Commission to perform a professional conduct review of McCloskey and King, concluded McCloskey had the conversation King described. The investigator, Barry MacKnight, retired Fredericton police chief, found McCloskey used words to the effect of "you don't have to tell them that." MacKnight found McCloskey made false statements at Oland's first trial and to Halifax police.

With his long experience and seniority, McCloskey should have been versed in proper protocol at a murder scene. It's unclear whether he had some other motive than curiosity. Saint John police chief John Bates put it that McCloskey was accused "for lack of a better choice of words, sort of a witness tampering." Bates retired in December 2017. He refused to give the reason he was retiring to the media, but the move came days after Saint John council voted to cut the police department by $1.25 million. Some councillors were surprised by Bates's resignation.

Said Gerry Lowe, "I made a couple calls and found out it was true. And then when I thought it all over, he got the $1.25-million budget cut, and I guess he felt that he couldn't run the police department the way he wanted to," the former-Saint John city councillor and now former provincial Member of the Legislative Assembly told a television news reporter. McCloskey followed Bates into retirement in April 2018, just months later.

Investigator Barry MacKnight recommended that McCloskey face five criminal charges. However, McCloskey was cleared after an investigation by Halifax police. This was supposed to be the subject of a hearing before the provincial police commission, but McCloskey retired in April 2018 before the hearing could take place. The commission only investigates officers on active duty.

The New Brunswick Police Association, which represents municipal officers, slammed the commission's investigation of McCloskey, and McCloskey himself struck back. He immediately launched a lawsuit against the New Brunswick Police Commission and its former executive director for alleged negligence in how they handled a conduct complaint against him in connection with the Dennis Oland murder trial. In documents filed with the Court of Queen's Bench in Saint John, McCloskey accused the independent civilian oversight body and Stephan (Steve) Roberge of failing to conduct the *Police Act* investigation without bias, deliberately engaging in unlawful conduct in exercising their public function and violating the public trust — Roberge had allegedly shared the MacKnight report with Oland's defence lawyers. McCloskey also accused the commission of breaching its duty to protect him from unwarranted disciplinary action and Roberge of damaging his economic interests through unlawful means.

CHAPTER TWENTY-EIGHT

The Lawyers and the Bill

Most people in Saint John expected the story wouldn't end with the guilty verdict in December 2015. And after a preliminary hearing, the jury trial that found Oland guilty, a successful appeal and a retrial that ended with a not-guilty verdict, they have been proved right. The Oland defence team appealed immediately after the first trial and most observers, even if most thought Dennis had done it, expected the family would eventually win — largely because they have sufficiently deep pockets to hire the best lawyers. Many expected Dennis Oland to get away with it — after all, money talks; these guys at the top are all buddies and take care of their own, don't they?

Money certainly does make a difference in mounting a successful defence. Nicole O'Byrne, a law professor at the

University of New Brunswick, said Oland had the resources to pay a defence team to follow up on every aspect of the case by hiring experts and by taking portions of the case to the Supreme Court of Canada for determination. Many Canadians who followed the case were surprised by Dennis Oland's conviction. There was skepticism among criminal lawyers, analysts and crime scene and forensics experts that justice had been served by the jury verdict. While a survey showed he was presumed guilty by the majority of New Brunswick's population in its three largest cities, close to one in four believed he was innocent and were deeply critical of the police investigation.

The Olands spared no expense in assembling Dennis's defence team. Estimates of the cost of proving his innocence ranged from three million dollars to as high as ten million dollars, depending on which legal expert you consulted. Either figure is well beyond the means of the average person wrongfully accused and convicted of a crime, so most would simply wind up in prison proclaiming their innocence while no one listens. After all, most convicted criminals say they didn't do it.

Lead lawyer Alan Gold, one of Canada's foremost criminal lawyers, once won three cases at the Supreme Court in a single year. He has been a commentator on high profile cases such as Conrad Black's fraud trial in 2007. *Toronto Life* magazine named him as one of "The Lawyers Other Lawyers Call," a guide to the most respected legal practitioners in the city. Gold has appeared as counsel before all levels of court in Ontario, other provinces, and for over fifty cases in the Supreme Court of Canada.

He is certified by the Law Society as a specialist in criminal litigation and was the first chairman of the Criminal

Litigation Specialty Committee for five years. In 1993, he was inducted into the American College of Trial Lawyers. He received the G. Arthur Martin Award for Contribution to Criminal Justice in 1997. Gold is a past president of the Criminal Lawyers Association of Ontario and a past-elected bencher of the Law Society of Ontario.

Fredericton lawyer Gary Miller, co-counsel at the first trial and who assisted in jury selection at the retrial before withdrawing from the case, is one of the most seasoned criminal attorneys in New Brunswick. He gained notice in 1984 as part of former Premier Richard Hatfield's defence team, winning Hatfield an acquittal on drug possession charges. In 2000, Miller also won a 'not guilty' verdict for the late indigenous leader Noah Augustine on a murder charge. He was made Queen's Counsel in 2012. Michael Lacy of Toronto was called in to replace Miller for the retrial. No reason was given for the change in the defence team. Lacy started his career with Gold over twenty years earlier as an articling student and then as an associate. Lacy explained in an interview,

> We have maintained contact over the years and have done other cases together. He is a mentor, colleague and friend. A fair amount of my practice involves appellate work. I have also appeared on appeals at the New Brunswick Court of Appeal.

Lacy had followed the initial trial. After Dennis's conviction, Gold asked him,

> Together with other experienced appellate lawyers, to assist on the appeal. This included getting our view of the charge to the jury and any of the

potential grounds of appeal. As an experienced appellate lawyer, Alan did not need our input, but in the interests of serving the client and ensuring there was no stone unturned he involved us.

I was not counsel of record but did work with the team in reviewing the trial record and contributing to the discussion as to how to frame the grounds of appeal. I attended the first day of the hearing of the appeal.

I was also interested in the bail decision and the ultimate appeal to the Supreme Court of Canada. I was the president of the Criminal Lawyers' Association, and the organization decided to intervene in the appeal — this is not unusual for the CLA, and whether I had involvement or not we would have done so. I was not originally scheduled to make the argument for our organization but the lawyer who was going to do so (my co-counsel Susan Chapman — now Justice Chapman) became ill the night before. That's how I ended up delivering the oral argument at the Supreme Court of Canada.

The Supreme Court of Canada decision was precedent setting. It resolved and provided clarification of the law regarding bail pending appeal for all people convicted of crimes. It is a decision that continues to get cited and quoted. Importantly, it makes the point that we have to maintain a robust system for bail pending appeal because trial Courts do not always get it right.

During the preparation for the new trial, Lacy remained in contact with Gold and the defence team.

I had gotten to know Dennis and his family through my involvement in the appeal. I also knew the lawyers involved.

Ultimately, I was asked if I would be interested in joining the defence team as counsel of record as second chair with Alan. It was a once-in-a-life-time opportunity to work with my mentor and a lawyer who is one of the best criminal defence lawyers in Canada on a case that had significant legal and substantive issues.

I cleared my schedule to be part of the case. It did not disappoint nor did the experience of working with Alan again.

Other lawyers on the team included James McConnell, a Saint John lawyer and Bill Teed, a lawyer representing the Oland family, who is also an Oland family friend and Rothesay neighbour. A public opinion survey conducted by the defence team of New Brunswick's three major cities — the provincial capital Fredericton, Moncton and Saint John — brought home to Gold's team just how solidified people were in their opinions on Dennis Oland's innocence or guilt. Without knowing anything or very little about the case, many who were asked believed they knew enough to pronounce a verdict. About 27 per cent of respondents found Dennis Oland guilty; and around 23 per cent declared him to be innocent. Half of those surveyed refused to answer at all. Dennis's lawyers interpreted such refusal to mean they thought he was guilty but were reluctant to say it.

Rumour had it in Saint John that Gold, who defended the Hell's Angels in 2004, makes one thousand dollars per hour. Although his rates aren't public, other lawyers estimated a legal bill reaching four million dollars for the Dennis Oland defence alone, including the preliminary hearing in December 2014. Some estimates are as high as ten million dollars. The Crown's cost was reported to be tallied at more than $1.56 million.

In the days following Dennis's acquittal, CBC News reported that the retrial had cost New Brunswick taxpayers nearly $930,000. That figure is in addition to the more than $637,000 expense of his first trial in 2015 and appeal in 2016. Of the costs, jury fees accounted for nearly $120,000. Court-related costs to the Saint John Police Force came to $7,561 in overtime for the retrial and $2,405 in overtime for the first trial. The retrial costs made public by the Department of Justice and Office of the Attorney General were not the final total.

CHAPTER TWENTY-NINE

Reasonable Doubts

Lawyer Alan Gold delved into reasonable doubt — the basis for Dennis Oland's acquittal in the second trial — and the burden of proof in an interview about the Conrad Black case with Douglas Bell, published in *Toronto Life* in the June 27, 2007 issue. A former newspaper publisher and author, Black was convicted in 2007 on four counts of fraud in U.S. District Court in Chicago. Two of the criminal fraud charges were dropped on appeal, a conviction for felony fraud and obstruction of justice were upheld in 2010, and he was re-sentenced to forty-two months in prison and a fine of $125,000. In 2018, Black wrote a glowing book about American president Donald Trump, and in May 2019 he was granted a full pardon by Trump.

Gold said then,

> *Reasonable doubt is undefinable. Our Supreme Court spent a lot of ink in a case called Lifchus stating that reasonable doubt cannot be defined, but only explained. They said: the standard of proof beyond a reasonable doubt is inextricably intertwined with that principle fundamental to all criminal trials, the presumption of innocence.*
>
> *The burden of proof rests on the prosecution throughout the trial and never shifts to the accused, a reasonable doubt is not a doubt based upon sympathy or prejudice; rather, it is based upon reason and common sense. It is logically connected to the evidence or absence of evidence; it does not involve proof to an absolute certainty; it is not proof beyond any doubt nor is it an imaginary or frivolous doubt; and more is required than proof that the accused is probably guilty — a jury which concludes only that the accused is probably guilty must acquit.*

In the same 2007 interview, Gold also issued a warning that may have some bearing on the 2015 guilty verdict in the Dennis Oland case:

> *Certain references to the required standard of proof should be avoided. For example, describing the term reasonable doubt inviting jurors to apply to the task before them the same standard of proof that they apply to important, or even the most important, decisions in their own lives. Equating proof beyond a reasonable doubt to proof to a moral certainty — qualifying the word doubt with*

236 Who Killed Richard Oland

236 Who Killed Richard Oland

adjectives other than reasonable, such as serious or substantial, which may mislead the jury; and instructing jurors that they may convict if they are sure that the accused is guilty, before providing them with a proper definition as to the meaning of the words beyond a reasonable doubt.

Gold advised lawyers that,

The more difficult the witness, the shorter your questions should be, because the length of your question is the length of leash the witness has. In terms of their answer, you keep a dangerous dog on a short leash. Use concrete, crystal clear words and short sentences to ask questions that don't leave room for debate; No words whose meanings can be negotiated. No words requiring judgment.

According to Gold, every witness falls into two categories in terms of what they've said.

What did they say that hurts me, and what did they say that helps me. Devalue what hurts, and inflate and expand what helps, he said. The same goes for what the witness hasn't said. Whatever the witness hasn't said that could hurt, don't go there. And if the witness hasn't said something that could help, bring that out and give it as large a presence in the testimony as possible. But always short, concrete, non-negotiable, non-argumentative, non-judgmental questions.

"Oh my god," gasped a woman reporter in the media

section of the courtroom on July 19, 2019, surprised into speech on hearing the decision to acquit by Justice Terrence Morrison of the Court of Queen's Bench of New Brunswick. Oland's face turned crimson at the news, and he kissed his lead counsel Alan Gold.

Despite the verdict, Greg Marquis, professor of the history of law at the University of New Brunswick and author of a book on the Oland case, *Truth and Honour, The Oland Family Murder Case that Shocked Canada* continues to believe Dennis Oland is guilty. Verum et honorem (Truth and Honour) is the Oland family motto. One can assume Marquis is being ironic in using it as the title of his book. Other reporters covering the trial shared Marquis's perspective.

"We were certainly aware of (CBC reporter) Bobbi-Jean MacKinnon's bias in her reporting right from the start," Dennis Oland said. He continued,

> *We had a mutual friend chat with her covertly to learn if the bias was real, and astonishingly Bobbi-Jean made it perfectly clear she had a strong belief that I was guilty . . . this was only a few weeks into the first trial.*

MacKinnon's book on the Dennis Oland trials, *Shadow of Doubt*, stops short of directly asserting guilt while it leaves little doubt about the matter.

A CTV television reporter commenting on the judge's not-guilty verdict said, "while they (police) may not have got their verdict, they (have no doubt they) got their man." By the time of Oland's acquittal in July 2019, Reid and his successor John Bates had retired but Bruce Connell, police chief at the time, said he would not reopen the investigation unless significant new evidence came to light. Connell said in a statement,

> *It is the function of the Saint John Police Force to complete an investigation, then turn the file over to the Crown prosecutor's office. The Crown decides if there is sufficient evidence to warrant a charge, as was done with this case. Our investigators worked closely with the Crown prosecutors assigned to this file, both during the initial investigation and the follow up.*

Observers who believed Dennis was innocent noted that Richard had many enemies who wanted him dead. "Richard was a bad cat," said Barbara Pearson, whose daughter attended the Rothesay Pony Club stabled at the Oland home. Then Mayor William Bishop described the man's funeral: "I don't know how to put this . . . the church was packed, but there wasn't a tear shed. People weren't disturbed emotionally."

Notwithstanding exoneration by the courts, despite the complete lack of real physical evidence against him and the flawed investigation by the police, Oland continues to be viewed by many in Saint John as a guilty rich man who got away with murder. Gold maintains his client has been the victim of police tunnel vision in the case and has called on the force to "reinvigorate" its investigation and "find the real perpetrators of this terrible, terrible crime."

Should new evidence come to their attention, police will consider it — not reopen the investigation as justice demands, but they will consider it if they decide it is warranted. The Olands, angered by this tepid response, released a statement through their lawyer Bill Teed, stating,

The family of Dennis Oland would certainly renew its offer of a reward, something that may provide the police with additional information or new evidence, which Chief Connell has suggested is required for further investigation to take place.

Notwithstanding this offer, we would have thought that the complete re-examination of the evidence by fresh eyes — a common step used by many police forces in reviewing old cases — would have been the obvious next step. Sitting and waiting for clues to be delivered to the police department is a very disappointing response. As a family, we believe our husband and father deserves better.

CHAPTER THIRTY
Psychology and Money

"It looks very much like amateurism. They don't see a lot of murder cases," Dennis Oland mused, in reflecting on the police investigation following his acquittal.

But it could have been human nature outweighing police training on the proper procedures for a criminal investigation. Social conditioning and preconceived bias may have played a significant role.

> *The Saint John police told Diana Sedlacek on July 7th [before they interviewed her] that I was the murderer. She was in Moncton, (and) police asked her to come to Saint John to be questioned. Right after that call, she called a friend of Dad's and he didn't answer the call, so she left a voice message*

telling him the police said, I'm the guy. We have that voice message; it was played in court at one of the pre-trial hearings.

The lead investigator when called to come in from holidays to start the investigation asked right away . . . who in the family did it? My lawyer Alan Gold feels the bias from the start (from the chief down) caused serious problems [for the defence]."

Dennis's body language, seen online in police-released video, was discussed widely and at length by case observers. His defensive attitude — averting his eyes, leaning away and fidgeting — convinced police interrogators, who pride themselves on being able to quickly sniff out a "tell" or a lie, that he was hiding the truth.

But the truth is, they're no better at discerning a falsehood than anyone else. When we meet someone who behaves weirdly or inappropriately, we are likely to jump to negative conclusions about them, even when there is little hard evidence to support our assumptions, says well-known journalist Malcolm Gladwell, who has researched and written a book on the subject. All of us are easily deceived, including the so-called specialists, says Gladwell in his book *Talking to Strangers* (New York: Little Brown and Company, 2019). Gladwell suggests prejudice and incompetence go a long way toward explaining social dysfunction in the West. We do not always realize that people whose backgrounds differ from ours may communicate in unfamiliar ways, he writes.

"There is zero evidence that this is a reliable indicator of lying," Gladwell says talking in an online video about the book, while purposely looking away, avoiding eye contact and fidgeting nervously with his hands. "And yet, I can show you study after study of surveyed cops in every corner of the world, and they all think that's lying."

Gladwell devotes a chapter in his book to the case of Amanda Knox, an American exchange student who spent almost four years in an Italian prison after being wrongfully convicted of murder because everyone, from the police interrogators to the prosecutors to the jurors, thought that Knox was guilty simply because she didn't behave like they thought someone who was innocent should behave.

Throughout it all, she didn't exhibit much sadness, grief or shock at her roommate's bloody murder. She saw blood on the bathroom floor mat but still carried on with a shower. She kissed her boyfriend outside the crime scene and performed stretches, cartwheels and yoga moves as they waited for the police to investigate. She wanted to remain living at the apartment afterwards — when most people would find it hard to stay long enough to pack their things.

Gladwell says Amanda Knox is a perfect example of someone who is mismatched — the kind of person we tend to get wrong when we try to deduce their thoughts based on their behaviour. Knox was ultimately acquitted of killing her roommate. Europe's top human rights court ruled she had been deprived of adequate legal aid during the police interrogation, and DNA evidence used to convict her was flawed.

The flawed investigative techniques used by the Italian police that led to her wrongful conviction mirrors what happened to Dennis Oland. Just as the Italian police misread Amanda Knox, the Saint John police misread Dennis Oland's behaviour. They also used a discredited interrogation method.

Dennis Oland said of his police interrogation, "The Reid technique, long proven to be the wrong way to interview/

interrogate, was strongly defended at trial by police."

The Reid technique that was used by Constable Stephen Davidson in questioning Dennis Oland is an accusatory process in which investigators, with little regard for the facts, tell suspects that the results of the investigation, even if it is far from complete, clearly indicate that they committed the crime in question. The interrogation takes the form of a monologue by the investigator instead of question and answer. It was developed in the 1950s by John E. Reid, an American psychologist, polygraph expert and former Chicago police officer.

The goal is to coerce a confession. The investigator spins a tale of how the crime went down and then offers the suspect a starring role and provides various psychological constructs as a justification for their violent behaviour. Dennis Oland's interrogators suggested that Dennis had serious problems with his father that justified what police said he had done. Critics of the Reid technique charge that it can elicit an unacceptably high rate of false confessions from innocent people caught up in a traumatizing situation. Oland did not confess.

"This was a premeditated murder. There is absolutely no way to have done this without planning," Dennis Oland said during an email discussion for this book.

> *But the crime scene investigation was a complete mess, so they tainted the ability to find things. Plus, when you spend more time investigating the interior of my car than the crime scene, that's pretty telling. Their focus from the start was clearly to find what fit their theory.*

In every court case, the high cost of litigation becomes a defining factor. The Olands' wealth left many New Brunswickers convinced that Dennis Oland would be acquitted. "There is a feeling that there is a two-tier justice system, that richer families get treated different," April Cunningham, a former reporter who covered the Richard Oland murder for the Saint John *Telegraph-Journal* told a Toronto reporter in the days following the murder.

Legal experts lined up to say the case proved how money makes a difference in mounting a successful defence. Nicole O'Byrne, a law professor at the University of New Brunswick, said Dennis Oland had the resources to pay a defence team to follow up on every aspect of the case, hiring experts and taking portions of the case to the Supreme Court of Canada for determination.

"All citizens enjoy the same constitutional rights, such as the right to be presumed innocent, however not all citizens have equal access to resources that may be needed to mount a successful defence," O'Byrne said in *Global News* television interview.

> *In an era when legal aid services are being cut and the costs of legal representation are continually rising, this case reminds us that access to justice needs to be for everyone and not just people with means.*

Kirk Makin, a former *Globe and Mail* court reporter, now co-president of Innocence Canada, a non-profit for individuals who may have been wrongfully convicted, says many people wrongfully convicted of crimes and later exonerated are poor people who can't afford the best defence. "A great many are homeless or otherwise rejected by society, having fallen through the cracks." Following Oland's exoneration, Makin commented,

Dennis Oland is a very fortunate man. The difference is profound between someone who has the means to get the best defence and pursue every avenue of appeal vigorously. The vast majority of people don't.

Making points to the case of Glen Assoun, who spent nearly seventeen years in prison after his 1999 conviction in the killing of Brenda Way in Halifax in November, 1995. Assoun, who has a Grade Six education, was forced to defend himself after he fired his lawyer appointed by Nova Scotia legal aid. He failed to find a replacement and Justice Suzanne Hood said he'd have to act as his own lawyer, telling him, "There are lawyers who come before the court who are doing their first trial; everybody has to start somewhere."

Assoun's case was finally dealt with by Justice Minister and Attorney General David Latimer. His conviction was overturned in March 2019. According to his lawyer, Sean MacDonald, founding partner of a small legal firm in Sydney Nova Scotia, lack of money played a major role in Assoun's conviction.

Saint John police made an issue of Dennis's erratic behaviour on July 6, 2011, leaving and then returning to the Far End office, alleging without any proof that he was confused and distracted because he was planning to attack his father for refusing to bail him out of a financial bind.

Asked, "Do you recall what was on your mind when you went to see your father that day?" Dennis replied in an email in February 2020,

> *I recall it being a typical drive at first, sort of the mechanical thing we all do when we just drive and think about other things perhaps not realizing how we actually arrived once stopped. Once on Canterbury Street I became awake to the fact parking was an issue and I later realized I had forgotten the Brice Will.*

This of course is the Worthington Brice Will that John Oland is mentioned within as his son. The will was significant to the Olands because it clarified the family's history prior to their arrival in Canada in 1865. The genealogical document that amused Richard and Dennis on their last visit together acknowledged that John Oland was the son of Worthington Brice and Grace Oland, but not an aristocrat. Brice and Oland's marriage was legal but Morganatic, sometimes called a left-handed marriage, between a couple of unequal social rank. Neither the wife nor offspring have a claim on the spouse's succession rights, titles or entailed property. The children are considered legitimate for all other purposes.

CHAPTER THIRTY-ONE
Dennis Oland
Speaks Out

The following is my question-and-answer interview with Dennis Oland, concerning the police investigation in Richard Oland's murder. Our communication took place over email on June 28, 2021:

Q) Diana Sedlacek — you were convinced that she had a major role in your father's death. She was a police informant and immediately accused you on July 7, 2011. What was behind this action? Why would she say these things? Had you had any interaction at all previously with her?

Dennis Oland) I have never spoken with her; I only knew her by reputation as being elitist and difficult. Of interest:

Diana was called by police around 8 p.m. (during my interrogation) and told that she needed to come in the next day for interview. After that call she immediately called one of my father's best friends. The call went to voicemail and that message was saved and given to us. In that call, Diana tells my father's friend that the police informed her they think I did it. I believe this knowledge very much impacted her interview and behaviour afterwards. Clearly, police had their minds made up already and they gave Diana a chance to plan out her police interview to her advantage.

The lack of proper investigation means a lot of information is lost. This is thin stuff, but I don't believe Diana had an alibi. Her husband only assumes she was on the property, he didn't see her. She said she never left her property all day, yet her cellphone pinged off different cell towers in the direction of Saint John.

It was clear Dad's/Diana's relationship was showing signs of strain with Diana's demands for marriage being ignored. Letters, emails, texts all showed very erratic behaviour, anger, threats, and a threat to kill my mother. A lot of bigoted, homophobic comments as well. One can see a pattern of possessiveness, control, lack of trust, demands, manipulation. She was pushing hard for dad to divorce my mother and buy a house with her. Dad was nonresponsive to these requests, and he let the few friends that were aware of the relationship know he was dealing with a crazed woman.

I believe (my memory isn't totally clear on this) that her cellphone records were in Eastern Standard Time and police were unaware they (her phone records) were an hour off.

There's other stuff but nothing that gets it out of the speculation bubble. I've no idea why she pointed her finger at me. Clearly, her thoughts were manipulated by what she had been told the night before. I'm guessing it was in her interest to do so. She certainly didn't know me from Adam.

Q) Are you aware of rumours in Saint John about Diana Sedlacek and her ex-husband Jiri Sedlacek? What was known about the couple prior to your father's death?

DO) Jiri was an immigrant from Czechoslovakia who became a senior executive in the Bata Shoe Company. The organized crime rumour comes from a startup company that didn't happen. The buyers were Ukrainian. No one lost money and my father was only acting as an intermediary. No one's feelings were hurt, no lingering upset. It was NB Govt that caused it to fall through. The rumour arose out of the word "Ukrainian." To some, Ukrainian equals bad guys. I don't have the correct details, but we explored this with those that were involved with the Ukrainians, and it was quickly evident they have a high opinion of them.

(Author's Note: Court documents from Can Sugar Inc.'s bankruptcy hearings show that total of $25 million was lost in the failed project including $17.5 million by the Ukrainian and Russian investors.)

Q) You told the police in your interrogation on July 7, 2011, that you believed Diana Sedlacek was responsible for your father's murder. Why was that?

DO) Complete speculation. Based solely on my belief she was demanding and difficult. A type that may not take rejection well. Research (like what I described above) after dad's death just seemed to point toward her as a suspect.

Q) The Saint John police investigation into your father's murder was controlled by one (Glen McCloskey) or a handful (including Greg Oram, Sean Rocca) of senior police officers from the morning of July 7, 2011, and on. Some police experts have described the Saint John Police Department as a para-military operation. Your view? Also, your family hired private investigators, ex-RCMP officers. What was their take on the Saint John police actions?

DO) Yes, we hired investigators and specialists. We had a comprehensive report done by ex-RCMP officer Neil Fraser of Halifax outlining all of the investigative failures and all examples of tunnel vision. He was blown away by how badly things were done.

I can't recall their words but the whole investigative team had great difficulty with how poorly the SJPF managed this. They very much wanted a police commission review. They weren't impressed with the "blue wall of silence" type stuff during first trial testimony. That changed during the second trial because we had all the interviews from the Halifax police investigation into McCloskey. They were more truthful with Halifax guys, and we were able to use that to get more truth from SJPF testimony. Way more cops admitted to investigative failings. Except McCloskey, Davidson, Gilbert and Copeland.

I don't know how I would label the SJPF. They weren't equipped to handle dad's case and they screwed it up so badly it will be a cold case forever. How much have they improved since then? We don't know. A comprehensive review was deemed unnecessary.

Q) The jury system: After your first trial several lawyers urged a change in the Canadian justice system to make the reasons for decisions by juries public. This would expose any jury tampering. In your view based on your experience should juries make the reasons for their verdict public?

DO) I think the biggest issue with juries for higher profile cases is easy access to media/social media. It is very easy to be swayed by those outside of the Court room and it's a known problem. Having a Judge politely ask you to not look at media/social media or be swayed by it is grossly insufficient.

Q) Do you think you were well served by your legal team? They called so few witnesses--only three at the first trial. There is some criticism that the lawyers let the case go long to inflate their fees. This led to criticism that only the rich can afford justice. This affected public opinion about your case. I am interested in your thoughts on this.

DO) We were all shocked with the guilty verdict . . . lawyers included. On paper the trial went perfectly for our side but clearly the jury didn't see it that way. Again, we were all completely shocked.

So yes, it was a mistake to not call more witnesses.

The assumption at the time was that my testimony was so effective more witnesses weren't needed. The ones to come after me (my mother, then wife Lisa and my uncle Jack) would have been able to affirm my testimony, particularly the dry cleaning. Had it been a Judge alone trial at that time the added witnesses would not have been necessary.

Any criticism of the length of the trials falls on the Crown . . . they call the witnesses . . . we had to cross examine them. The actions of my lawyers, their work ethic, wisdom, behaviours, kindness etc. were all above board. We tried hard to get the Crown to limit the number of witnesses, or have agreed statements of fact for some but for the most part they refused.

But yes, there was opinion that only the rich can afford justice. I don't disagree with that statement. I saw a lot of men in prison who would have benefitted from a having a good lawyer. But that's not the only problem with the Criminal Justice system. But many confuse this with the rich being guilty and just using their money to buy themselves freedom by paying someone off. That falls in the category of conspiracy theory.

Another issue is the Crown and police in Saint John are too close to each other and work too closely together. There should be a more arm's length relationship. This was made clear when the NS Attorney General's office wrote to the NB Attorney General to point out findings of improper behaviour regarding McCloskey. The NB Crown office refused to take the matter to the law society. It was emails from Crown (Patrick) Wilbur trying to assist McCloskey in not having to testify. The reason given was so that no one would know how many times he went

into the crime scene (author: *or that he was there at all*).
Crown Wilbur acted inappropriately.

Q) The police have closed their investigation despite the
fact the murder is unsolved. Given the New Brunswick
Police Commission probe into the police actions have
stalled, what do you/your family think should be done
now?

DO) We are at a standstill now. We've hit a wall! Where
do you go next? We don't know . . . so far, there isn't a
next . . . we've been shut down. Hiring a private investigator has its limits. The work that wasn't done by SJPF
regarding Diana (Sedlacek) and others is a major barrier
now. The police/crown tactic was clear . . . no evidence
to point the finger elsewhere because they didn't bother
to properly look. The police/crown turned it into "if not
Dennis then who else could it possibly be . . .?" It was
poor police work or intentionally stubborn police work to
not explore other pathways.

There are many glaring examples of work not being
done. As the chief said at the time "dotting I's and
crossing T's" . . . well clearly that wasn't happening.
Do you know the police had no idea I was on surveillance
video in several spots until we pointed this out to them
in 2015? They essentially had no video evidence to base
their theories on. The video evidence proved my version
of events (save for forgetting the third visit) so they then
changed tactics. How do you miss me walking down the
street across from dad's office . . . nuts!

I really think there needs to be a proper review. This
can't keep happening to others.

254 Who Killed Richard Oland

Q) The effect on the family/community: How have the events post 2011 affected you (your relationship with Lisa), your children, mother, and sisters and the rest of the Oland family? You received strong support throughout the ordeal. Is this still helping?

DO) Our lives are forever changed. Mental health trauma, financial ruin for me, ruined my marriage, took 10 years of my life away.

My father's life was taken from him in a most horrific way. He was still fairly young. He was healthy and active and enjoying life . . . that was all taken from him. It's so completely sad for all of us. Dad was a force and his grandkids never got to see the full extent of that. The impact on the community is this: For some it's Dennis got away with murder. The mean world of social media has shown that.

Dennis was wrongly convicted due to poor police work and a serious murder is unsolved.

Saint John lost a dedicated community champion, and I lost my dad.

CHAPTER THIRTY-TWO
The Mystery Lives On

Richard Oland's brutal murder created a mystery that remains unsolved to this day: who killed Richard Oland and why? The comfortable life of an elite New Brunswick society family ended that day. Even worse for the family, members of the 150-year-old Oland brewing dynasty, suspicion immediately fell on Richard's only son, Dennis, although he was not charged for another two years. And as if all that wasn't bad enough, Dennis was convicted by a jury of his peers in a Saint John courtroom in 2015 and sentenced to twenty-five years in prison with no chance of parole for ten years.

A successful appeal, a second trial and an acquittal in 2019 should have brought relief to the beleaguered family. But the fact is that many, maybe even most, people in Saint John and beyond still believe him guilty — just another silver-spoon kid who got away with murder thanks to the family's great wealth.

"I don't know how he did it, but I still believe he did it," Judith Meinert, a court regular at the trial, said years after the acquittal. In the wake of the killing, the café crowd indulged themselves over lattes and espressos in endless speculation about what happened that warm summer night in July 2011. They spent hours dissecting circumstantial evidence, motive and opportunity. Two books and a television series on the case stop just short of declaring Dennis Oland's guilt. Despite Justice Terrence Morrison's lengthy written decision, police continue to believe they got the right man but the wrong verdict and refuse to reopen the investigation.

For the police it's all about the path of least resistance. If someone presents as the obvious suspect, that's who they will arrest — just so they can arrest someone.

Most murder cases are built on circumstantial evidence. In this case there wasn't really any evidence at all, circumstantial or otherwise. The defendant had an airtight alibi based on time stamped video footage. Dennis Oland was in the building, but video evidence showed him depart unscathed and bloodless.

The rush by the Saint John police to accuse Dennis Oland — the tunnel-vision investigation — raises serious questions about police intent. In the eyes of some observers, the police themselves have become suspect in the murder as a result of their clumsy and heavy-handed tactics.

The police actions on the day Richard Oland's body was found raise obvious questions. Was the contamination of the crime scene and the overlooking of possible forensic evidence at the entrance and exit to Far End Corporation part of a deliberate plan to conceal evidence of the killer or killers?

American writer Kyle Ann Ross, author of *Taserized: Neighborhood Walk ends in Police Brutality* (2012), recounts being mistaken by police for a criminal. She was tasered three times in custody and has become a harsh critic of police interrogation and investigation tactics. The book is her account of being mistaken by police for a burglar and/ or drug dealer when out for a walk in Asheville, a city of 93,000 in North Carolina's Blue Ridge Mountains in 2005. In December 2015, she weighed in on the Oland case in an email response to an article in *Atlantic Magazine* about the investigation.

Ross wrote in her letter to the magazine editor,

> *There is no way on earth a man can be axed 46 times with blood spurting everywhere in pools and tablespoons and pints that a son would have three little spots on his jacket.*
>
> *C'mon, I am starting to wonder if the police investigators have been corrupted by the drug lords and cartels. How could a "seasoned" investigator even mention this possibility. Your country is like our country. The USA and Canada are becoming similar by charging after the innocent and closing a case without examining details and using details like those that came from a worker in the building (Anthony Shaw) who now is "done co-operating." Who scared the daylights out of this worker? Wow for all the security camera footage they have of an innocent man where is the security camera footage and witness testimony from the person who saw the*

BLOOD covered suspect leave the building? I was just wondering.

Listen, if Dennis had a dad who would give him five hundred thousand dollars he did not need to kill for money. He could get another loan. I am very sorry to hear that even though we in the USA are closer to Mexico and we here have judges and police and Federal agents corrupted by the Cabals and Cartels, well now I see you in Canada are suffering too.

Dennis has had to prove his innocence, and in the eyes of too many he has yet to do that. This is patently unfair to Dennis Oland and his family, who deserve closure, and ultimately to the justice system itself. The justice system is designed to have results that are acceptable to the public. When the judge's decision is publicly derided as it was in the Dennis Oland case by the Saint John police, that undermines trust.

There were no witnesses to the crime, no murder weapon, no fingerprints, no DNA, no motive and no confession. Problems with the investigation emerged within minutes of discovering the body on the morning of July 7, 2011 and help to explain the lack of hard evidence. While working on the crime scene, officers used the bathroom before it was tested for blood or fingerprints, and they roamed around the office with bloodied gloves. The blood spatter expert didn't show up until four days after the murder, by which time the body had been removed and spatter had dried and flaked.

The back door wasn't tested for fingerprints. Some police witnesses couldn't remember if the back entrance had steps down to the ground. The three steps had been in place since at least 1999, the building's owner John Ainsworth confirmed. The back alleyway, a possible escape route, wasn't photographed until three years after the crime. Police investigators didn't interview some witnesses for a year and a half after the murder. Some witness statements disappeared.

There are many other suspects the police could have investigated to find the real killer. Diana Sedlacek moved to New Brunswick in 2003, and quickly became romantically involved with Richard Oland. Their affair ended with his murder. She informed the police within a day of his death that she thought Dennis killed his father. He, in turn, without knowing she had accused him, suggested to police during his July 7, 2011, interrogation that she might be responsible. Oland compared her to a scorned woman like the psychopath played by Glenn Close in the movie *Fatal Attraction*. Police liked her theory better.

Also on the table but ignored by the police is the contract killing theory — a Russian mafia hit. One source speculated Richard Oland had dealings with organized crime that got out of hand. Port cities are targets for import and export of illegal goods and services, and Saint John is a port city. The Can Sugar refinery debacle raises questions related to this theory. Was the refinery a cover for drug smuggling and human trafficking? Canada Border Services Agency only inspects 3 per cent of container ships in Saint John.

Richard Oland had willingly lent his name to the re-establishment of a sugar refinery in Saint John. Perhaps when the project failed, he was expected to cover the losses. He had the means to make whole the losses to investors. According to the theory, he refused to do so since he had not even put money into the project; nonetheless he paid the price. Experts in organized crime see this as a plausible scenario, fitting the Red Mafia's *modus operandi*. They befriend independent businesses and businessmen like Oland to help set up ways to launder money. And to intimidate other businessmen who might be tempted to resist their overtures, twenty-first-century contract killings are brutal.

Can Sugar fit the description of a company funded by money of uncertain sources. Oland's accountant Robert McFadden assisted with the refinery's bankruptcy proceedings and provided details of the business failure. Death by Red Mafia is a theory worth investigation by police. With the exoneration in 2019 of Dennis Oland, the question remains — who did kill Richard Oland?

Immediately after Dennis Oland's acquittal and through the years that have followed, the Saint John police won't admit they got the wrong man. They refuse to re-open the case unless someone comes forward with new information.

"The Saint John police has no update to provide on the Richard Oland case," wrote Staff Sergeant Sean Rocca, communications director for the Saint John Police Force, in response to a repeated request for an interview for this book with Saint John police chief Robert Bruce — the fifth person to hold the top job in eight years. Police chiefs regularly hold the position for a decade, so this many in such a short time is unusual.

Bill Reid, Saint John's chief of police at the time of Richard Oland's murder, retired in early 2015 after thirty-seven years with the police force, including seven years as chief. John Bates, formerly the police chief in Stratford, Ontario, was appointed to the position in August 2015, and took over the job in November of that year. Bates surprised many when he announced his retirement in early 2018, after less than two years in the position.

Bates was replaced by Bruce Connell, who had retired in 2014 after thirty years of service in the Saint John force. Connell, a former deputy chief, came out of retirement to serve as interim chief in April 2018. Stephan Drolet, appointed in February 2020, retired the following February, citing personal reasons a few days short of a year in the job. Robert Bruce became chief in July 2021.

On the afternoon of July 11, 2011, four days after Richard Oland's body was discovered, Chief Reid held a press conference calling the death a homicide.

He stressed that they were in the "very long process" of fact-finding. "It can always be said that you've got tunnel vision in an investigation if you're focusing on one person or a specific thing . . . the analogy here is that we're using a funnel."

"We do not want to make a mistake."

Postscript

The aftermath of Richard Oland murder was devastating for his son, wife and family. As Dennis Oland was preparing with his legal team for his second trial for second degree murder, his marriage with Lisa was unravelling. During the final weeks of his retrial, Lisa was sometimes absent from court, and observers noticed that Dennis wasn't wearing his wedding ring.

While his legal ordeal was resolved when he was exonerated on July 19, 2019, his homelife was disintegrating, and the winter of 2020 ended with the final collapse of their marriage. On Monday, February 17, having just turned fifty-two, Dennis Oland moved out of their home at 58 Gondola Point Road to live with his mother at nearby 5 Almon Lane. Five weeks later, on March 23, Dennis and Lisa announced they were separating after a decade of marriage.

Then in June, Lisa applied for a restraining order, alleging her husband was prone to intimate partner violence. The allegations came in an application for an emergency intervention order, which Lisa filled out on June 10, 2020, at a shelter for abused women in Saint John. Lisa's application under the Intimate Partner Violence Intervention Act was issued by an emergency adjudicative officer on the day it was filed. The officer imposed a publication ban on the details of the complaint.

"I am not sure what he will do, but he has PTSD and has had many episodes where he is not controlling his actions and becomes aggressive," Lisa alleged in the document. "It is getting worse because he is less and less in control. He is not getting a reaction from me, and he can't handle it . . . I am not safe in my own house."

Chief Justice Tracey DeWare of the Court of Queen's Bench, reviewed the emergency intervention order on June 11, 2020, the day after it was issued, and ruled there was insufficient evidence to confirm the order without holding a hearing. On June 17, Dennis Oland appeared in family court in Saint John to face allegations of domestic violence. When court began, however, Justice DeWare announced the hearing might not proceed.

"We're hoping not to proceed. That is the goal," confirmed Lisa's lawyer, Margaret Layden. "The parties have reached an agreement," she said, as her client looked on from the front right-hand row, with a woman by her side, and Dennis Oland sat alone on the opposite side of the empty courtroom. Layden and Oland's lawyer, Tracy Peters of Moncton, jointly requested that the emergency order be set aside as part of the interim agreement on the family court dispute.

264 Who Killed Richard Oland

Lisa was seeking an interim order to prevent Dennis Oland from selling their home in Rothesay and three adjacent properties. The four parcels, which cover just over two hectares, had been assessed by Service New Brunswick to be worth $732,800. She was also seeking a freezing of family assets, ownership of the house and its contents, spousal support, an equal division of marital property and debt, as well as a restraining order.

With Justice DeWare presiding, it was agreed Lisa would have interim possession of the home and its contents. The two agreed not to contact each other, except through Oland's lawyer or any other agreed-upon third party. In setting the intervention order aside, DeWare upheld a publication ban on the details of Andrik-Oland's complaint. A fall hearing was scheduled for November 10, but it was subsequently removed from the docket when the estranged couple reached an out-of-court settlement. The details remained private.

Media outlets set out to have Andrik-Oland's allegations against Oland released. On December 23, 2020, lawyers argued before Justice DeWare for nearly six hours. David Coles, a lawyer for the CBC and *Telegraph-Journal*, argued the details should be released, while lawyers for both Andrik-Oland and Oland argued the publication ban should remain in place.

It wasn't a happy new year for either side. In early 2021, Deware ruled the media, and the public may obtain a copy of the transcript of Andrik-Oland's application for an intervention order. The adjudicative officer had no jurisdiction to impose a publication ban on the details in the first place. She ruled maintaining that ban would be "inappropriate and not in conformity" with the open-court principle.

Also, in January 2021, the couple's house, an English Country architectural style built in 1930, was listed for sale at $750,000. "Grand First Olde Rothesay, Original, traditional heritage family home," the MLS description stated. It sold in seven weeks to a local family for an undisclosed amount.

In May, they lost the appeal to retain the publication ban on the intervention order, and the allegations of domestic conflict made news headlines. It was revealed the order included her handwritten notes alleging Oland was an angry, violent man who was losing control and suffering from post-traumatic stress disorder.

In her notes, Andrik-Oland recounted an incident during a visit to a Toronto hotel in June 2018. The couple got caught up in a marital dispute that led to a 911 call and the police knocking on their hotel room door.

"People in the next room called police," the notes said. "Dennis used a belt to tie my hands behind my back; there was a physical altercation." The alleged incident happened five months before Oland's second murder trial was set to begin, and Andrik-Oland says because of that she told police, "everything was OK."

In the same section of Lisa's notes with her account of the hotel incident, she also refers to a "beach incident" in September 2019, when Oland allegedly bound her hands and feet with rope and pulled her down a dirt path. She alleged her husband threw her over his shoulder and dropped her headfirst toward some rocks. Headlines on the allegations reported "a lot of blood."

Dennis Oland's lawyer, Bill Teed, declined to comment when asked about the allegations. Oland said only that he suffered mental anguish that ended his marriage.

Dennis Oland's refusal to give his side of the divorce clouded public opinion. His silence created the public perception that perhaps he was prone to bursts of rage as the Saint John police had alleged. Perhaps he was guilty after all of murdering his father despite the court verdict; it even raised doubts for many of his supporters.

However, police incident reports tell a different story. The evening before Lisa went to the women's shelter and filed for an emergency restraining order, she had called Rothesay police. Three officers came to 58 Gondola Point Road at 9:40 p.m. on June 9, 2020. In his report, Constable Matthew Marsh notes, "Caller advised her husband is in their house and he is not supposed to be. She is sitting out in her car as she does not want to have a confrontation with him."

Officers Sebastien Lee and Nick Dupuis were also present. Marsh noted, "All in order when we arrived. Dennis Oland was looking for his laptop." Marsh wrote that there was no court order stating that he was not allowed in the home. "Both left and will be staying elsewhere."

Dennis explained in a June 2023 email for this book that the incident on June 9, 2020, involved both him and his son Henry and a few of Henry's friends. There were two reports filed by police about that night, Oland wrote.

The first report/incident is a result of my son and friends. When the police were called [by Andrik Oland to 58 Gondola Point Road], my son called me to assist. Thus, I was present from when the police arrived until they left.

It's clear there was no bad behaviour on my part. The allegations are all about [Lisa] seeking sole possession of the home/restricting my access and preventing sale. Prior to any allegations, our side was seeking a hearing on possession of the home/ forcing sale . . . this was an end run on that.

The police report on the hotel altercation during their Toronto getaway weekend also tells a much different story. In fact, according to the report, Dennis called police, not the people in the room next door. Police constables Diana Croll and Alex Li responded to a 911 call to the Hotel Continental on Bloor Street West. Croll's narrative states as follows,

On 2018.06.09 at approximately 0436 hrs, a 9-1-1 call was received with no one speaking to the call taker. The call taker could hear a male voice and a female voice in conversation.

The conversation overheard included the male voice saying, "you tell me you hate me all the time," and the female crying and saying, "I wish I was dead." The call ended and the call taker was not able to reach anyone on a ring back as the only contact info listed was the main phone number for the Hotel Intercontinental.

In speaking to hotel staff, they advised that the manager on duty received an email that a 9-1-1 call originated from room 641 and he would be in touch with the residents. Shortly afterwards the manager called back to advise that he spoke to the residents of room 641 and they advised they mistakenly dialed 9-1-1 instead of 4-1-1 for information.

Due to the emotional state of the conversation overheard and the potential for a domestic

situation, police attended to speak to the residents of room 641. Officers arrived at 0453 hrs and spoke to the manager. He advised that he only spoke to the residents over the phone, he did not attend the room. PC Li and PC Croll attended room 641. Before knocking on the door officers listened and could hear a conversation between a male and female. The only words that could be heard were an argument about shoes, something along the lines of "I don't want your fucking shoes" and a short time later a male saying "when you get so emotional like that . . .

There was no shouting or sounds of a struggle. Officers knocked and a male answered the door wearing boxer shorts. He advised that he and his wife were the only occupants of the room, and they were having a discussion. He invited officers into the room.

The male put on a shirt and shorts while the female spoke to officers wearing a hotel robe. The hotel room was clean and orderly with 2 suitcases and shopping bags present. PC Li spoke to the male in the hallway while PC Croll spoke to the female in the room. The male produced a New Brunswick driver's license and identified himself as Dennis OLAND. Similarly, the female identified as Lisa ANDRIK-OLAND.

The female told police that they have had a stressful few years and that recently the stress has been difficult to handle for her emotionally. She advised that she felt overwhelmed tonight and the emotional outburst she had is what was overheard on the 9-1-1 call.

She advised that she believes her husband was trying to call 4-1-1 although does not know what information that he was seeking. She advised she does see a therapist regularly. She was adamant that no assaults or threats had occurred and that she was not feeling like killing or harming herself. She advised that she had a glass of wine earlier in the evening but that was all. She advised that her husband was in the middle of a well-known court case that had been on-going for 7 years and the stress had taken its toll on her mentally. They visit Toronto periodically in order to 'get away' for a few days and be anonymous in the big city.

The male initially told police that he was trying to call 4-1-1. When confronted with that illogical explanation, he admitted that he did intend to call 9-1-1. He advised that he and his wife had been out all day and had been at a local restaurant where they consumed an amount of alcohol. When they arrived back at the hotel room his wife got upset and highly emotional. He knows that she has some on-going mental health issues and is diagnosed with depression and PTSD. He called 9-1-1 as he was worried that he might not be able to calm her down and feared she may hurt herself if she was so upset. He then decided that he did not require police or ambulance as she got herself under control.

The male advised police that he had been convicted of murder but was going through an appeal process and currently on bail pending a new trial for Second Degree Murder. He went on to

270 Who Killed Richard Oland

> *tell officers that since the 9-1-1 call his wife had calmed down and he no longer feared for her safety or immediate emotional state.*
>
> *He advised that no assaults or threats or criminality of any kind occurred that night. Both parties appear 10-60 with no bail conditions listed for the male party. There were no allegations or evidence of any criminality nor did the officers believe either party to be apprehendable under the Mental Health Act. Saint John Police Service was contacted regarding Mr. OLAND's bail conditions and Sgt SIMMONS confirmed that OLAND is not on conditions to stay within New Brunswick but can travel within Canada.*

The family trait for privacy, which was also very much in evidence in the months immediately after Richard's murder in 2011, has coloured events that took place after Dennis Oland's exoneration. The Olands prefer that private matters not be discussed publicly.

"I am very reluctant to answer your questions directly. In particular, the divorce and media stories are just a can of worms I don't wish to open," Dennis Oland wrote in an email.

> *I've not spoken publicly at all on this. . . . I think your journalist friends would agree . . . men are at a disadvantage when defending against abuse accusations against women. Back when this was in the media, I sent a letter to my friends and family with my side of the story and backstory. I didn't care to court public opinion . . . just wanted my friends in the loop . . . that's it and I'm happy I did that.*

There have been other developments since the exoneration. The Saint John building where Richard Oland was murdered and where his company Far End Corporation continued to operate for more than a decade after his death was sold by its owner John Ainsworth in late April 2021. The red brick Italianate-style commercial building at 52 Canterbury St. in the city's uptown core came back on the market for $950,000 in 2023. According to the MLS description, the three-storey heritage 1891 building was "situated in a bustling area with plenty of foot traffic and a strong sense of community." Far End Corporation has relocated to Rothesay.

Author's Note

I arrived in Saint John in October 2018 for the start of Dennis Oland's second trial. Convinced by this time that he had been wrongly convicted, I planned to write about the case. Jury selection had begun when an abrupt halt was called to the proceedings while the court looked at possible jury tampering. Court did not resume for two weeks.

My husband was with me and with time to spare, we went exploring all that the city had to offer and the wild and rocky beauty of the Bay of Fundy. We met a man with a Maritimes history as captivating as that of the Moosehead Breweries dynasty I was in the midst of covering. His business dealings connected him to the richest families of New Brunswick and to the grittiest and most hardened dockworkers at the Port of Saint John.

What he had to say and what he believed to be the fate of Richard Oland pulled the cover back on dark secrets, leading me to a new line of inquiry (as depicted in my reconstruction in Chapter One).

There was no fly on the wall or security camera in Richard Oland's office at 52 Canterbury Street (even if that is what the police told Dennis) on the night he was killed. My theory of his murder by a contract killer for losses in a failed sugar refinery is an educated guess constructed on the available evidence. Any mistakes are my own.

Timeline

The following is a detailed description of the Richard Oland story. The chronology begins in 1981, when Richard loses a battle for succession and left the family business, Moosehead Breweries, and establishes his own companies. It sets out a timeline of his final days, the murder, the police investigation and his son's trials.

* * *

1981 – Richard Oland loses his father Philip Warburton's support for succession with brother Derek to lead Moosehead Breweries Ltd. With his father's backing, he starts a trucking company, Brookville Transport.

1985 – Oland organizes the 1985 Canada Summer Games in Saint John with five thousand volunteers.

1997 – Battered by hard times in the truck transport business, Richard Oland sells Brookville Transport to Laidlaw Bulk Carriers, Woodstock, Ont. and focuses on investments and his land development company, Kinghurst Estates Ltd., from his Far End Corporation office.

1997 – Richard Oland is appointed an Officer of the Order of Canada for his contributions to New Brunswick and to Saint John.

2000-2011 – Richard Oland, a serial philanderer, carries on overlapping extra-marital affairs, most notably with investment banker Hilary Brock (the Olands' neighbour in Rothesay), Lesley Oland (Dennis Oland's first wife) and a Saint John realtor, Diana Sedlacek. The affair with Sedlacek began in late 2003 and continued until Richard's murder in 2011. It's not clear when the other two began.

The Brock relationship was also still going on when he was killed.

2000 – 'Lantic Sugar closes its Saint John refinery and consolidates its operation in Montreal.

2002-2003 – Richard Oland is a leading supporter of local businessman John Cardwell in his effort to replace 'Lantic Sugar with a new sugar refining venture. With federal and provincial support, the city's economic development agency, Enterprise Saint John, backs Can Sugar Inc. Its principals are Russian/Ukrainian with a $17.5 million investment. Oland's role involves assists in making introductions to local bankers, provincial government officials and federal officers at The Atlantic Canada Opportunities Agency.

Fall 2003 – Can Sugar has fifty-five employees and an annual two million dollar payroll. It also adds to the economy by using local trucking and other service companies. Management and production problems lead to serious financial difficulties.

Toronto couple Jiri and Diana Sedlacek move to Saint John with their son. Jiri, seventy-five, is retired, a former executive with global shoe manufacturer Bata Corporation. He describes himself as "international." Diana, fifty-four, a real estate agent with RE/MAX, and Richard Oland, sixty-one, begin an affair that continues for eight years until his 2011 murder.

January 2004 – Can Sugar goes bankrupt, owing more than $25 million. Its two main shareholders, Sergei Ryazanov and Alex Chernyak of Toronto, acting for a group of East Bloc investors, lose their $17.5 million investment. Tapped as a potential angel investor, Richard Oland declines to provide the financing needed to keep the company going. He lends his accountant Robert McFadden to help shepherd the company through bankruptcy proceedings.

2005 – Dennis Oland and Lesley Oland separate. Divorce proceedings begin the next year.

2007 – Richard Oland, former vice-president of Moosehead Breweries, takes a buyout of his shares in Moosehead for $36 million and settles years of legal wrangling with his brother Derek, president of Moosehead.

2008/2009 – Dennis Oland and Lesley Oland's divorce proceedings are ongoing. Richard Oland steps in with a $500,000 loan to ensure Dennis doesn't lose the family home. Dennis marries Lisa Andrik in 2009.

2011

Dennis Oland is in less dire financial straits than the previous year, though still living in the red. He bounces a mortgage interest payment of $1,666.67 to his father. The payment clears a few weeks later, though Richard Oland's assistant Maureen Adamson later testifies her boss was unaware of the NSF cheque.

June 20: Richard Oland goes to Block Island, Rhode Island to compete in a sailing race week.

June 25: Richard Oland flies back to New Brunswick on a Grand Manan-based charter plane to attend a family gathering to celebrate the 100th birthday of a Rothesay relative, his wife Connie's cousin Marg Bourne. At the event he makes plans to get together with Dennis to talk about a genealogy project when he gets back from his fishing trip.

June 26: Richard Oland joins friends for a fishing trip at the Miramichi Fish and Game Club on the northwest branch of the Miramichi River.

July 4

Richard returns from the Miramichi to hold a fundraising

276 Who Killed Richard Oland

meeting with Roman Catholic Bishop Robert Harris for a ten million dollar new roof for the cathedral. In "a great mood," he goes out for dinner with Connie and her visiting family.

Richard calls or texts with Diana five times:

11:20 a.m.: Diana Sedlacek texts Richard, "Richard Richard!!!!! It's 2 long now--Hate this waste of time!!!! You're always wasting OUR time OUR life."

Two seconds later she sends another text: "Where are U???? Are u not coming back 2day????"

3:03 p.m.: "What's happening now? Are U here? Want 2C you"

Diana and Richard have two brief phone chats, each lasting less than two minutes.

5:56 p.m.: Sedlacek sends two more texts.

10:10 p.m.: Richard calls back.

July 5

July 5 – Diana phones or texts Richard ten times.

Between noon and 9:00 p.m. – Richard does not contact Diana.

9:02 p.m.: Diana Sedlacek texts Richard: "Kisses Snuggle me up I need your body."

9:19 p.m.: Richard texts Diana: "Snuggle up kkk in bed."

July 6 — Day of the murder

Richard has his first day back at Far End Corporation after his holiday.

9:08 a.m.: Richard is having breakfast when Diana Sedlacek messages him about an upcoming trip to Portland, Maine: "Morning Lixxxx on Golden Gun. Drvn 2gym--Did Zu find note? re Our Trip?"

9:09 a.m.: Richard Oland texts back: "Have in [office] just up kkk."

9:10 a.m.: Diana: "Kissssss wen U get ther text it -- mmm kisss."

Richard puts his phone aside to talk with his houseguest, Jack Connell, who has just sat down at the table. Connie, Jack's sister, joins them.

9:50 a.m.: Richard's assistant Maureen Adamson calls him to remind him that he has a meeting at his Far End Corporation Office.

En route to the office in his 2009 BMW, Richard Oland calls Diana Sedlacek. She is in a spin class at a Quispamsis gym and doesn't pick up.

12:01 p.m.: Richard Oland texts Diana Sedlacek about three possible dates for their trip to Portland Maine: "3 options all ex St. Stephen nb. Option 1 lv jul 11 return Jul 15 11 am; Option 2 lv 15 pm return 3:00 jul 19; Option 3 lv Jul 20 at 4 pm return 24th. All should be 4 nites, would prefer option 2 or 3."

Sedlacek is driving and pulls over to the side of the road to text a reply: "I agree 2 or 3 let me think"

Lunch is a takeout pizza brought in from Boston Pizza by Adamson.

12:45 p.m.: Dennis Oland, at work a few streets away at his CIBC Wood Gundy office, reminds his daughter in a text to thank her grandfather for his donation to her sports team to help send them to a meet in Newfoundland.

1:57 p.m.: Diana Sedlacek replies to Oland's text: "Let's leave at Noon on Fri. 15th we can arrive early enough in Portland--so leave 15th come back on 19th." Occupied with a backlog of work, Dick doesn't get around to reading Sedlacek's message.

2:41 p.m. and 2:51 p.m.: Dennis Oland sends emails to Richard on a stock split and a RRIF. Richard Oland has one million dollars invested with CIBC Wood Gundy managed by Dennis.

4:42 p.m.: Apparently having forgotten about Diana Sedlacek's message, Richard Oland makes entries to his electronic calendar regarding trips to Portland Maine, July 11, 15 or 20.

4:44 p.m.: Richard disconnects his iPhone 4, fully charged, from his computer and lets any calls and texts go to voice mail.

5:08 p.m.: CCTV security cameras at Dennis Oland's Wood Gundy office record him leaving the building wearing a sports jacket and lighter-coloured pants.

5:15 p.m.: When Dennis gets to the top of the stairs at 52 Canterbury, he realizes he's forgotten some of the documents related to Oland family history that he wanted to show his father. He decides to drive back to his office only to realize on the way there he doesn't have a pass card that would allow him to use the elevator after hours.

5:26 p.m.: CCTV security cameras at Thandi's restaurant clock Dennis Oland's silver VW Golf parking on the west side of Canterbury Street near the green painted street door at No. 52 with its brass plaque, Far End Corporation.

5:30 p.m.: Robert McFadden and son Galen, summer intern at Far End, leave Richard Oland's office for home, recorded on the same camera. McFadden nods to Bill Adamson who is parked at the curbside on Canterbury Street waiting to pick up Maureen, his wife. Adamson sees Dennis Oland enter Richard's building for the second time carrying a red reusable grocery bag with something light in it.

5:44 p.m.: Maureen joins Bill in their car. In talking about the day, she tells him that Dennis had come by to discuss genealogy with his father.

6:12 p.m.: Dennis Oland sends his sister Lisa Bustin a text message mistakenly meant for his wife Lisa saying he was at his father's office doing "history stuff" and is heading home. He is seen walking down Canterbury Street looking relaxed and depositing a red grocery bag in the rear hatch of his car by Thandi's security camera across from his father's office.

6:14 p.m.: The camera at Thandi's restaurant records Dennis Oland driving South on Canterbury (a one-way street) then looping around to return to Far End Corporation. Dennis is going to his father's office for a third time to retrieve a family camp logbook that Richard had borrowed for the last year. He delivers it to his mother's house the next morning, leaving it in the hall, unmarked by any blood.

Dennis Oland later said in an email interview for this book that he found his father was standing, presumably getting ready to go out when he came back into his office to pick up the logbook. They leafed through it together for a few minutes, reminiscing and laughing about some of the entries.

6:21 p.m.: Dennis Oland leaves the Far End office and is seen on Thandi's CCTV camera in his car. He heads home to Rothesay, a twenty-to-twenty-five-minute drive.

6:44 p.m.: Diana Sedlacek texts Richard's iPhone, U there?? from her home on Darlings Island, which was not answered. Richard Oland's iPhone pings off the tower in Rothesay, indicating it is on and receiving texts.

Subsequent calls and text do not reach the phone, indicating it was switched off after 6:44 p.m.

6:44 p.m.: A couple in their car on Renforth Wharf see

Dennis at the wharf around this time but do not see him throw anything into the water. A woman sees him pick something up and put it in a red bag.

Dennis later says he doesn't really remember but thinks it might have been a beer can.

6:45 p.m. – 7:15 p.m.: Diana phones Richard on his cellphone five times.

7:19 p.m.: Diana texts Richard again: "You've turned your phone off!! Why!!!!!!?????? Your not at office & don't tell me you have a 'Bus' mtg cause U don't --So tell the fucking truth!!! Cause I'm sitting here not doing suspicious things & I hav a lot of men who would love 2 b with me!!!!!! Do stop this fucking around! And answer the damn phone! I wil call at your house."

This and subsequent texts and a dozen or so unanswered calls go to voice mail.

7:15 p.m. and 8:01 p.m.: Diana phones the Far End office.

7:35 – 8 p.m.: Dennis Oland, who has changed from his work clothes into a light blue golf shirt and tan shorts, is seen on CCTV shopping at two different stores in Rothesay — Kennebecasis Drugs in Rothesay and then at Cochran's Country Market, where he and Lisa chat with Dennis's aunt Jane Toward, Richard's sister. Dennis cradles a melon in his left arm as he pays at the counter for his groceries.

7:35 – 7:45 p.m.: Cheryl Johnson, a lawyer with the firm Gorman Nason, overhears an argument while working late in her office across the alley from Richard Oland's office.

Johnson later gives police a statement that she heard two men arguing with raised voices between 7:35 p.m. and 7:45 p.m. She is never called to testify. When I track her down by phone at her office in 2016 and explain I am calling to ask about what she heard on July 6, 2011, she says "I'm not interested. I'm sorry," before hanging up. Her voice was weak. I thought she sounded terrified.

Richard is cut down by someone wielding a two-headed drywall hammer, one flat head with a cross hatch pattern and one head with a sharp blade. Blood, bone and brain matter fly in all directions, coating the walls, floor, furnishings, boxes of papers and items on his desk. His glasses fall to the floor and his fingers are broken as he suffers forty-five blunt and sharp force blows to his head, neck and hands. He falls face down. He is quickly unconscious and dies within minutes.

7:30 – 8:00 p.m.: John Ainsworth, the building's owner, and Anthony Shaw, a friend who happened to come by, are working in the print shop, Printing Plus, one floor below Richard's office. They hear "a crash and loud, quick pounding thumps" that continue for about ten seconds. Neither goes to investigate.

Ainsworth and Shaw, in separate interviews, estimate the loud noises went on for about ten seconds between 7:30 p.m. and 8:00 p.m. A walk-in job is used as a time measure as they remember scanning and emailing a document for a customer time stamped at 8:11 p.m.

Ainsworth later changes his version of events. He claims in court the noises may have been much earlier, anytime between 6 p.m. and 8 p.m.

7:40 p.m. – 8:35 p.m.: Local businessman Gerry Lowe,

a director on Saint John's economic development board, goes for dinner with a woman friend to Thandi's restaurant. Surveillance video clocks him arriving at 7:40 p.m. and leaving at 8:35 p.m. Looking through the restaurant's large glass windows, he sees a man — someone he doesn't know — exit 52 Canterbury Street and walk towards King Street, the city's core. It's a narrow one-way street with perfect visibility that sultry summer evening.

Although Lowe gives a police statement as to what he witnessed in the days following the murder, he isn't called to testify until Dennis Oland's retrial in 2018-19.

8:09 p.m. – 9:16 p.m.: Dennis, in Rothesay, exchanges email messages with a client.

8:19 p.m. – 10:01 p.m.: Dennis talks on his cellphone with Mary Beth Watt, co-owner of a sailboat, *Loki*, with his wife, Lisa, about some repairs he is going to make to the boat's motor the next morning. He exchanges texts with a friend.

9:00 p.m.: Ainsworth and Shaw close their print shop below Richard Oland's office and leave.

10:30 p.m.: Dennis is on CCTV video buying milk at the Irving convenience store on Marr Road in Rothesay near his house.

11:12 p.m.: Diana sends the last text of the evening: "Pathetic!"

Sedlacek later says that on the evening of July 6, she and her husband Jiri, then eighty-three, were both at home at their six-acre property on Darlings Island on the Kennebecasis River, an eighteen-minute drive northeast of Rothesay.

July 7 — The day the body is found

8:08 a.m. – 8:23 a.m.: Dennis, wearing his navy blazer, is recorded by CCTV video at Kent Building Supply in Rothesay. He runs errands at several stores.

Estimated 8:45 a.m.: Maureen Adamson, Richard Oland's personal assistant, arrives at work and is surprised to find the door to the office is partially ajar, the lights and air conditioner are on, the blinds are drawn, and a television is on with the sound on mute, tuned to CNBC, an American business network. Richard Oland must have been watching the news when he was interrupted.

She is assaulted by a terrible smell. She sets down her Tim Horton's tray of coffee and rushes downstairs to the print shop for help. According to Preston Chiasson, a friend of the owner John Ainsworth, Maureen Adamson comes into Printing Plus shortly before 9 a.m.: "She seemed panicked, and she said, 'I see feet upstairs.'"

"I immediately thought Richard was in trouble," says Chiasson, and he rushed with her upstairs. John Ainsworth watched them go.

Adamson points to the feet. "I saw Richard on the floor, slaughtered," Chiasson says. "As soon as [Richard] came into view, I stopped moving. It was immediately apparent there was nothing I could do." He carefully turns around and walks out of the room without touching anything.

8:54 a.m.: Chiasson calls 911 from the office foyer and says, "There's a man down." He describes what his head looks like and adds that Maureen is in a "bad, bad way."

Constable Duane Squires, on the force since November 2006 and cadet trainee Trinda Fanjoy from the Atlantic Police Academy are on patrol in their police cruiser a couple of hundred metres away from Oland's office when they take a call for "male not conscious, not breathing."

8:56 a.m.: Squires and Fanjoy are the first responders on the scene. Chiasson is waiting on the sidewalk. He points and says, "second floor."

Squires and Fanjoy rush into the building and up the stairs into Oland's office. Squires recognizes the metallic odour immediately as a decaying body.

Squires "observe[s] a deceased male, laying on the floor." Man has "severe injuries" to his head, and blood around him is coagulated. There is also lots of blood spatter. He notes a remote control on the floor, as well as a set of keys in the blood above Oland's head. Oland's feet are underneath the desk area, where Squires notes a garbage can that was knocked over.

Cadet Fanjoy keeps notes of the comings/goings of everyone at the crime scene.

Paramedics Philip Comeau and Christopher Wall arrive. Squires tells them they don't need any equipment, there is nothing they could do.

Within one minute, Comeau advises Squires that rigor mortis has set in, the male has been deceased for "quite some time." Squires guards the scene.

Comeau will later describe the pungent smell permeating the stairwell as "the odour of death." It assaults the nostrils and sticks in the back of the throat. "It kind of lingers in the air, stays with you for a couple of hours."

9:01 a.m.: Comeau declares "time of no resuscitation."

9:22 a.m.: Acting Sgt. Stan Miller arrives on scene, a twenty-one-year veteran of the Saint John Police Force. Miller views the body "for about 20 seconds and notes it had been there for a while."

Miller then goes to Boston Pizza (because there's a box in the garbage can.) and Thandi's restaurant to get surveillance footage from its two security cameras that face toward Oland's office building.

Miller canvasses other uptown Saint John businesses over the following days for security video.

9:37 a.m.: Diana Sedlacek drives past 52 Canterbury St. on her way to a hair appointment at a nearby salon. She texts Oland: "What the hell is going on with you?????????" She keeps calling and texting and there's no response.

9:39 a.m.: Coroner Andrew Cavanagh and Staff Sgt. Mike King arrive. King's cellphone rings. Chief Bill Reid wants to know what's going on. It is the first time the chief has called King at a crime scene in his thirty years of service.

Chiasson later says the police arrived quickly. An officer — "a big, tall guy" — sits him down and starts asking questions.

At his print shop, John Ainsworth puts the time that he heard noises overhead the previous night at 8 p.m. At 11 a.m., at the police station in his official statement to police, he confirms the time with Constable Don Shannon as "sometime about an hour before we left, which was around nine o'clock."

Anthony Shaw is at the print shop and is questioned by Constable Stephen Davidson in the presence of Ainsworth. He estimates the time of the noises as, "it was around eight-ish."

In October 2011, under oath, when asked when he heard the noises, Ainsworth said it was 7:45 p.m. He would later change his story at the preliminary hearing on August 20, 2014, to hearing noises between 6 p.m. and 8 p.m.

In 2015, under cross-examination by the defence's Gary Miller, Ainsworth denied changing his story to help the police frame their case against Dennis Oland. "Was it made apparent to you that based on your and Mr. Shaw's statement that the noises were around eight o'clock, that it was not helpful to the police case against our client?"

"Not at all." Ainsworth went on to make repeated denials. A private investigator working for the Oland defence team questioned Ainsworth on July 27, 2011, about the noises and he told the investigator, "around 7:45 p.m.; about an hour before we left . . ."

10 a.m.: Dennis Oland calls his assistant to tell her he will not be coming into the office as he is working on the boat.

10:18 a.m.: Sgt. Mark Smith of the SJPF forensic identification team arrives at the crime scene and then goes to the police station to get his equipment. He takes three hundred photos of the crime scene. His photos show that blood on the floor covers a significant area — probably a full square metre, with blood spatter extending beyond that. Oland's glasses are found under his left arm. The photos reveal a bloody shoe print. Smith is the only person with full protective clothing on — body suit, booties, latex gloves, but he compromises his protective actions when he later wears the booties on the street during a break.

10:52 a.m. – 11:07 a.m.: Sgt. Dave Brooker, the head of the major crime unit (MCU), arrives with Inspector Glen McCloskey, who oversees the criminal investigations division of the MCU. It's a desk job that involves allocating personnel and equipment resources. McCloskey is not assigned to the investigation team. He later testifies he was there out of curiosity.

11:00 a.m.: Diana Sedlacek arrives at Richard Oland's office saying she has an appointment with him. Police tell her there is no access to the building, so she calls Connie at home to ask what happened. Dennis would later describe her as "yelling" at his mother over the phone. Connie calls Robert McFadden, and he tells her about her husband's death. Sedlacek sends emails to Maureen Adamson and Robert McFadden asking what happened. Neither responds.

11:50 a.m.: Cadet Fanjoy is asked to look for Richard Oland's BMW. She finds it in a parking lot at the corner of Carmarthen and Princess streets and reports that there is nothing unusual about the vehicle.

12:00 p.m.: Around noon, Sgt. Merle Smith allows officers Dave Brooker, Glen McCloskey and Mike King into the crime scene to observe the body. The three officers are not in protective gear. For King, it is his second walk through the crime scene.

McCloskey leaves and then returns to the scene with Sgt. Greg Oram. Oram conducts lie-detector tests. They walk through the office without proper gear. They move in close to the body, and McCloskey remarks to Oram that he hopes it was suicide. McCloskey crouches on the edge of a table and moves around to two other locations in the office area as Oram walks over to the window and touches a window blind.

Sgt. Mark Smith is still processing the crime scene. Smith leaves them alone unobserved when he goes for more equipment. When Smith returns, he tells them to leave.

12:30 p.m.: Dennis Oland is at the Royal Kennebecasis Yacht Club working on his wife's sailboat when his uncle Jack Connell calls shortly before 12:30 p.m. and tells him to go to his parents' house. "Something bad happened. It's your father."

12:52 p.m.: Diana Sedlacek texts: "Richard why the police at your office and car in lot--trying to reach everyone--What has happened PLEASE I love you God be with My Love--praying praying."

12:53 p.m.: Police have Oland's car towed away.

1:00 p.m.: Constable Rick Russell is off work and on vacation when he receives a call from Chief Bill Reid appointing him the lead investigator in Richard Oland's homicide. He quickly comes in, arriving at 52 Canterbury Street between 1:00 p.m. and 1:30 p.m. Climbing the stairs, he doesn't go past the foyer into the office crime scene itself. He sees that Sgt. Mark Smith is forensically processing the scene and retreats to the street, staying 10-15 minutes and chatting with other officers.

He later testified as to the reason he didn't go into the crime scene: "I didn't want to contaminate, at that time there's no value in me going in." He would retire a few months later.

Russell returns police headquarters to "prepare for a wave of information." He assigns officers to conduct various interviews.

1:10 p.m.: Diana sees Richard Oland's BMW being towed away to the police garage. Later that afternoon she drives to Moncton. Called by the SJPF to come in, she arrives late that evening and is questioned by police. She tells Constable Charles Breen she believes Richard Oland's family knew of their affair.

2:00 p.m.: Three police officers visit Richard Oland's home, Far End House, at 5 Almon Lane in Rothesay to inform the family that he has died in his office. They offer few details. "All of us made inquiries as to what happened to our father. They wouldn't provide answers," Dennis Oland said despite being asked "repeatedly."

2:30 p.m.: Two employees from Brenan's Funeral Home, Sharlene MacDonald and Adam Holly, arrive at the crime scene with a folding stretcher. Constable Duane Squires, asked to assist with removing Oland's body, stands in the pool of coagulated blood near the upper portion of the body. He is wearing gloves and booties over his shoes, which he removes before helping to carry the body out "because they were pretty covered in blood."

The body, in a body bag and on a stretcher, is maneuvered down the narrow staircase to Canterbury Street. On the street there is a three-vehicle convoy, the coroner, the police forensic van and the funeral home van.

Curiously the police and two funeral directors overlook a much easier exit through the double doors to the alley. At ground level, the alley was clearly visible through the office foyer's large window beside the door. The alley is wide enough for several vehicles. It would have been the logical way to remove the body.

2:45 p.m.: Officer Squires canvasses residences and businesses in the area around Oland's office, asking people if they saw or heard anything suspicious. By that time, most people have heard that Richard Oland is dead, and many people Officer Squires approaches ask him questions.

The funeral van is driven to the Saint John Regional Hospital morgue.

3:03 p.m.: Oland is pronounced dead at 3:03 p.m. The body is placed in the police locker in the morgue to await the autopsy on July 8.

3:20 p.m.: Cadet Fanjoy and other police search for a possible murder weapon. She is with Constable Don Shannon. Two other officers are also searching, along with Mike Horgan from the canine unit and his dog Leo. They check parking lots, alleys, back stairs, and empty lots, combing through the bushes, the grass, and dumpsters. They don't find anything.

6:00 p.m.: Dennis Oland is the last member of the family to answer questions at the police station. Constable Stephen Davidson starts the interview that continues for two and a half hours before a break. Lead investigator Rick Russell is forceful in trying to get his mother and wife to go home but they refuse and wait for Dennis.

6:55 p.m.: Payman Hakimian, crime forensic analyst with Fredericton RCMP's tech crime unit since 2007, arrives at the crime scene, called in to assist by the Saint John Police Force. He waits until 9:00 p.m. to begin work as Sgt. Mark Smith is still processing the scene.

Meanwhile at the police station, Dennis is confused about some of his actions coming and going that day. He explains he forgot to bring a genealogy document and started back to his office for it. Then on leaving his father's office, he forgot to take an item for his uncle and then went back to retrieve it. He tells the police he wore a navy blazer to the meeting with his father, not his brown one.

More than two hours into his questioning, Constable Stephen Davidson cautions Oland against making incriminating statements and advises him that he has the right to call a lawyer. Oland leaves the room to call the family lawyer, Bill Teed, who advises him to stop talking. It's not clear whether Teed advised him that he had the right to leave.

8:25 p.m.: Davidson exits Dennis Oland's interview room. He is replaced by Keith Copeland — a veteran, more intense and accusatory. Copeland plays bad cop. He employs the Reid technique of questioning, a method that is aimed at extracting a confession by the interrogator suggesting the suspect is basically a good person and by coming clean can ensure a reduced penalty. Copeland suggests Oland was a normal guy under tremendous pressure who just snapped.

Curiously, Copeland claims he had been sitting in an unmarked police car at Renforth Wharf, catching up on paperwork, on the evening of July 6, when Dennis Oland appeared on his way home. Dennis, who had been mostly silent up to this point, protests, "You're sneaky."

11:00 p.m.: After five hours, Dennis is allowed to leave the police station in the brown shoes and light brown pants he said he wore the day before to his father's office.

At Dennis Oland's retrial, Retired Constable Russell testified there was a briefing after Dennis Oland left the police station on that day following his interview with Constable Stephen Davidson, who took over as lead investigator in the case when Russell retired. Crown prosecutor P.J. Veniot asked if he was involved in any decision regarding the surveillance of Dennis Oland. Russell said a decision to track Dennis Oland was made by Inspector Glen McCloskey and Sgt. David Brooker who then informed him of it.

Upon leaving the station, Dennis is placed under surveillance for one week.

July 8

Morning: Lisa Oland drops off Dennis's brown Hugo Boss jacket and several dress shirts for cleaning at VIP Dry Cleaners in Rothesay.

The dry cleaner, Yang Hwan "Steve" Nam, tells police days after Lisa Oland drops off the garments that he didn't notice any stains on the jacket or any of the other items in Lisa and Dennis Oland's order.

Morning: Five divers search the water around Renforth wharf.

More than two years later, they reported they were looking for an undisclosed item that "would not have been in the water for a long period of time." "Nothing suspicious in nature was located," court documents released to the public on September 6, 2013, state.

4:30 p.m.: The forensic autopsy is performed on Richard Oland at Saint John Regional Hospital morgue by Dr. Albert Fraser— the first examination of the body in any detail — along with pathologist Dr. Ather Naseemuddin, who later testifies his surgical gown became covered in blood.

Prior to the autopsy, Smith and Constable David MacDonald, assisted by a morgue attendant, examine the body under forensic light. They take digital photographs and tape the clothes for hair and fibres. They swab the victim's hands and check the fingernails. They find thirty-one hairs, including two on his fingers. The body is washed, and x-rays taken. A penile swab is collected, and blood, urine, and vitreous fluids are extracted to test for drugs and alcohol.

Naseemuddin begins the autopsy. He works until almost midnight. The police officers make notes. Injuries are photographed and documented. There are forty wounds noted to the head and six sharp force injuries to the hands. X-rays show fractures to the skull and finger bones on each hand. The toxicology test indicates ethyl alcohol in the urine (23 milligrams per decilitre), consistent with a drink taken within an hour or hours before death.

In cataloguing the wounds, the pathologist notes fourteen skull fractures. On the left posterior of the skull is a traumatized area the size of man's fist, penetrating the brain. There are five blunt-forced wounds to the skull in a round, cross-hatched pattern. There is an orbital fracture on the left eye socket.

Naseemuddin does not offer an opinion on the murder weapon.

Smith returns to the police station and examines the logbook for blood using a forensic light and a blood screening test. It is clean.

July 9

Saint John police tell reporters they think Richard Oland knew his killer.

A Roger's technician assisting Saint John police investigators to locate Richard Oland's iPhone calls Richard's phone and receives a "roaming error" message. A roaming error means the iPhone was out of Rogers' service jurisdiction but that it was on and in working order, though it had been turned off since 6:44 p.m. on July 6. Had Dennis taken his father's phone and thrown it into the water as police believed, it would not have been in working order on July 9 when the error message went out.

A telecom expert who helped solve a kidnapping case for the police in B.C. by locating an active cellphone said in an interview for this book that with the technology available at that time, the Saint John police should have been able to locate the phone anywhere in the world. The police never found Richard Oland's iPhone.

Forensics officer Sgt. Mark Smith performs extensive testing on some geometric patterns found in the blood around Oland's body. He initially thinks they are boot prints left by one of the officers who helped remove the body, but upon reviewing photos of the crime scene, he realizes the marks were there before the body was removed.

Smith sends photographs to SICAR (Shoeprint Image Capture and Retrieval) database in Ottawa, in hopes they would be able to determine the make and model of the footwear that left the impressions. The attempt is fruitless because of a lack of detail and unique identifiers, according to Smith.

Smith also turns his attention to the washroom outside Oland's second-floor office. It has been used by police for the previous two days during the crime scene investigation.

He finds a paper towel in the wastepaper basket that appears to have a blood stain on it, but there is "nothing else of note." The blood stain is identified as intern Galen McFadden's who was working in the office on July 6 and got a paper cut.

The washroom is the second area other officers have touched before Smith can gather evidence. Smith had planned to test the deadbolt on a door located in the foyer outside Richard Oland's office for fingerprints. But by the time he gets to it, the door has been opened by officers including Glen McCloskey and therefore contaminated, "negating" his plans, he says in court later.

It is a contained crime scene – two rooms, a hallway and a washroom — yet Smith "overlooks" photographing the back door on July 9.

He would go on to testify: "It was always in the plan to do that at some point, but it wasn't completed" until July 23, 2015 — four years after Richard Oland's murder, and shortly before Dennis Oland's first trial.

Glen McCloskey drops by the crime scene, his third visit.

He later tells the court this final visit to see if he could provide any resources.

July 10

RCMP blood spatter expert from Halifax, Sgt. Brian Wentzell, notes blood has dried by then and is flaking away from the floor.

July 11

Police tell the media that Richard Oland was the victim of a homicide and that it does not appear to be a random act.

July 12

12:00 p.m.: Richard Oland's funeral is attended by about 450 family members, friends and several prominent Saint John citizens at Our Lady of Perpetual Help Church in Rothesay.

Meanwhile, Smith continues his forensic examination of Oland's office. He swabs a computer to determine who the last user was. He tests the left key of the computer mouse, as well as the enter key and space bar, following a conversation with the tech crime experts at the RCMP forensics lab in Fredericton.

This computer sitting on a spare desk was being used by Galen McFadden, who was helping Oland with the family tree project he was working on that summer by scanning old photographs and documents.

July 14

Dennis Oland's silver Volkswagen Golf is seized by police. It does not appear to have been cleaned recently.

Smith takes seventeen hours to process Oland's car, which is secured in the police garage. It appears clean on the outside, but the interior has dirt and debris on the floor, as well as papers on the dash and around the console area, a pair of women's shoes in the back seat and numerous items in the trunk, including plastic cups, a sail cover, a lawnmower blade, dog toys and a red reusable grocery bag containing some documents.

Smith uses a special forensic light and magnifying glass to search the inside for "anomalies," then does some preliminary tests for blood. He swabs eleven areas, including the door latches, the trunk release button, the steering wheel, the headlight and signal light switches, the emergency brake and the passenger seat. A week later, July 21, 2011, swabs from the car are sent to the RCMP lab in Halifax for forensic testing.

Smith subsequently tries two other procedures, spraying the floor, pedals, and the fabric seats with other chemicals, but all come back negative for blood.

Some items are seized from the car, including a receipt from an Irving station in Saint John's north end, which is found in the passenger side door and is from around the time Richard Oland's body was discovered.

Smith also reviews video surveillance of Dennis Oland taken on July 6, 2011, to see what shoes he was wearing that day, and creates impressions of six pairs of footwear seized from his home to compare the tread marks to those at the crime scene.

"My results were the same, insufficient detail to be able to come up with any kind of meaningful comparison," he later says.

12:00 – 8:00 p.m.: A squad of twenty police officers search Dennis Oland's Rothesay home. Police seize fifty-seven items from the property, including legal papers, bank statements, garbage bags, bedding, clothing including a brown jacket, dryer lint, a purse and a "note in a purse" and bathroom wastebaskets. They search outbuildings and dig up the lawn.

Saint John police later bring in Grant Fredericks who operates Forensic Video Solutions in Spokane, Washington, to examine video of Dennis Oland to make sure the jacket they seized from his home was the one he wore to his father's office. After going to great lengths and expense, Fredericks would later advise the jury that he cannot say with certainty the jacket Dennis Oland was seen wearing in the surveillance videos is the same one police seized from his closet.

Police obtain a total of seventeen judicial authorizations to search for evidence in the murder case, including one for Oland's home on July 13, 2011 and one on August 11, 2011, to search his computer at CIBC Wood Gundy, where he worked as a financial advisor.

August

Joy Kearsey, an RCMP forensics expert, begins to prepare eleven blood and DNA reports related to the Dennis Oland case. The scope of work balloons so that by August 2013, her report totals fourteen hundred pages.

Kearsey tests eighteen areas on the inside and outside of Dennis Oland's brown sports jacket. She tests other articles of clothing and bedding from his home, swabs taken from his Volkswagen Golf, the red grocery bag seized from his trunk, his cellphone, samples from the crime scene and autopsy and Richard Oland's clothing.

At the end of it all, she doesn't find any of the victim's DNA on Dennis Oland's possessions.

Kearsey later testifies that four hairs found on Richard Oland's hands couldn't be tested for DNA because they did not have roots with the cellular material. Defence lawyer Michael Lacy told me in an interview for this book that those hairs belonged to the victim. He didn't explain how the defence knew that.

October

Robert McFadden won't give interviews to reporters. He says that police have advised potential witnesses not to speak to the media. The police offer no explanation for the lack of progress in the investigation to find Richard Oland's killer(s).

Constable Sean Rocca, on the Oland investigation from the first day, is assigned as the Oland case file co-ordinator.

November

November 9 and 17: Saint John police forensics Constable David MacDonald examines Dennis Oland's sports jacket, magnifying it five hundred times, and finds four "areas of discolouration," on both sleeves and the chest area. He tests a red- and brown-coloured spot on the inside right cuff with a Hemastix for blood and gets what he later describes to the jury in 2015 as a "weak positive" result. He does not test any other areas of the jacket.

November 25: MacDonald drives the jacket to the RCMP lab in Halifax. The warrant on the jacket has lapsed and this is illegal.

December

A Freedom of Information (FOI) legal challenge is launched by the media to unseal the sealed search warrants.

The Crown argues initially that the search warrants and related documents should remain sealed because they contained evidence that only the person or persons responsible for Oland's death would know.

December 6: RCMP Sgt. Brian Wentzell, forensics officer, examines the jacket under magnification. He identifies five areas where there might be blood and then puts it in the lab freezer. He does not do any blood tests himself but requests the tests done by another RCMP lab.

Three specks match to Richard Oland's DNA. One of the bloodstains on the right sleeve does not contain enough of Oland's DNA to meet the RCMP's minimum requirement for comparison to Oland's blood sample taken at the autopsy.

In the aftermath of his father's murder, Dennis travels extensively. Neither the police nor the Oland family reveal much information about what happened to Richard Oland or who may be suspects in his murder.

2012

August 16: Heavily redacted portions of five search warrants and related documents in the Oland case are released after the New Brunswick *Telegraph-Journal* and the CBC asked the provincial court in Saint John to make them public.

The documents show that the police believe Richard Oland was murdered. The documents are the first of a trickle that amasses to hundreds of documents released sporadically until Dennis Oland is arrested a year and three and a half months later.

October: Jiri Sedlacek claims to learn of his wife's affair with Richard Oland in a media report shown to him by his lawyer.

October 26: Constable MacDonald transports the brown jacket back to the RCMP lab.

November: Investigators meet with the Crown to lay a case against Dennis Oland, but the prosecutors say there isn't enough evidence.

December 29: The police follow Robert McFadden, Richard Oland's accountant, to an East Side Mario's restaurant and seize a straw for a DNA sample.

2013

February 14: On Dennis Oland's birthday, Constable MacDonald retrieves the brown jacket from the Halifax RCMP.

May 17: More court documents are released to the media that indicate police suspect Dennis Oland murdered his father.

July: Dennis flies to Baltimore, MD, to buy a boat.

Mid-October: The Crown approves criminal charges against Dennis Oland.

November 12: In a spectacle for the media, Saint John police, with sirens and flashing lights, arrive at a car wash in Rothesay to arrest Dennis Oland. Police disregard an offer from Oland passed to them by his lawyer Gary Miller that he would present himself to police voluntarily on request.

2014

Some months before the preliminary hearing on the charges

against Dennis Oland, Inspector Glen McCloskey tells Staff-Sgt. Mike King in a private conversation that he doesn't have to say in court that McCloskey visited the crime scene.

May 12: The preliminary inquiry for Dennis Oland begins. A publication ban is imposed on all evidence presented during the hearing.

Summer: Released on bail, Oland spends much of the summer sailing with Lisa on their forty-two-foot yacht.

December 12: After his preliminary hearing, which lasted thirty-seven days and heard from forty-two witnesses, Judge Ronald LeBlanc's decision orders Dennis Oland to stand trial on a charge of second-degree murder in his father's death.

Family members issue a statement saying they know Dennis is innocent. "Throughout this ordeal our faith in him continues to be absolutely unwavering," the family says. "We are devastated that we will have to endure a trial, but we know Dennis will be found innocent in an objective and fair process in a court of law."

2015

February: VIP Dry Cleaners' Steve Nam and his wife and co-owner Jin Hee Choi are interviewed by the Saint John police about their findings in July 2011 when they cleaned Dennis Oland's brown jacket. They tell the police there were no stains.

March – September: At pre-trial hearings, trial Judge Jack Walsh makes several rulings on the admissibility of evidence. He grants the Crown's request to do further testing on the brown jacket but refuses to admit two pay stubs and two letters from Dennis to his father from 2003.

After their search warrants have expired, police obtain personal information from Oland's work computer. The

Crown wants to enter the evidence. Walsh refuses, pointing out that the evidence was obtained in violation of the search and seizure provisions of the Charter of Rights.

Walsh maintains that "whether one characterizes it as carelessness or negligence, police did not pay sufficient attention to the requirements of the judicial orders. However, Walsh ultimately rules there was "lawful authority for the forensic examinations of the things seized under the house warrant."

While there were errors and omissions in the applications police had used to get both warrants issued by a provincial court judge, they aren't enough "in their nature and number" to invalidate either warrant, he says.

March 30: In a pretrial motion, the defence argues against the Crown's application to conduct more DNA tests on pieces of Dennis Oland's brown jacket. The Crown argues it now has a "more discriminating" test, Identifiler Plus, which compares fifteen areas of DNA. Joy Kearsey's tests used Profiler Plus, which compared nine areas of DNA.

April 7: In a 16-page ruling, Judge John Walsh agrees with the Crown's request for more testing. He orders the DNA extracts to be released for further analysis and the defence be provided with the results.

May: RCMP blood analyst Tom Suzanski retests DNA taken from three bloodstains on the jacket. His findings support DNA expert Joy Kearsey's findings that the bloodstains match Richard Oland's DNA.

August 13: Lead prosecutor John Henheffer steps aside a few weeks before the high-profile trial is to begin for health reasons. He is replaced on the prosecution team by P.J. Veniot from Miramichi who had retired but comes in for the trial.

September 8: Dennis Oland pleads not guilty to second-degree murder. Jury selection begins at a hockey arena in Saint John. It's a media circus with five thousand citizens called in for screening as potential jurors.

Constable Sean Rocca screens the jury candidates illegally for prior involvement with the police. The Crown prosecutors later claim they were unaware of Rocca's actions.

September 10: Fourteen jurors — eight men and six women — are chosen, as well as two alternate jurors.

September 16: The trial, scheduled for sixty-five days, begins in Courtroom 12 at the Court of Queen's Bench. Crown attorney P.J. Veniot tells the jury Richard Oland died from no fewer than forty blows to his head and neck. It lasts thirty-seven days and involves forty-four witnesses. There are more than five hundred exhibits collected in the case.

October 13: In his testimony at Dennis Oland's murder trial, retired Saint John police officer Mike King makes allegations of misconduct against his supervising officer Glen McCloskey.

King also testifies McCloskey had a box of exhibits related to the Oland investigation in his office that he wanted King to deliver to the RCMP in Fredericton, which is not the "normal procedure."

October 14: On the stand, Glen McCloskey denies any intent of wrongdoing at the crime scene. When asked about a box of evidence related to the Oland case having been in his office, McCloskey says he can't recall.

Saint John police chief John Bates directs the force's professional standards unit to open a probe into King's allegations. The Saint John Board of Police Commissioners and the New Brunswick Police Commission (NBPC) have both been advised, Bates writes in an emailed statement to local media outlets. McCloskey remains on active duty.

October 20: Former Fredericton police chief Barry MacKnight is appointed by the NBPC to investigate the allegations against McCloskey. MacKnight's investigation is postponed under the Police Act until the conclusion of the Dennis Oland trial.

October 23: Constable Stephen Davidson says during cross-examination that he was aware that a former officer was allegedly asked to alter his testimony about the case, but he didn't do anything about it.

November 3: Justice John Walsh gives the jury instructions on evidence that suggests there was an inadequate police investigation in the case. He says it is up to the jury to decide whether that evidence alone or in combination with other evidence creates doubt of guilt.

November 10: Diana Sedlacek arrives at court in a black pant suit, wearing large dark sunglasses and a black, white and grey printed shawl draped around her blonde hair. The courtroom is so full that the sheriff's deputies must bring in extra chairs. She tells the court that she tried repeatedly to contact Richard Oland by cellphone and text message the night before his body was found, but she never got a reply.

Sedlacek testifies she never told her husband Jiri Sedlacek, (eighty-seven at this time) about her eight-year affair with Richard Oland. Her version is that he found out when police questioned him. She says she saw Oland about three times a week at his Far End Corporation office, testifying, "often after church on Sunday, we would pop in there for a bit."

The Sedlaceks later split up. Diana moves to Victoria, BC in 2013.

November 10: Jiri Sedlacek testifies that he met Dick and

Connie Oland around 2003. The two couples, along with other friends and acquaintances, socialized at each other's homes eight or ten times over the years until 2011. The retired Bata Shoes executive, who had been director of corporate development for the global company, says he found Oland an interesting man, well-travelled. He says the last time he saw him was at Christmas mass in 2010. "We shook hands."

Sedlacek says he was at home with his wife on Darlings Island on the day and evening of the murder, July 6, 2011.

Sedlacek claims he found out about his wife's affair in October 2012, when his lawyer showed him a newspaper article naming Diana as Oland's mistress.

In cross examination, defence lawyer Alan Gold points out that it is hard to believe Sedlacek didn't know about an eight-year relationship as his wife went away on trips with Oland. It's a good motive for murder, Gold argued.
He claims he never even suspected the affair.

Asked if police had seized his bank records, phone records or the GPS on his vehicle, Sedlacek says no. In the course of their investigation, SJ police questioned him twice, he says.

November 24: An expert in DNA analysis testifies that a brown sports jacket seized from the home of Dennis Oland tested positive for blood, and DNA samples match the profile of Richard Oland.

November 25: The Crown concludes its case with its forty-fourth witness, Tom Suzanski, an expert in DNA analysis who worked on the case at the RCMP lab in Ottawa. Suzanski confirms the chances of it not being Richard Oland's blood on Dennis Oland's brown jacket are one in twenty quintillion, a figure that has eighteen zeroes.

November 26: The defence launches its case, arguing that over the forty-two-day trial, the Crown has not proved beyond a reasonable doubt that it was Dennis Oland who committed this "dastardly deed."

Patrick Laturnus, a blood spatter expert from Ottawa, retired from the RCMP, testifies the person who killed Richard Oland would have had a significant amount of blood on their hands and clothes. Laturnus says the killer would have bent over the victim during the strikes, "so it follows and it's logical" a "significant amount," of blood would land on the killer's hands, face and upper body. If Dennis Oland's brown sports jacket had been worn during the slaying, it would have had "so much blood" on it, the blood would have been visible in the video footage the Crown showed the court, Laturnus stresses.

December 1: Dennis Oland testifies for two days in his own defence. Gary Miller takes him through the July 6, 2011 timeline according to the video footage of his arrival and departure from his father's office. Asked by Miller if he killed his father, Dennis replies, "No. No, I did not."

December 2: Dennis Oland testifies he made a mistake when he told police that he was wearing a navy blazer the last time he saw his father. He was confused. In fact, he had been wearing it on the morning of July 7, 2011, on the day of his police interview, as seen in the Kent Building Supplies security video. He chokes back tears and wipes his eyes, telling the courtroom he misses his father.

December 3: The defence closes its case after calling only three witnesses.

December 14: Closing arguments are presented. Defence lawyer Alan Gold says the jury should reach a verdict of not guilty based on Dennis Oland's testimony and the weak circumstantial evidence presented by the Crown. Crown attorney P.J. Veniot says Dennis Oland was the last person to see his father alive and had opportunity to kill him.

December 15: Justice John Walsh takes more than a day to deliver his final instructions to the jury, repeatedly emphasizing the need for caution and common sense as jurors assess the evidence presented during twelve weeks of testimony. Walsh expresses bewilderment at the police actions: "The police applied for and obtained a general warrant to forensically examine the various items seized under the house warrant [including the brown sports jacket] and then, inexplicably, allowed it to lapse before conducting the examinations contemplated."

Police did not pay sufficient attention to the requirements of the judicial orders, "whether one characterizes it as carelessness or negligence," he says. However, Walsh ultimately rules there was "lawful authority for the forensic examinations of the things seized under the house warrant."

While there were errors and omissions in the applications police had used to get both warrants issued by a provincial court judge, they wasn't enough "in their nature and number" to invalidate either warrant, he says.

December 16: Walsh concludes his jury charge, and jurors retire to begin deliberations.

December 19: The jury find Dennis Oland guilty of second-degree murder.

December 22: The Saint John Board of Police Commissioners asks the NBPC to investigate the Saint John Police Force's handling of the Richard Oland murder investigation.

The independent provincial oversight body is now conducting two separate investigations: Glen McCloskey and the police force.

2016

January 29: The NBPC suspends its investigation into the Saint John police pending Dennis Oland's appeal of his murder conviction.

The NBPC also suspends Barry MacKnight's investigation into Glen McCloskey's alleged misconduct.

February 11: Dennis Oland is sentenced to life (twenty-five years) in prison with no chance of parole for ten years.

February 17: Dennis Oland is denied bail pending appeal.

March: Halifax Regional Police Serious Incident Response Team (SiRT) is asked by Saint John police to investigate King's allegations against McClosky.

April 6: Steve Roberge, executive director of the New Brunswick Police Commission, tells news media that MacKnight, who was carrying out the NBPC's McCloskey investigation, has found some red flags.

Roberge says suspending the commission's Police Act investigation is common procedure in a case concerning police criminal misconduct.

Saint John police chief John Bates says he asked Halifax Regional Police to take over because the allegation was "beyond the purview" of the NBPC.

The NBPC says its probe into the Saint John police's overall handling of the Oland murder investigation will resume at the conclusion of the criminal investigation into McCloskey.

July 31: Dennis Oland is attacked in jail by two convicted murderers who plead guilty to the assault.

Since there is no trial, we can't know if this was an intimidation effort by organized crime elements, but at least one family member of the Oland's had been "warned" not to talk about the murder.

September 16: Alan Gold, a high-profile lawyer hired by the Oland family to defend Dennis in his first trial, finds out in a telephone interview for this book about Richard Oland's affair with Lesley Oland (Dennis's first wife). For whatever reason, this information was withheld by his co-counsellors.

October 3: Saint John police announce that Halifax Police Serious Incident Response Team (SiRT) clears McCloskey of any criminal wrongdoing in the Oland murder after an eight-month investigation, which included consultation with the Nova Scotia public prosecutions service.

McCloskey is still facing an investigation into his conduct by the New Brunswick Police Commission under the provincial Police Act.

October 24: The Court of Appeal of New Brunswick overturns Dennis Oland's second-degree murder conviction and orders a new trial. The basis for the decision? The trial judge did not properly instruct jurors regarding one key piece of evidence: the brown jacket Dennis Oland wore the night of the murder with traces of blood matching his father.

October 25: Dennis Oland is granted bail pending a new murder trial.

December: Two months after the SiRT report cleared McCloskey, MacKnight submits his report to the NBPC, which concludes that McCloskey made false statements at Oland's 2015 trial. In his report, which was not made public at the time, MacKnight recommends McCloskey face criminal charges.

2017

July 13: The Supreme Court of Canada decides not to hear appeals on the decision by the New Brunswick Court of

Appeal to grant Dennis Oland bail even though he was previously convicted to second-degree murder.

2018

April 30: McCloskey retires from the Saint John police after twenty-seven years because of the accusations resulting from his conduct in the Oland case. The NBPC investigation of McCloskey is dropped because the commission only has the authority to discipline active officers.

May: The NBPC's probe into Saint John police conduct in the Oland murder investigation is also put on hold when the provincial government announces that retired RCMP assistant commissioner Alphonse MacNeil would review the policies, practices and procedures of the commission itself.

October 15: Dennis Oland enters a not guilty plea in his retrial.

Gary Miller, one of Dennis Oland's defence team of lawyers, steps down, just as his retrial gets underway in Saint John with jury selection again at the hockey arena in Saint John. Miller is replaced by Michael Lacy of Toronto.

Miller tells reporters he can think of only one other case in his forty-one-year career where he represented a client at both trial and retrial. "It wasn't this kind of case where there's issues all over the place," he says without elaborating. Constable Sean Rocca screens one thousand potential candidates for the jury selection process, using a method outlawed by the Supreme Court of Canada.

October 16: Oland murder case goes under *voir dire*.

November 7: Trial is adjourned for two weeks while unspecified legal issues are addressed.

November 20: A mistrial is declared in the second murder trial of Dennis Oland. Justice Terrence Morrison dismisses the jury because of "improprieties." Police had tried to weed out any jurors who had previous encounters with police and might be biased. The jury is dismissed with thanks, and the trial proceeds with a judge alone.

In a statement after the mistrial, defence lawyer Alan Gold explains Saint John police overstepped limits on jury investigations. Gold says the Supreme Court of Canada has made it clear that jurors' privacy "disallowed any police database searches into the private lives of jurors in order to find out any and all contacts they may have had with the police." But Gold says the errors by Saint John police didn't stop there and asked that the New Brunswick Police Commission's inquiry into the force's conduct in the Oland murder investigation, which had been put on hold pending the jury trial, now be resumed.

November 21: Dennis Oland retrial proceeds with opening arguments. The trial is expected to last until mid-March.

December 18: The MacKnight report, which was under a publication ban, becomes public when it is decided Dennis Oland's retrial will go ahead without a jury. The report recommends charging McCloskey for five breaches of the Police Act: two counts of discreditable conduct, and one count each of deceitful behaviour, neglect of duty, and being party to a breach of the professional code of conduct._

The report was included in court documents sought by Oland's defence lawyers at pre-trial hearings as they prepared for his retrial.

The documents include prosecutors' emails about McCloskey and another officer's tour of the crime scene. The defence alleges the Crown conspired before the first trial to conceal the fact McCloskey had gone through the crime scene.

December 27: The New Brunswick Police Association accuses the police oversight body of being "out of control," and alleges the NBPC is being run in an "abusive, authoritarian fashion" illustrated by the way it probed McCloskey's actions during the police investigation into the murder of Richard Oland.

2019

January 3: NBPC announces Steve Roberge is no longer employed by the province of New Brunswick. Roberge is terminated by the commission, largely for having shared MacKnight's report with Dennis Oland's lawyers.

January 8: Saint John police officer Sgt. Greg Oram is called as a witness for the first time in relation to the case, despite having thought he would participate in the 2014 preliminary hearing and 2015 trial.

January 31: Robert McFadden, Richard Oland's accountant and long-time business associate, takes the stand, where he gives the trial a picture of the victim.

McFadden says Richard Oland's holdings were worth about thirty-six million at the time of his death, and he was the owner and sole director of three companies dealing with investments and real estate. There are now two directors of those companies because of the murder: Dennis Oland and McFadden, the trustees and co-executors of Richard Oland's will.

The accountant says he arrived at Oland's office around 9 a.m. on July 6, 2011.

McFadden says under questioning from prosecutor P.J. Veniot, "We had a meeting planned with some insurance fellows who wanted to sell a life insurance policy to Richard." He already had a life insurance policy worth about eight million dollars. The beneficiary was his investment company, the Far End Corporation.

It was a "cosmic coincidence" that life insurance agents were trying to sell Oland a new policy just hours before his death, says defence lawyer Michael Lacy.

The accountant tells the court about travelling with Oland "to scout out sailboats."

"I also travelled with him for races in the United States and the Caribbean."

Banking officials from CIBC also take the stand to detail lending activity involving Dennis Oland. Oland had increased the $75,000 line of credit he was given in 2010 to $163,000 in March 2011. Richard Oland had loaned Dennis $538,000 in 2008 and 2009, to buy out his ex-wife's share of their house in their divorce.

"He (Richard Oland) viewed it as a loan," McFadden says of the $538,000. "He just wasn't worried about collecting it."

McFadden says he was aware of Richard Oland's affair with Saint John real estate agent Diana Sedlacek. He tells the court Dennis asked him on one occasion, at least a year and a half before the murder, to tell his father to "cool it" because word of the affair was getting out.

McFadden says he did not pass on the message to Richard Oland.

April 15: McCloskey sues the NBPC and its former executive director, Roberge, for alleged negligence in how they handled a conduct complaint against him in connection with the Dennis Oland murder trial.

In documents filed with the Court of Queen's Bench in Saint John, McCloskey accuses the independent civilian oversight body and Roberge of failing to conduct the Police Act investigation without bias, deliberately engaging in unlawful conduct in exercising their public function and violating the public trust.

McClosky also accuses the commission of breaching its duty to protect him from unwarranted disciplinary action and Roberge of damaging his economic interests through unlawful means.

"As a result of the negligence of the defendant Roberge and defendant NBPC, the plaintiff has sustained significant economic loss as he was forced into an early retirement," the court document states.

The case against McCloskey was dropped when he retired because the commission only has the authority to discipline active officers.

McCloskey wants the court to quash MacKnight's report and declare it "did not meet the reasonableness or the correctness standard."

July 19: Dennis Oland is acquitted by Judge Terrence Morrison. Saint John police chief Bruce Connell announce the police will not be reopening the case, barring new evidence.

December 12: In his 80-page report, NBPC consultant Alphonse MacNeil makes twenty-two recommendations, including the creation of an independent agency to investigate deaths, injuries or other serious incidents arising from the actions of police. Six Canadian provinces already have a civilian watchdog — Nova Scotia, Quebec, Ontario, Manitoba, Alberta and British Columbia.

December 13: In a report, Alexandre Deschênes concludes the commission breached McCloskey's privacy on two instances by disclosing his personal information to Oland's defence and the Crown on July 4 and 12, 2017.

2020

February 17: Dennis Oland moves out of his SevenAcres home.

March 23: Dennis and Lisa announce they are separating after a decade of marriage. He moves in with his mother, news reports say.

June 10: Lisa files an application for an emergency intervention order. Dennis faces allegations of domestic violence in Saint John Court. The marital dispute is settled out of court in December.

2021

January: The couple's house is listed for sale. It sells in seven weeks to a local family for an undisclosed amount.

The Saint John building where Richard Oland was murdered goes on the market.

May 4: The Canadian Press reports Lisa Andrik-Oland, Dennis Oland's ex-wife, applied for a restraining order on June 10, 2020, alleging her husband was prone to intimate partner violence and was suffering a "mental breakdown."

The allegations were contained in an application for an emergency intervention order that Lisa Andrik-Oland filled out at a shelter for abused women in Saint John, NB. The document, protected by a publication ban until May 2021, includes her handwritten notes alleging Oland was an angry, violent man who was losing control and suffering from post-traumatic stress disorder. Dennis Oland's lawyer, Bill Teed, declines to comment when asked about the allegations. Dennis says he suffered mental anguish that ended his marriage.

2023

February: The New Brunswick government announces it has

reached an agreement with Nova Scotia to allow that province's Serious Incident Response Team to open an office that would investigate serious incidents involving the police in New Brunswick.

In a statement, the New Brunswick government says the deal solidifies an agreement in principle reached in September 2021. Since then, officials from New Brunswick and Nova Scotia have been working together to "ensure the appropriate legislative and policy frameworks are in place" to allow the team to operate in New Brunswick.

Sources

Books

Charlesworth, Hector. *More Candid Chronicles*. Toronto: MacMillan, 1928.

Donovan, Kevin. *The Billionaire Murders: The Mysterious Deaths of Barry and Honey Sherman*. Toronto: Penguin, 2019.

Galeotti, Mark. *The Vory: Russia's Super Mafia*. New Haven, CT: Yale University Press, 2018.

Gladwell, Malcolm. *Talking to Strangers*. New York: Little, Brown and Company, 2019.

Gray, Charlotte. *Murdered Midas: A Millionaire, His Gold Mine, and a Strange Death on an Island Paradise*. Toronto: HarperCollins, 2019.

Haliburton, G. Brenton. *What's brewing: Oland, 1867 – 1971, A History*. Glen Margaret, NS: Four East Publications, 1994.

MacKinnon, Bobbi-Jean. *Shadow of a Doubt: The Trial of Dennis Oland, 2nd edition*. Fredericton, NB: Goose Lane Editions, 2018.

Marquis, Greg. *Truth and Honour; The Death of Richard Oland and the Trial of Dennis Oland*. Halifax: Nimbus Publishing, 2019.

Pitts, Gordon. *The Codfathers*. Toronto: Key Porter Books, 2005.

Ross, Kyle Ann. *Taserized: Neighborhood Walk Ends in Police Brutality*. Baltimore, MD: Police Brutality and Prosecutor Misconduct Books, 2023.

Sawler, Harvey. *Last Canadian Beer: The Moosehead Story*. Halifax: Nimbus Publishing, 2009.

Winn Sneath, Allen. *Brewed in Canada: the Untold Story of Canada's 300-year-old Brewing Industry*. Toronto: Dundurn Press, 2001.

Key Court Decisions

Humphrey, Stacey. *Production Order to Rogers Communications* (PDF). Court of Queen's Bench of New Brunswick. July 9, 2011.

R. v. Oland, 2017 SCC17, [2017] 1 R.C.S.250

R. v. Oland (D.J.), 2015, 446 N.B.R.(2nd) 317 (TD); 2015 NBQB 247.

Periodicals, Magazines

Campbell, Meagan, "The murder trial that took New Brunswick by storm," *Maclean's*, December 30, 2015.

Holloway, Andy, "Derek Oland: Lifetime Achievement, 2011 Entrepreneur of The Year," *Financial Post Magazine*, December 6, 2011.

Kimber, Stephen, "Spilled secrets: The Richard Oland murder mystery," *Atlantic Business Magazine*, January/February 2013.

Köhler, Nicholas, "Murder and a maritime dynasty: The death of Dick Oland has a province worried and wondering," *Maclean's*, July 28, 2011.

Light, Matthew, and Gavin Slade. "Crime and criminal justice after communism: Why study the post-Soviet region?," *Theoretical Criminology*, first published April 30, 2015.

McIlvenna-Davis, Dylan, "Gangs and Gulags: How Vladimir Putin Utilizes Organized Crime to Power his Mafia State," *Berkeley Political Review*, December 16, 2019.

Wilbur, Patrick, Canada's online legal newspaper *AdvocateDaily.com*.

Wright, Julia, "Blood, Beer, and the Maritime Rumour Mill: The Dennis Oland Murder Trial," *VICE newsletter*, published Nov 30, 2015.

Newspaper articles

Bissett, Kevin. "Dennis Oland Charged in Father's Death," *HuffPost*, Associated Press, Nov. 13, 2013.

Bissett, Kevin. "Oland murder trial opens with details of beating, accused's financial woes," *The Globe and Mail*, The Canadian Press (Saint John), Sept. 16, 2015.

Bissett, Kevin. *'Family tragedy of Shakespearean proportions': Oland gets life for murder*. The Canadian Press, Feb. 11, 2016.

Bissett, Kevin. "Dennis Oland murder trial jury selection almost complete," (Saint John), Sept. 9, 2015.

Bissett, Kevin. "Dennis Oland murder trial set to begin in September, take 65 days," (Saint John), Feb. 2, 2015.

Bissett, Kevin. "Dennis Oland's second-degree murder trial: Nov. 24," (Saint John), Nov. 24, 2015.

Bissett, Kevin. "Dennis Oland's charter rights violated by police, judge ruled," (Saint John), Dec. 20, 2015.

Bissett, Kevin. "Saint John police under investigation for how they handled Oland murder," (Saint John), Dec. 22, 2015.

Bissett, Kevin. "No bail for Dennis Oland as he waits to appeal conviction in father's murder," (Saint John), Feb 17, 2016.

Brenan's Funeral Homes & Crematorium, "Richard Henry Oland – Obituary," (Saint John).

Canadian Broadcasting Corporation, "Blood stain expert continues testimony at Oland murder trial," (Saint John), Oct. 16, 2015.

The Canadian Press, "Supporters line up as Dennis Oland faces sentencing for murder," Feb. 11, 2016.

The Canadian Press, "Head of N.B. police watchdog leaves amid controversy over Oland murder probe," posted Jan. 3, 2019.

The Canadian Press, "Dennis Oland, charged with murder in father's death, granted bail," (Saint John), Nov. 18, 2013.

CTV Atlantic, "Defence questions police handling of evidence at Oland trial," Nov. 16, 2015

The Globe and Mail, "New Brunswick police commission to probe police handling of Oland murder," (Toronto), Nov 23, 2018.

MacKinnon, Bobbi-Jean, "Blood on Dennis Oland's jacket focus of murder trial today," *Canadian Broadcasting Corporation* (Saint John), Oct. 19, 2015.

MacKinnon, Bobbi-Jean, "Crown seeks leave to appeal overturning of Dennis Oland's murder conviction," *CBC News* (Saint John), Jan. 3, 2017.

MacKinnon, Bobbi-Jean, "Dennis Oland became suspect in father's murder same day body was found," *Canadian Broadcasting Corporation*, posted Oct. 21, 2015.

MacKinnon, Bobbi-Jean, "Dennis Oland charged with 2nd-degree murder in dad's death," *Canadian Broadcasting Corporation*, posted Nov. 13, 2013.

MacKinnon, Bobbi-Jean, "Dennis Oland as father's killer an 'inescapable conclusion', Crown argues," *CBC News*, Dec. 14, 2015.

MacKinnon, Bobbi-Jean, "Dennis Oland gets life in prison for killing father, Richard Oland," *CBC News* (Saint John), Feb. 11, 2016.

MacKinnon, Bobbi-Jean, "Dennis Oland gets new 2nd-degree murder trial, as appeal court cites judge's error," *CBC News*, Oct. 24, 2016

MacKinnon, Bobbi-Jean, "Dennis Oland murder trial hears suspected weapon was drywall hammer," *Canadian Broadcasting Corporation*, posted Oct. 22, 2015.

320 Who Killed Richard Oland

MacKinnon, Bobbi-Jean, "Dennis Oland not guilty of murder in retrial over 2011 death of multimillionaire father," *CBC News* (Saint John), July 19, 2019.

MacKinnon, Bobbi-Jean, "Dennis Oland pleads not guilty to 2nd-degree murder," *Canadian Broadcasting Corporation*, Sept. 8, 2014.

MacKinnon, Bobbi-Jean, "Dennis Oland preliminary inquiry may hear from 60 witnesses," *CBC News* (Saint John), posted May 26, 2014.

MacKinnon, Bobbi-Jean, "Dennis Oland's brown jacket was handled by officer without gloves," *Canadian Broadcasting Corporation*, *CBC News* (Saint John), Nov. 02, 2015.

MacKinnon, Bobbi-Jean, "Dennis Oland's car, shoes, bag all tested negative for blood, jury hears," *Canadian Broadcasting Corporation* (Saint John), posted Oct. 07, 2015.

MacKinnon, Bobbi-Jean, "Dennis Oland's mother, Connie, shares 'living hell'," *Canadian Broadcasting Corporation* (Saint John), posted Feb. 16, 2016

MacKinnon, Bobbi-Jean, "Deputy chief denies suggesting officer lie about Richard Oland crime scene," *Canadian Broadcasting Corporation*, posted Oct. 14, 2015.

MacKinnon, Bobbi-Jean, "Documents shed new light on Oland murder investigation," *Canadian Broadcasting Corporation*, posted Sept. 06, 2013.

MacKinnon, Bobbi-Jean, "Judge at Dennis Oland murder trial is a leading legal expert in DNA," *Canadian Broadcasting Corporation* (Saint John), Dec 11, 2015.

MacKinnon, Bobbi-Jean, "Jury selection in Dennis Oland's murder trial begins in Saint John," *Canadian Broadcasting Corporation* (Saint John), Sept. 08, 2015.

MacKinnon, Bobbi-Jean, "Officers ought to have known how to protect Oland crime scene, trial hears," *Canadian Broadcasting Corporation*, posted Oct. 06, 2015

MacKinnon, Bobbi-Jean, "Richard Oland survived only 'minutes,' murder trial hears," *Canadian Broadcasting Corporation*, posted Oct. 09, 2015.

MacKinnon, Bobbi-Jean, "Richard Oland was considering changing will, life insurance, jury hears," *Canadian Broadcasting Corporation* (Saint John), posted Nov. 03, 2015.

MacKinnon, Bobbi-Jean, "Why Dennis Oland was found not guilty of murder at his retrial," *CBC News* (Saint John), July 20, 2019.

O'Kane, Josh, "Oland investigation puts Saint John in eerie calm," *The Globe and Mail*, July 21, 2011.

Pitts, Gordon, "Derek Oland: Raising a Glass to 50 years with the Family Brewery," *The Globe and Mail*, originally published Sept. 7, 2012; updated May 8, 2018.

Pearson, Heide. "Graphic testimony of Richard Oland's autopsy heard by Saint John jury Friday," *Global News*, posted Oct. 9, 2015.

Telegraph-Journal, "How a city councillor ended up being mentioned in the Oland trial," Jan. 10, 2019.

Videos and Other Sources

First half of videotaped statement, never seen by jury, made public by judge. "RAW: Dennis Oland's police statement," *Canadian Broadcasting Corporation*, Oct 22, 2015.

Second half of videotaped statement, never seen by jury, made public by judge. MacKinnon, Bobbi-Jean, "Dennis Oland pressured to confess to father's murder by police," *Canadian Broadcasting Corporation*, posted Feb 11, 2016.

Nova Scotia Archives, 6016 University Avenue, Halifax, Nova Scotia.

The Oland Murder: A four-part series on the murder of millionaire Richard Oland and the retrial of his son Dennis. CBC Docs, posted Feb 10, 2020.

Connie Oland. *Character reference letter to Justice John Walsh*. January 16, 2016.

Dennis Oland. "I Saved a Good One," online blog for Volvo Dealer. 2014.

Oland Family Fonds. Archives Catalogue. Dalhousie University, Halifax, Nova Scotia.

Acknowledgments

The writing process begins with an idea. This book came out of a holiday dinner party. Dennis Oland was found guilty by a jury of murdering his father on Dec. 19, 2015, after a trial that lasted months and made national headlines. So close to Christmas, the case was a topic for discussion around the table. What struck me was that all were surprised by a guilty verdict and felt the prosecution had failed to prove its case.

In the new year, a straw poll of friends and acquaintances across the country found each had followed the Moosehead beer family murder with interest and expressed opinions about how the police conducted the investigation. When a prominent New Brunswick couple, whom I thought would be able to shed some light on the case, failed to return my call, I decided to look into it. Early on in my research, I noticed watching video of the police interrogation that Dennis Oland is left-handed, and that based on the pathologist's evidence the killer was most likely right-handed as Richard Oland had been killed by a fatal blow to the left side of his head. Here was a story that became this book.

My first thanks go to all those who gave their time to speak with me and who trusted me to get it right. If you are in Saint John, be sure to check out diner Slocum & Ferris in City Market, Canada's oldest farmers' market in a lovely old building in the city's heart. With luck you'll meet The Red Ball Kid, Ralph Willett, who knows who's who and knows a lot about the city's history.

Thanks also to the Public Archives of Nova Scotia, and the Dalhousie University Archives where the voluminous

Oland fonds consisting of donations made from 1978 to 2012 by various members of the Oland family, including Richard Oland are among the most studied by business students, the archivists say.

This book began with a series of articles for the Chronicle Herald in Halifax, and I am grateful to journalists Brian Ward, David Ramsay and Bruce Lantz for their fine editing skills.

There were many technical and legal matters from how cellphones work to police procedures and practices, and cyber security. I thank the experts who gave freely of their time and specialized knowledge. I am especially grateful to Joe Chu, a former Vancouver police officer and now a security consultant; Anwar Visram, CEO of Visram Security, and Geordie Cree, principal of Decision Point Cyber Security Advisors Inc.

I thank Mark Fenton, former internet investigator for the Vancouver Police Department and an expert who trains law enforcement in global internet searches, who probed the internet on my behalf including the dark web for crucial information about the case.

I am fortunate to be publishing a book with Jim Lorimer of Formac Lorimer, a skilled journalist and editor. Jim and his team were endlessly helpful and patient with the drafts it took to bring the book to completion. Looking back, I was amazed at the effort. Special thanks to editor Ghislaine Sinclair and Susan Joanis, copy editor and law school graduate, for their careful eyes and helpful contributions.

My thanks to early readers. A special thank you to Ken Cuthbertson for his friendship, being an early reader and for his writing advice and counsel.

I wrote most of the manuscript during Covid lockdown with my husband Paul Brettle's full support, enthusiasm for all drafts and kind encouragement. To our daughters, Paige and Meghan, thank you for always being willing to talk about Mom's book, and never growing bored or impatient.

Index

A

Adamson, Bill, 32, 50, 278
Adamson, Maureen
 as Richard's assistant, 28, 29, 33, 37, 150–51, 183
 discovery of Richard's body, 39–41, 49, 71, 282–83
 on Richard's last day, 31, 32, 50, 113, 142, 143, 277, 278
 participation in the investigation and trial, 187, 275, 287
Ainsworth, John
 as Richard's landlord, 29, 51, 179, 259, 271
 on Richard's last day, 49, 114, 123, 195, 281, 282, 283, 285
 participation in the investigation and trial, 184–85, 285–86
Alward, David, 53
Assoun, Glen, 245
Atlantic Canada Opportunities Agency (ACOA), 24, 84, 200, 274

B

Bates, John, 226, 237, 260, 303, 308
Baumeister, Gregory, 180–81
Bentenuto, Luciano, 205
Bishop, William, 61, 88, 89, 238
Black, Conrad, 229, 234
Brice, Worthington, 246
Brock, Hilary, 43, 99, 273–74

Brooker, David, 71–72, 223, 286, 287, 291
Bruce, Robert, 260, 261
Bustin (Oland), Lisa, 22, 32, 45, 47, 64, 66, 67, 94, 96, 152, 278
Butt, David, 79–80, 164–65, 166–67

C

Can Sugar Inc., 24, 94, 126, 188, 193, 197–205, 249, 259, 260, 274
Cardwell, John, 23–24, 188, 199, 201, 203–4, 274
Carson, Steve, 202
 cellphone (Dennis Oland's), 73, 121
 cellphone (Richard Oland's)
  location of, 34, 36, 74–75, 114–16, 117, 118, 121–22, 125, 135, 183, 187, 189
  messages received on last day, 33–34, 35, 126, 188, 278, 280
  roaming error, 34, 126, 181, 293
Chernyak, Alex, 199, 204–5, 274
Chiasson, Preston, 40, 71, 283
CIBC Wood Gundy, 21, 31, 32, 49, 68, 90, 120, 150, 155, 277, 278, 297
Coles, David, 76, 264
Connell, Bruce, 237–38, 239, 261, 314
Connell, Jack, 22, 28, 32, 122, 277, 287
Copeland, Keith, 250, 290–91

Court, Ivan, 58
Croll, Diana, 266–70
Cunningham, April, 244

D

D'Angelo, Frank, 212–13
Darrah, Pat, 54, 55
Davidson, Stephen, 46–47, 70, 72, 76, 180, 243, 250, 285, 290, 291, 304
Day, Joseph, 201
DeWare, Tracey, 263–64
DNA evidence
 on Dennis's jacket, 69, 117, 119, 145–46, 148, 150–51, 158, 182–83, 297, 305
 testing at crime scene, 180, 299
 testing of Dennis's car and clothing, 50, 73, 118–19, 297–98
 use in murder trials, 130, 242
Dow, Patty, 159
Drapeau, Ernest, 164–66
Drolet, Stephan, 261

E

Edwards, Murray, 197, 201
Enterprise Saint John, 24, 84, 198, 199, 202, 274

F

Fairweather, Gordon, 83
Faloon, Gary, 202
Far End Corporation
 as beneficiary of Richard's life insurance policy, 29, 313
 as crime scene, 36, 39–40, 49, 72, 113–14, 135, 178–79, 221, 257

Dennis's visit to, 32–33, 46, 245, 278, 279
office space, 28, 204, 271, 273, 277, 280, 304
as Richard's company, 27, 30, 67, 83, 106, 124, 276
Fineberg, Martin, 100
footprint (found at crime scene), 179–80, 293–94
Fraser, Albert, 143–44, 181, 292
Fraser, Neil, 250

G
Galeotti, Mark, 199
Gallant, Brian, 194
Gill, Sylvie, 188, 189
Gladwell, Malcolm, 241–42
Glennie, Peter, 201
Gold, Alan D.
at first trial, 72, 78, 112–12, 118, 121–22, 136, 142, 149, 150, 158, 221–22, 229–30, 305, 306–7
at the retrial, 180–81, 182, 184–85, 189, 230–32, 237
commentary on reasonable doubt, 234–36
commentary on the case, 82, 165, 188, 221, 238, 241, 311
knowledge of Richard's affair with daughter-in-law, 89, 97–98, 309
Gottlieb, Myron, 212
Graham, Gordon, 29
Grant, Mcgregor, 57

H
Harris, Robert, 54, 275

Hatfield, Richard, 129, 230
Henheffer, John, 130, 302
Hicks, Christopher, 161–62
Hoeksema, Gerry, 57
Hood, Suzanne, 245
Howard, Gary, 84
Howard, Steven, 206–7, 208

I
Irving, Brian, 202

J
jacket, brown sports (Dennis Oland's)
blood spots on, 69, 119, 135, 145, 148–50, 158, 182–83, 187, 298, 299, 302, 305, 306, 309
Dennis's incorrect claim of which jacket he wore, 47, 49–50, 117–18, 145, 147, 163–65, 186–87, 290, 306
drycleaning of, 116–17, 146, 150, 290, 291, 301
handling by police, 118, 120, 146, 147, 148–49, 151, 297, 300
Johnson, Cheryl, 36, 123, 195, 280
Johnson, Eric, 153–54, 155–57
jury selection, 128–29, 170, 171, 172–75, 230, 303, 310

K
Kenney, Ann, 200
Ketcheson, Sarah, 200
King, Mike, 71–73, 180, 221–23, 225, 285, 287, 301, 303, 308
Klyuev, Dmitry, 208

Knee, Jill, 182
Knox, Amanda, 242

L
Lacy, Michael, 95, 172, 174, 176, 222–23, 230–32, 298, 310, 313
Lafrance, Dan, 198
'Lantic Sugar, 23, 193, 197–98, 201, 203, 205, 274
Latimer, David, 245
Laturnus, Patrick, 149, 150, 306
LeBlanc, Michael, 54
LeBlanc, Ronald, 70, 110, 112, 113, 115–18, 301
Legere, Allan, 130
life insurance policy (Richard Oland's), 29, 312–13
Light, Matthew, 205–6
loan from Oland for Dennis's divorce settlement, 48–49, 75, 88, 135, 152–53, 313
Lord, Bernard, 129, 201
Lordon, Denis, 163
Lowe, Gerry, 37, 177–78, 179, 190, 192–95, 226, 281–82

M
MacDonald, David, 69, 145–46, 147–49, 292, 298, 300
MacDonald, Sean, 245
MacKinnon, Bobbi-Jean, 237
MacKnight, Barry, 225–26, 227, 304, 308, 309, 311, 312, 314
Makin, Kirk, 244–45
Marquis, Greg, 159, 237
Marriott, Aaron, 162–63
McAlary, Shirley, 41, 59, 66, 202